THE SURGEON'S BATTLE

CIVIL WAR AMERICA

Caroline E. Janney and Aaron Sheehan-Dean, editors

This landmark series interprets broadly the history and culture of the Civil War era through the long nineteenth century and beyond. Drawing on diverse approaches and methods, the series publishes historical works that explore all aspects of the war, biographies of leading commanders, and tactical and campaign studies, along with select editions of primary sources. Together, these books shed new light on an era that remains central to our understanding of American and world history.

A complete list of books published in Civil War America is available at https://uncpress.org/series/civil-war-america.

THE SURGEON'S BATTLE

How Medicine Won the Vicksburg Campaign and Changed the Civil War

Lindsay Rae Smith Privette

THE UNIVERSITY OF NORTH CAROLINA PRESS

Chapel Hill

© 2025 The University of North Carolina Press

All rights reserved

Designed by Jamison Cockerham
Set in Arno, Scala Sans, and Fell English
by Jamie McKee, MacKey Composition

Cover art: After Winslow Homer, "The Surgeon at Work at the Rear during an Engagement" (from *Harper's Weekly*, July 12, 1862), Harris Brisbane Dick Fund, 1928, The Met, 29.88.3(2).

Manufactured in the United States of America

LIBRARY OF CONGRESS CATALOGING-IN-PUBLICATION DATA
Names: Privette, Lindsay Rae Smith author
Title: The surgeon's battle : how medicine won the Vicksburg Campaign and changed the Civil War / Lindsay Rae Smith Privette.
Other titles: Civil War America (Series)
Description: Chapel Hill : University of North Carolina Press, [2025] | Series: Civil War America | Includes bibliographical references and index.
Identifiers: LCCN 2025013282 | ISBN 9781469690261 cloth alk. paper | ISBN 9781469690278 paperback alk. paper | ISBN 9781469683799 ebook | ISBN 9781469690285 pdf
Subjects: LCSH: United States. Army of the Tennessee—Medical care | United States. Army. Medical Department—History—19th century | Medicine, Military—Mississippi—Vicksburg—History—19th century | Vicksburg (Miss.)—History—Siege, 1863 | Vicksburg (Miss.)—History—Siege, 1863—Environmental aspects | United States—History—Civil War, 1861–1865—Logistics
Classification: LCC E621 .P95 2025 | DDC 973.7/75—dc23/eng/20250416
LC record available at https://lccn.loc.gov/2025013282

Portions of chapters 3 and 5 appeared, in somewhat different form, in Lindsay Rae Privette, "Contaminated Water and Dehydration during the Vicksburg Campaign," in *American Discord: The Republic and Its People in the Civil War Era*, ed. Lesley J. Gordon, Megan L. Bever, and Laura Mammina (Baton Rouge: Louisiana State University Press, 2020), 99–115. Portions of chapter 5 also appeared, in somewhat different form, in Lindsay Rae Smith Privette, "'A Hard Place to Be Well': Soldiers' Health and the Environment during the Vicksburg Campaign," *Journal of Mississippi History* 86, no. 3 (Fall/Winter 2024).

For product safety concerns under the European Union's General Product Safety Regulation (EU GPSR), please contact gpsr@mare-nostrum.co.uk or write to the University of North Carolina Press and Mare Nostrum Group B.V., Mauritskade 21D, 1091 GC Amsterdam, The Netherlands.

To Dad,

my first history teacher

Contents

List of Illustrations ix

Acknowledgments xi

Introduction 1

1 DOWN THE MISSISSIPPI 11

2 THE GOLGOTHA OF AMERICA 37

3 THE KILLING MARCH 67

4 THE SURGEON'S WAR 93

5 THE VICTORIOUS ARMY 121

Epilogue 151

Notes 155

Bibliography 181

Index 203

Illustrations

FIGURES

Map of Chickasaw Bayou   29

Wartime sketch of Chickasaw Bayou   31

Location of Grant's canal   41

The USS *Nashville*   44

The Head of the Canal   49

Wartime sketch of a search party   105

Resection diagram   107

"Shebangs" east of Wexford Lodge   142

Rear of Union siege lines   145

MAP

Union military operations against Vicksburg   70

TABLES

2.1. Disease in the Department of the
Tennessee, winter 1862–1863   63

4.1. Casualties treated by Union surgeons   99

5.1. Disease in the Department of the
Tennessee, February–May 1863   125

5.2. Disease in the Department of the Tennessee,
May–July 1863   134

Acknowledgments

This book has been nearly ten years in the making. During that time, my life has changed dramatically. I have gone from graduate student to tenured professor, moved across several states, and lived through a global pandemic. I became a wife. I am who I am today, in part, because of the people who took the time to invest in me, to think with me, and to love me. This is my attempt to say, "Thank you."

First and foremost, I thank those who have shaped me as a scholar. I began my academic career at Baylor University, and it was there that I first met Mike Parrish. Not only did his classes show me the importance of understanding the present in light of the past, but his insights demystified the world of academia for this first-generation college student. I am forever grateful for his guidance, which ultimately led me to pursue my graduate work at the University of Alabama. While there, I had the privilege of meeting George Rable, who has had, perhaps, the greatest influence on my work. We spent hours in his office examining my writing, trying to deepen my analysis, and perfecting my editing skills. It was during one of those meetings that he first gave me the idea to write a study on medical care at Vicksburg. Quite simply put, this book would not exist without his patient instruction. But there are so many others at the University of Alabama who shaped my thinking and writing in equal measure, among them Steve Bunker, Lisa Lindquist Dorr, Kari Frederickson, Erik Peterson, Josh Rothman, and Jenny Shaw. Lesley Gordon was a wonderful addition to the faculty in my last few years and brought another element of Civil War expertise. Ellen Pledger and Morta Riggs were always around for a laugh when stress ran high. I am also honored to add John Marszalek to the list of people who read and offered feedback on this study in its earliest form.

Writing a book is no small feat. Fortunately, as this study became more complex, so did my network. The Southern Association for the History of Science and Medicine, the Society of Civil War Historians, and the Society for Military History proved important outlets to present and workshop my research. I am grateful for those who took the time to engage with my ideas and offer feedback. Comments and support from Kari Boyd-Weisenberger, Daniel Burge, Dillon Carroll, Mike Flannery, Sarah Handley-Cousins, Caroline Janney, Mark Johnson, Jonathan Jones, Adam Petty, Angela Riotto, K. T. Shively, Diane Miller Sommerville, Katie Thompson, Lauren Thompson, Dave Thomson, Susannah Ural, Trae Wellborn, and Terry Winschel have gone a long way in driving this project forward. I am thankful for Judkin Browning's generosity as both a colleague and a friend. In June 2020, I joined John Heckman and Peter Carmichael for a discussion on medical care during the Vicksburg Campaign as part of the Tattooed Historian's Facebook Live series. It was one of my first opportunities to speak nationally about this book, and it was during that interview that Pete urged me to give greater consideration to the role that emotions played in this story. His encouragement heavily influenced the revisions I made to chapter 4 and, I believe, resulted in a more compelling study. I add my voice to other scholars who will remain indebted to Pete for his ideas, his engagement, and, above all, his kindness.

This project has been fundamentally and irrevocably shaped by the members of my Civil War writing group: Megan Bever, Laura Davis, Angela Elder, Jonathan Lande, Laura Mammina, and Evan Rothera. I consider them all a source of inspiration and am privileged to have them as a guiding influence. Additionally, I am thankful for the encouragement and thoughtful criticism provided by Carrie Janney and the anonymous readers of the University of North Carolina Press. I also want to express my heartfelt thanks to Mark Simpson-Vos for guiding me through the publication process, as well as the rest of the team at UNC Press, including Thomas Bedenbaugh and Madge Duffey.

Of course, any work of historical scholarship succeeds or fails at the feet of the historical record. Early research for this book was made possible through grants and fellowships funded by the Reynolds-Finley Historical Library, the Ulysses S. Grant Presidential Library, the US Army Heritage Education Center, and the University of Alabama. Furthermore, archivists at the Abraham Lincoln Presidential Library, the State Historical Society of Iowa, the Library of Congress, the Mississippi Department of Archives and History, the National Archives and Records Administration, the Old Courthouse Museum, the University of Pennsylvania, Vicksburg National Military Park, and the Wisconsin Historical Society worked tirelessly to answer all my questions and make records accessible. A special thanks to Elizabeth Hoxie Joyner, Glenna Schroeder-Lein, and Ryan P. Semmes for their patience and thoughtful advice.

When I joined the faculty at Anderson University, I had no way of knowing what an amazing set of colleagues I was getting. I am especially grateful to the Faculty Development Committee, which offered financial support during a critical period of revisions for this project. Furthermore, the library staff, including Melanie Croft, Kenzie Barnett, Fred Guyette, and Darlene McKay, went above and beyond to help obtain much-needed resources in order to finish this book. I feel especially privileged to have administrators who have supported my research, including Ryan Neal, Nathan Cox, Wayne Cox, and Roger Flynn. Amiable colleagues make my work more enjoyable. Thanks go to Ryan Butler, Jennifer Campbell, Tanya Cordoba, Tori Dalzell, Jayson Evaniuck, Sue Kratko, Zach Lang, Allan Wilford, and Kathrine Wyma. And, of course, a special thanks goes to Lynneth Miller Renberg, who has been a cheerleader of sorts, not only encouraging me but offering tangible feedback despite the fact that my work takes place nearly 500 years after her own field of study.

We humans are social creatures, and I would be amiss to neglect the people who make my life rich. Little did I know when I packed my bags and moved to Waco in the fall of 2007 that I would find a lifelong friend in Amanda Costello. To Kimberly Bobbitt, Jennifer Chapman, Valori Waggoner, and Rachel Zitzman, you know how much your friendship means to me. I tell you regularly, but now you have it in writing. Ryan Gregornik and Abbie Holmes, you have blessed me with some of my favorite memories from graduate school. To my faith family at Graceview Church, and in particular the Millers' home group, thank you for every time you asked me about this book and listened while I talked excitedly about people who have been dead for over a century. Thank you to Vince and Tina Privette, who have welcomed me as part of their family.

I am grateful for your support. And to Dexter and Joy Smith, who have always encouraged me to embrace the things that I love most, thank you for following me into this world that was unfamiliar to us all and never wavering in your faith that we would come out the other side.

And finally, Anthony. In some ways, I have known the people captured in these pages longer than I have known you. And yet, I hardly remember a time when I didn't know you. Thank you for the years. Thank you for the laughter. Thank you for knowing when I shouldn't take myself too seriously and when I simply needed a hug. Thank you for your faith. I am, and shall always remain, your *Beloved*.

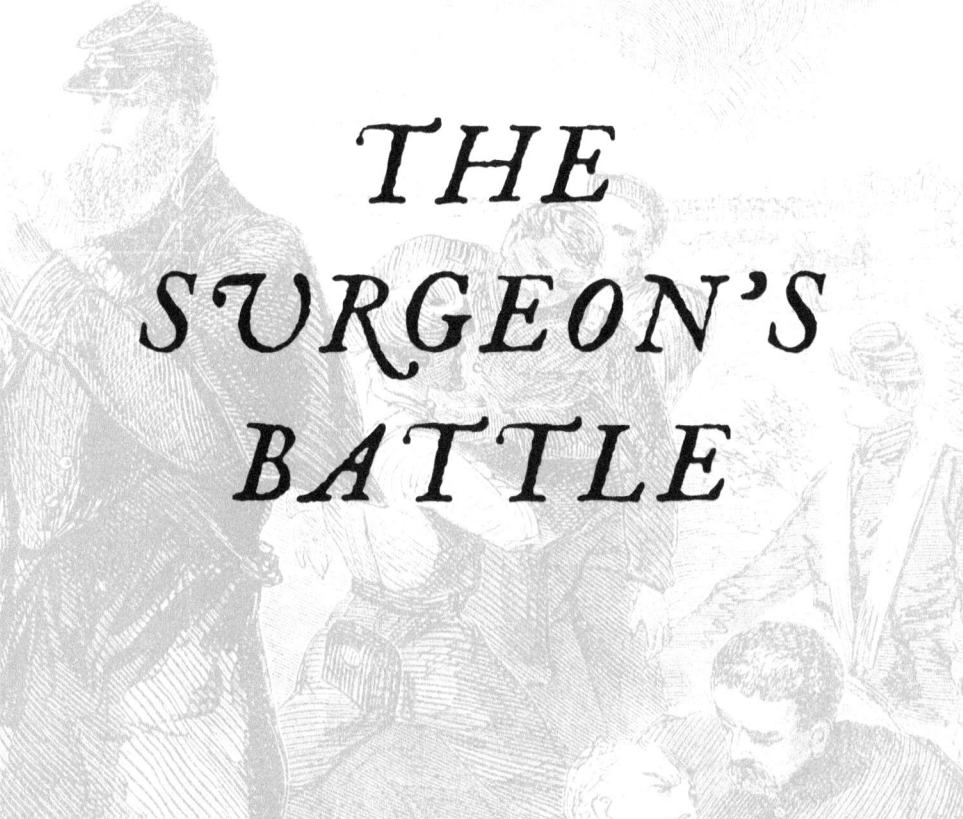

THE SURGEON'S BATTLE

Introduction

The siege of Vicksburg officially ended on July 4, 1863. That morning, Confederate forces stacked their arms while Union troops prepared to enter the city. In town, an advance guard raised the American flag over the Warren County Courthouse. For many Union soldiers, that first march through Vicksburg was a surreal experience. They had, after all, spent the better part of seven months trying to take the Confederate stronghold, and here they were: the victors. However, that march also granted them the first opportunity to witness the destruction that accompanied their triumph. "When we beheld the emaciated condition of the women and children at the entrance of their cave dwelling, along the roadside, on our way in, we didn't feel a bit like cheering," recalled soldier James Mahan. Instead, soldiers opened their haversacks and gave away whatever eatables were inside: "It was pathetic to see them gnaw the hard bread."[1] In addition to the emaciated bodies of city residents, soldiers were shocked at how sickness had consumed the town. "Until my ride through Vicksburg, I never had seen a hospital city, for such it seemed to be," wrote Wisconsin surgeon Christopher Blackall. "Two of its streets formed a continuous row of hospitals, every house being thus occupied while in the yards between[,] double rows of large tents were filled with sick or wounded men."[2] In all, 5,400 soldiers were included on the Confederate sick list. Of those, 2,400 were left behind when their comrades were paroled and sent home during the first weeks of July.[3]

Confederate bodies, of course, were not the only ones broken by the siege. Sickness had spread across the battlefield in equal measure. Within the Union army, cases of remittent and intermittent fever spiked. Diarrhea and dysentery tore through the ranks, and soldiers succumbed to the blistering sun and sweltering temperature. "I was taken with the chills the day after the fall of Vicksburg," sixteen-year-old Chauncey Cooke wrote to his mother, "but I ain't alone, there are thousands along this river of death.... There are only about 100 of our regiment fit to do duty."[4] Division and corps hospitals overflowed with the bodies of sick and wounded men. A constant stream of ambulances jostled through the hills and ravines to carry the worst cases north for evacuation. But if Union and Confederate bodies were equally taxed by the siege, the Union and Confederate medical corps were not equally up to the challenge. Within the city, Confederate efforts to care for and repair broken bodies floundered for want of medicine, space, and personnel. Union efforts, by contrast, prevailed.

Supported by an intricate system of transportation lines and aided by extra supplies provided by relief organization such as the United States Sanitary Commission, Union commanders and medical officers coordinated their efforts to meet the healthcare challenges produced by the siege. Medical officers monitored camp sanitation and supply distribution, oversaw patient triage, performed surgery, changed bandages, administered medicine, and organized an increasingly complex hospital system that stretched from the front lines at Vicksburg to general hospitals in Memphis. Commanders, in turn, granted the medical corps space within the army command to perform their duties with order and efficiency. Together, their efforts were integral to sustaining the Army of the Tennessee's fighting strength, not just through the siege but through the campaign that preceded it. Consequently, the fall of Vicksburg was as much a medical victory as a tactical one. Vicksburg's surrender was the triumph through which medical officers, and commanders, proved themselves responsible stewards of soldiers' bodies.

This book traces the evolution of Union medical care in the Vicksburg Campaign. In doing so, it offers a new understanding of the scientific limitations, logistic challenges, and interpersonal conflicts that shaped the campaign and siege. To successfully conduct the campaign and secure Vicksburg, commanders and medical officers in the Army of the Tennessee had to overcome three obstacles, the first of which was rooted in the tension between medical providers and their patients. The second quarter of the nineteenth century had been so characterized by a spirit of egalitarianism and a growing skepticism of professional and intellectual authority that many states had eliminated medical licensing laws and the recognition of local medical societies. This meant that physicians' authority to practice medicine was dependent on their medical degree, the value of which had eroded because of proprietary policies, poor regulation, and a lack of experiential training. As a result, several unorthodox medical sects flourished in the antebellum years, offering alternative options for patient care. Of course, there had been prewar efforts to reform the medical profession and legitimize its authority. Members of the orthodox medical community established professional organizations to define ethical practice, sought to improve education, and embraced new scientific theories. Yet on the eve of the Civil War, middle-class, working-class, and rural Americans—those who disproportionately filled the ranks of Civil War armies—remained wary of physicians' expertise and skill. Consequently, the war, having initiated a transition in which responsibility for soldiers' health and medical care transferred from the domestic domain of the family to the impersonal hospital system of the army, exacerbated popular anxieties regarding medical care and consent. Soldiers resisted this loss of bodily autonomy.[5]

With its professional authority already tenuous, the medical corps's competence was further compromised by a near endless string of embarrassing failures during the first year of the war. For the most part, Civil War surgeons were not members of the regular army. Instead, they were volunteers who had practiced, prior to the war, as civilian physicians. However, the responsibilities of a civilian practitioner were dramatically different from a military surgeon, and because there was little formal training, medical officers faced a steep learning curve. This included knowledge about camp sanitation, medical treatment, and combat surgery but also extended to their ability to regulate the emotional toll caused by the sights and sounds of the field hospital. Furthermore, having begun the war with an undermanned and inexperienced corps of medical officers, the US Army Medical Department was further plagued by an archaic supply structure incapable of meeting the demands of modern combat. As a result, the field medical service was often marked by inefficiency.[6] Battlefield evacuations stalled during combat, supplies ran low, and surgeons succumbed to the chaos. Off the battlefield, the medical corps fared no better. Outbreaks of measles, typhoid, and smallpox swept through training camps while dysentery plagued campaigns. Soldiers fell victim to fever, their bodies racked with chills and contorted with pain.[7] In the years to come, Maj. Gen. William T. Sherman would observe that "war is hell," but this hell was not the result of enemy fire. Instead, soldiers' suffering was seemingly produced and prolonged by the carelessness and incompetence of their own surgeons and commanding officers. Soldiers questioned whether there was any nobility in such needless suffering.

Like their medical officers, most Civil War soldiers were volunteers, having enlisted only to discover that the rigors of military discipline sharply contrasted with their idea of personal liberty. The growing dissonance between soldiers' expectations and the emerging realities of their wartime service generated tension between enlisted men and their commanding officers.[8] This strain was rooted in a democratic culture that valued freedom, liberty, and individual autonomy. However, the tension extended beyond the relationship between soldiers and their commanding officers. It was also present in their relationship with the medical corps. Just as soldiers chafed against the expectation that they should willingly submit to their commanders' military authority, so too did they resist the expectation that they should blindly submit to their surgeons' medical authority. Consequently, soldiers' willingness to voice their frustration and criticize their medical officers not only challenged the professional expertise of the medical corps but did so publicly. Their letters, along with frontline reports, were circulated widely through the Northern press, generating outrage over the condition of soldiers' health and the quality of their medical care. This, in turn, gave rise to the second obstacle that threatened to undermine the Army of the Tennessee's efforts to take Vicksburg: civilian intervention.

Growing fears that military officials could not—or would not—safeguard soldiers' bodies led to increased involvement from Northern civilians, reformers, and other noncombatants. In some cases, these individuals acted as concerned citizens writing missives to their congressional representatives on behalf of their loved ones. In other instances, state governments attempted to intervene with resources earmarked exclusively for their soldiers. Of particular note were relief organizations such as the United States Sanitary Commission and the Western Sanitary Commission, which endeavored to provide the army with additional supplies, manpower, and expertise in an effort to improve the quality of soldiers' health and medical care. Of course, none of the civilians involved in these efforts would have described their actions as interference, and that is certainly not how they were interpreted by the rank and file. But for the high command and medical corps, civilian involvement was often seen as more hindrance than help.[9] By offering competing medical services such as evacuation and hospital care, state governments and civilian relief organizations weakened the army's ability to track soldiers' movements, monitor their recovery, and return them to the field. In doing so, they not only threatened officers' authority over their command but also undermined the medical corps's ability to care for sick and wounded soldiers.

Nevertheless, Union officials could not simply ban civilian involvement in the war effort. The donations raised and distributed by relief organizations were vital to soldiers' welfare. Each new crate of clothes, bedding, bandages, and food helped to reduce the financial and logistic strain on the Quartermaster Department. It was only when civilian relief efforts competed with the army for control over soldiers' bodies that conflict occurred. The relationship between civilian organizations and the US Army could excel when it reinforced the supremacy of military authority and served to support the army's primary objectives. To this end, medical officers faced additional pressure from military officials to develop and execute an efficient method for collecting, treating, and rehabilitating sick and wounded soldiers that would mitigate the need for civilian intervention.

Finally, there was the environment. The scholarship dealing with the evolution of the Union field medical service has focused mostly on the eastern theater, largely because the Army of the Potomac was at the center of the army's medical reforms.[10] However, over the years scholars have demonstrated that the war effort varied dramatically between the eastern, western, and trans-Mississippi theaters. And, indeed, the medical corps's evolution at Vicksburg did not simply mirror the experiences of medical colleagues in the East. The fight for Vicksburg was heavily shaped by the region's demanding geography: jagged bluffs, deep ravines, putrid swamps, and a vicious river.

The Mississippi Alluvial Plain—otherwise known as the Lower Mississippi River Valley—is one of the largest forested wetland systems in North America. The floodplain consists of 22 million acres and reaches from Cairo, Illinois, in the North to the Gulf of Mexico in the South. It extends up to 150 miles across at its widest point.[11] As a meandering river, the Mississippi River has an extremely unstable channel that alters its path in accordance with silt deposits and erosion.[12] Consequently, the region's topography serves as a quiet testament to the river's ultimate power. The cyclical flooding and retreat of the river waters carved features into the landscape that were often unseen but nonetheless serious obstacles for an invading army. Oxbow lakes appear when the river overflows its banks, as it did nearly every spring, carrying with it silt and sand that formed rings of natural levees as barriers. Abandoned river channels created a series of interconnected waterways—rivers and bayous—bordered on either side by natural levees that were often navigable by steamboats. Here, in the space between the river channel and bayou, there were closed-off pools of stagnant waters. Some of these backswamps drained during the low-water seasons of late summer and winter, but many of them did not. Regardless, these swamps are home to thick undergrowth and serve as the breeding ground for alligators, snakes, aquatic birds, and countless fish.[13]

Though bordered by swamps and bayous to the north and west, the city of Vicksburg is built upon higher ground. The floodplain's eastern boundary is marked by a line of bluffs, and in 1863 those bluffs met the river channel at Vicksburg. This was the terrain that gave the city its significance, not only as a port connecting river traffic flowing north to south with railroad lines moving goods east to west but also as an important site for river defense. The specific bluffs that ground Vicksburg are part of the Loess Hills, a unique sedimentary deposit that extends roughly ten to fifteen miles inland to the east. Loess's basic properties are seemingly contradictory. Though highly porous, the soil, if left undisturbed, is relatively impermeable. When compromised, however, loess is subject to rapid erosion. While the original landscape was likely a series of gently undulating hills, centuries of runoff water—exacerbated by deforestation and agricultural development—had created the deep gullies and jagged ridges that made up the city's eastern border by 1863.[14]

When combined, these geographic features made Vicksburg strategically valuable, easy to defend, and difficult to conquer.[15] But while they proved a strategic challenge for commanding officers attempting to take the city, they were also a medical challenge for surgeons. By the middle of the nineteenth century, the Lower Mississippi River Valley had become notorious for its unhealthy environment. The region's subtropical climate, which is marked by temperate winters, hot summers, and high humidity, facilitated the spread of mosquito-borne illnesses.[16] The sick season, which began in late summer, was marked by endemic malaria and sporadic outbreaks of yellow fever to the extent that sickness—or rather the microorganisms that caused it—dominated military operations in the region. But they were not the only such environmental threats to soldiers' health. Considering the blistering sun, unforgiving heat, limited rainfall, and incessant flies, it is clear that the natural world was just as important to Vicksburg's defense as the Confederate batteries.[17] In this regard, the demands of practicing medicine in the Army of the Tennessee were shaped both by the army's immediate environment and by its military objective. For medical officers, the campaign and siege for Vicksburg was a race to capture the city before the army's overall stamina collapsed.[18]

By combining sources such as soldiers' accounts, military correspondence, and official records with medical reports, surgeons' records, and *The Medical and Surgical History of the War of the Rebellion*, this study seeks to integrate the scholarship on Civil War medicine with environmental history, soldier studies, and traditional military history. Doing so offers a much fuller account of the challenges faced by members of the field medical service as well as their achievements. For almost a century after the war, scholars steadfastly characterized Civil War era medical care as an abject failure by highlighting the devastating disease toll. With bacteriology in its infancy and germ theory a few years away, Civil War surgeons had limited means to effectively treat and cure various ailments.[19] But when the focus shifts away from disease and toward the medical corps's other responsibilities such as evacuation, triage, recordkeeping, and surgery, the narrative becomes more complex.

Since the early twenty-first century, there has been a notable shift in scholarship as historians have challenged the traditional narrative of failure. These studies argue that the medical corps's scientific, surgical, and managerial work played a significant role in the profession's development. However, in doing so, they have focused largely on the wards of Northern general hospitals, the surgeon general's office, or the Army of the Potomac. Of the works that do consider the evolution of medical practices in the camp and field, few extend the study beyond the adoption of the tiered hospital system at Fredericksburg in December 1862. By expanding the geographical and chronological focus, scholars might consider how medical practices were adopted—or adapted—throughout the army. This is particularly significant when considering the topographical and climatic differences between the eastern and western theaters.[20]

This approach offers insight into the intricate relationship between commanding officers, enlisted men, and members of the medical corps. While many studies have highlighted the tension between enlisted men and commanders, newer works have examined the strained interactions between soldiers and their medical officers.[21] By pressing beyond a simple emphasis on the power relationships created by the military hierarchy, this study emphasizes how interpersonal conflict shaped military operations. Commanding officers, struggling to achieve their objectives, pressured medical officers to privilege strategy over health. Soldiers, fearing that their suffering was futile and avoidable, rarely distinguished between the authority wielded by commanding officers and that by members of the medical corps. Finally, medical officers found that they were bound to two professions: one military and one medical. Unfortunately, war and medicine often had competing interests.

Ultimately, the campaign and siege of Vicksburg demonstrates that while Civil War field medicine was influenced by the national conversation regarding soldier care, medical reform, and noble suffering, it was also shaped by military leadership and the specific environment. The process by which the Army of the Tennessee grappled with its health care challenges was not linear, nor was it always successful. After a failed naval bombardment in the winter of 1862, military commanders retreated north and waited for winter. During a December assault across the Chickasaw Bayou, the medical corps employed new procedures for collecting, treating, and evacuating wounded soldiers. Unfortunately, these efforts were overshadowed by the Union defeat. Abandoning plans for a direct assault, the Army of the Tennessee spent the next three months attempting to dig a canal among the swamps and bayous of eastern Louisiana. Soldiers watched bitterly as the command's health deteriorated with no victory in sight. The campaign came with the spring thaw, a rapid 200-mile march through the Mississippi countryside that ended on the outskirts of the Confederate fortifications.

During the Vicksburg Campaign, the Army of the Tennessee experienced unprecedented isolation. Ironically, this isolation became the army's greatest asset. Without interference from the outside world, military discipline became more flexible. Soldiers were afforded a greater opportunity to care for their own bodies and to provide their own food and comfort. And even as they continued to draw sharp distinctions between noble sacrifices and gratuitous suffering, they enjoyed physical and emotional benefits from foraging. Furthermore, the medical corps proved itself more than capable of caring for the army's physical needs. Medical officers established field hospitals, distributed supplies, and provided for soldiers' long-term care without compromising their efficiency. The campaign finalized their transition from civilian practitioners to skilled and resilient veterans of the medical service. Ultimately, the army's physical condition coupled with its battlefield success limited public criticism; relations between the army and civilian relief organizations gradually became more cooperative. And though tension would remain, Vicksburg was a turning point.

At its core, *The Surgeon's Battle* is a story about sacrifice. It is about soldiers' deteriorating health and their broken bodies. It is about physicians' efforts to heal their patients and learn something in the process. It is about generals who tried to move rivers and race mosquitoes. Above all, it is a story about men who wanted their suffering to matter. Unfortunately, not everyone agreed on the sacrifices necessary to capture the River City. Vicksburg was a formidable opponent, guarded by a hostile terrain and unforgiving climate. Prolonged exposure to the region's environmental threats was just as dangerous as Confederate guns. To gain the city, Federal troops would have to defeat more than their human enemies.

I

Down the Mississippi

On a dreary December day in 1862, Indiana corporal Reuben Scott stood on the deck of the *J. S. Pringle*, taking in the scenery. "We had heard of the great Mississippi," he would later write, "but this was our first view of the great river, with which our subsequent history is to be so closely associated."[1] Scott's steamer was one of fifty-nine transports that left Memphis on December 20 destined for the murky waters of the Chickasaw Bayou. Their goal was to launch an assault against the northern bluffs guarding Vicksburg, Mississippi, and capture the last Confederate stronghold on the river. Unfortunately, the city would not be easily attained. As the gallant parade of steamers and gunboats pushed their way downstream, soldiers found themselves surrounded by a curious mixture of cultivated farmland and wilderness. There were "white cotton-fields by the side of dark bayous and palm," observed Lt. William Jordan, all under "tall cypress trees festooned with Spanish moss."[2] As the transport moved east up the Yazoo River, the landscape became even more desolate. Catching the first glimpse of the Chickasaw Bayou, Ohioan Frank Mason described it as a "deep, tortuous, sluggish stream," interspersed with land that alternated between dense woods and open fields. By December, the ground was "soft and miry, from the last autumn rains."[3] It was here, among the tangled forest and churning waters, that soldiers disembarked and began preparations for the coming assault, but as the sun sank beneath the horizon a heaviness descended upon them. To Scott, it was as if a "great thick wall of darkness hemmed us in." With no other option, he and his comrades prepared for sleep, lying "down by the roots of the tall cypress trees . . . while the wintry winds moaned a tune of loneliness" above their heads.[4]

For the western soldiers who found themselves camped along the Chickasaw Bayou, the woods and fields, lakes and swamps of the Lower Mississippi River Valley merged into an untamed wilderness that dramatically contrasted with the orderly fenced farmland with which they were so familiar. It was unsettling.[5] Here, the river ruled the land, regulating life in the region, including that of humans. Even in the stillness of winter, when the water was low, the trees testified to the river's threatening power. "The ground from the bayou back to the boats was very low," wrote Schuler Coe of the 1st Illinois Light Artillery; "at high water [it] was entirely overflowed to the depth of twelve or fifteen feet as we could see by the watermarks of the tree."[6] And the same terrain that tested soldiers' perception of order and safety created logistical problems for their commanders and medical officers. In order to even launch the assault, Maj. Gen. William T. Sherman had to contract an enormous fleet and lead a seven-day expedition into the swamp. Even now, as Scott and his comrades prepared for sleep, officers were planning an attack across the 100-yard bayou filled with chest-deep water.

While Sherman's officers were looking for ways to get soldiers to the battlefield, Medical Director Charles McMillan was making arrangements to evacuate casualties. Even in the most favorable conditions, the medical corps's job seemed insurmountable. It was a daunting task to offer medical care to thousands of wounded and dying soldiers in a timely manner. But the bayou made everything more difficult. There were few roads and no permanent structures. Everything seemed covered in mud and vine. But McMillan pressed on, issuing orders and urging his officers to observe "prompt and careful compliance." He reminded his men that they shouldered a weighty responsibility not to squander the army's human assets. And they would, in fact, be held accountable—if not by their patients, then by their "much sacrificing friends at home."[7]

The battle at Chickasaw Bayou came at a pivotal moment in the Union war effort. After more than year and a half of fighting, victory remained elusive and progress disjointed. In the East, Union attempts to capture the Confederate capital at Richmond were consistently thwarted. Western armies produced better results. By the end of 1862, Union forces had occupied most of western Tennessee and were set to secure the Mississippi River, if only Vicksburg would fall. But for many Americans, the army's success was not exclusively measured in territory lost and gained. It was also measured in bodies—diseased, maimed, infected, and dead bodies. By this measure, the war was a failure.

Beginning with Manassas, disorganization, supply mismanagement, and a shortage of reliably trained personnel characterized the medical corps's performance on the battlefield. Consequently, the Medical Department came under fire for its apparent inability to reliably care for sick and wounded soldiers. As the war progressed, criticism grew. By the spring of 1862, civilians and soldiers alike were increasingly frustrated by the department's unwillingness to change its archaic procedures. Some attempted to intervene, investing their time and resources in reform organizations in an effort to allay the Medical Department's deficiencies and alleviate soldiers' needless suffering. This interference, as it was viewed by many officers, spurred the department into action. With the appointment of a new surgeon general in April 1862, the department spent the rest of the year embracing a series of reforms intended to increase efficiency and strengthen the medical corps's battlefield performance. However, it was not enough for these policies to simply exist. They had to work. And in December of 1862, they would be tested at Chickasaw Bayou.

When war first broke out in April 1861, there was little indication that the conflict would eventually become one of the bloodiest in the nation's history. Most Americans assumed that the rebellion would be short-lived, and little effort was put into practical training for soldiers or surgeons. In fact, the US Army Medical Department made so few preparations that Surgeon General Clement A. Finley bragged on June 30 that the department had completed the fiscal year under budget.[8] Under ordinary circumstances, Finley's frugality might have been heralded as an administrative triumph. But these were no ordinary circumstances. In the two and a half months since the fall of Fort Sumter, 75,000 men had volunteered for service in the Union army. These men were organized into companies and then regiments, placed under the command of a colonel, and appointed a surgeon and an assistant surgeon. Unfortunately, the Medical Department had little control over who these volunteer physicians were. Instead, state governors were granted the opportunity to appoint medical officers for each regiment, and they often deferred to the colonels. The result was a chaotic recruitment process with no standard qualification guidelines. Volunteer medical officers came from a variety of educational backgrounds, employed an array of therapeutic practices, and, in many cases, had limited exposure to surgery and surgical techniques. They were ill-prepared for the challenges of combat medicine, and the Medical Department's conservative approach to mobilization left them with almost no resources to bridge the gap.[9]

The army's poor planning and preparation became painfully apparent on July 21, when Federal forces clashed with Confederates near Manassas, Virginia. With no formal training, limited supplies, and no clear strategy for casualty removal, the battlefield quickly collapsed into chaos. In the aftermath of the disaster, hastily written reports and editorials lambasted the Union army's conduct. Reporter William Howard Russell was deeply ashamed of the "disgraceful conduct of the troops," lamenting that "the retreat . . . at Centreville seemed to have ended in a cowardly rout—a miserable, causeless panic."[10] Surgeons' performance was equally scrutinized. They were, after all, supposed to care for soldiers' bodies, alleviate suffering, and heal the wounded. But in each circumstance, surgeons failed. Soldiers marched into battle underfed and dehydrated. They sustained devastating injuries but were left to languish in the sun. Many died needlessly, forgotten and overlooked, from injuries that were easily treatable.[11] Scenes depicting medical negligence were carefully—and elaborately—described in the Northern press, characterizing medical officers as inefficient, careless, and heartless and generating public outrage against the medical corps.[12]

The medical disaster at Manassas was the first indication that the war would yield an unprecedented amount of destruction to the human body and that the antebellum Medical Department was incapable of managing the carnage. And yet, despite public outcry that demanded the Medical Department improve its procedures for evacuating, transporting, and caring for wounded soldiers, not much changed. Surgeon General Finley remained steadfast in his commitment to tradition. For some Americans, however, Finley's refusal to make any significant alterations to the department's supply and evacuation procedures was unacceptable. If the surgeon general refused to reform the department from within, they would attempt to force the change themselves.

In early 1861, a group of civilian reformers appealed to the president for permission to create a new commission dedicated to bearing "upon the health, comfort, and morale of our troops, the fullest and ripest teachings of Sanitary Science in its application to military life."[13] Noting the success of a similar commission created by the British government during the Crimean War, reformers proposed to use volunteers as agents of inquiry to consult on the prevention of disease as well as on the efficiency of all military hospitals. On June 13, 1861, President Lincoln signed an executive order approving the creation of the United States Sanitary Commission (USSC). Although the USSC was created prior to the Battle of Manassas, it gained prominence after the Union defeat. Ultimately, the commission would set standards for camp and hospital inspections as well as organize a national donation distribution program. Its work granted the USSC a considerable amount of political power, which commission leaders leveraged to pressure government and military officials into adopting various reforms.[14]

The USSC was not the only sanitary commission operating in the United States during the war, however. A few months after Lincoln signed his executive order, Maj. Gen. John C. Frémont, commander of the Department of the West, appointed the Western Sanitary Commission (WSC) to aid casualties in the western theater.[15] Although the USSC and the WSC had similar objectives, they were not the same organization. The USSC was headquartered in Washington, DC, and distributed its volunteers and supplies across the entire army, while the WSC focused specifically on the western theater. In reality the commissions were rivals. Unable to understand why a western commission was necessary, the United States Sanitary Commission initially tried to absorb the WSC as a subsidiary but was ultimately shut out by both Frémont and John Strong Newberry, the WSC's secretary.[16] For Frémont, the Western Sanitary Commission was an important resource for the Department of the West, which was far from Washington, DC, but quickly developing its own need for hospitals, supplies, and personnel.

While some military officials believed the civilian sanitary commissions an important resource for supplementing the Medical Department's supplies, knowledge, and personnel, others feared that the commissions' involvement on the battlefield would undermine the authority of the United States Army. The fall of Fort Donelson in February 1862 offers early insight into growing tension between army officials and the civilian sanitary commissions. Upon hearing of the battle, Newberry solicited donations, commissioned transport, and led an expedition of relief workers and physicians to the fortification in northwestern Tennessee. Arriving at local field hospitals shortly after the battle, Newberry wrote that "we found the cabin floors thickly crowded with the wounded men, and others were constantly arriving from the various places where they had been deposited when taken from the field of battle. When received they were laid side by side in juxtaposition, part on the floor and part on mattresses." Many of the soldiers had not yet been given medical care. Their wounds lingered, undressed and unwashed, days after the fighting. Others were just then being treated. They were "receiving such care as could be given them by men overburdened by the number of their patients, worn out by excessive and long-continued labor." There was no clothing, no blankets, no bandages for dressings. Surgeons worked with limited access to medicine and stimulants and had "nothing but corn meal gruel, hard bread, and bacon, to dispense as food."[17]

The US Sanitary Commission's arrival flooded field hospitals with much-needed supplies. Having raised nearly $3,000 in donations, commission members poured "into the two [army] hospital boats a constant stream of bedding, clothing, surgical dressing, medicines, stimulants, and food." These hospital stores were eagerly received by surgeons and assistant surgeons, who immediately employed the resources to ease the suffering of wounded and dying soldiers. However, the army's medical director did not welcome the commission with the same enthusiasm. "It would be impossible by any description to give an adequate idea of his arrogant, insulting manner," Newberry fumed. Now that the donations had arrived at the front, the medical director and Newberry disagreed over who had the authority to distribute them. While USSC members anticipated the right to manage the resources themselves, the medical director disagreed. He demanded that the commission turn over all hospital stores to his purveyor and that physicians and nurses, having traveled the distance to offer their service, place themselves under the direction of "Dr. B., a civil surgeon from Cincinnati." Newberry and his team found these conditions too objectionable, and, having felt themselves greatly insulted, the commission members decided to turn over the stores and leave.[18]

Newberry was shrewd when recounting the event. He drew a distinct contrast between the operating surgeons, who made "an earnest appeal for all our sympathies, all our efforts, all our stores," and the medical director, whom he characterized as "ungenerous," "unkind," and "cruel."[19] According to Newberry, surgeons and assistant surgeons were not entirely to blame for the army's poor medical care. They did not intentionally neglect their patients but were instead overworked, overburdened, and undersupplied. The same could not be said for their superiors, many of whom privileged their own authority at the expense of soldiers' lives. Their doing so, according to Newberry's report, not only justified the WSC's existence but also emphasized its importance. While the commission's donations made tangible improvements to soldiers' medical care, its presence at the front would play an essential role in advocating for soldiers' health.

Newberry's report, however, oversimplified the growing conflict between civilian reformers and the United States Army. The medical director's behavior was not just selfish or autocratic; it aligned with a growing concern about the division of responsibility between the sanitary commissions and the Medical Department. Despite the fact that both the WSC and the USSC asserted a commitment to work "in cooperation with the [Medical] Bureau" and to "not interfere, but to strengthen the present organization," both the secretary of war and the surgeon general viewed the organizations with suspicion, believing that they threatened to undermine the army's authority over sick and wounded soldiers. The concept of cooperative health care might have been attractive, but, they feared, it was impractical. The medical director at Fort Donelson could not allow civilian volunteers to independently enter his field hospitals, distribute supplies, and treat patients without conceding at least some of the responsibility for soldiers' health care. Doing that would establish the WSC as a legitimate authority over soldiers' health in direct competition with the medical corps. That competition might not be noticeable when commission members and medical officers agreed on the best course of treatment, but it would be disastrous when they disagreed.

The implication of this threat was fully realized in April 1862, after Confederate forces launched a surprise attack against Union troops near Shiloh Church in southwestern Tennessee. In a scene reminiscent of the chaos at Manassas, Federal evacuation of the battlefield broke down. This time, in response to the crisis, the Western Sanitary Commission, the United States Sanitary Commission, and several state governments sent hospital steamers to aid the wounded. These boats, along with ones commissioned by the army, clogged the waterways around Pittsburg Landing, accepting the overflow from field hospitals.[20] Their presence, however, added to the mayhem as scared and wounded soldiers flocked to the water's edge, desperate to board. "The wild confusion of that scene cannot be expressed," wrote one witness; "the hurry, the excitement, and the miseries of war all mingled together in that narrow space. Men and munitions of war were being landed, the wounded embarked, and the dead trampled over as of no account in that struggle for life."[21] Filled with men in varying states of physical and mental duress, these boats shuttled the soldiers away from the battlefield and their command.

After the crises at Fort Donelson and Shiloh, the Northern public became even more convinced that the WSC and the USSC were essential to the preservation of soldiers' lives. After all, the Medical Department was clearly inept and plagued by bureaucratic inefficiency, chronic supply shortages, and antiquated leadership. As one early supporter of the USSC wrote, "The evils themselves were so glaring, the danger from them to the health and efficiency of the army so imminent and the Government apparently so helpless to provide an adequate remedy that it was determined by some enlightened men ... to try the experiment of infusing some of the popular enthusiasm and popular sympathy into the cumbrous machinery of Government."²² This narrative, which focused on the Medical Department's failures and highlighted the USSC's humanitarian work, was instrumental to generating civilian support for sanitary reform. Commission agents leaned in, promoting their work as an opportunity for Americans to safeguard the lives and bodies of their sons, brothers, and husbands and to ensure that soldiers sacrifice only what was absolutely necessary.²³

For military officials, however, civilian intervention was a threat to the Union war effort. For one, the army's inability to control its own evacuation weakened discipline and created opportunities for desertion. General Sherman, who commanded a division at Shiloh, was convinced that few of the soldiers carted away from Pittsburg Landing needed much care. Instead, he believed that soldiers used their illness and injury as an excuse to escape the terror of battle. His suspicions were shared by the medical director of the Army of the Ohio as well as by Patrick White, an artilleryman from New York. "I never saw so many sick men as there were at this battle," White remarked. "In fact, everyone wanted to go to the hospital."²⁴ After Shiloh, Sherman estimated that there were 57,000 soldiers unaccounted for. Four months later, 2,000 were still missing. "I know full well the intense desire to get home," Sherman admitted to his brother that August, "but any army will be ruined by this cause alone."²⁵ From his perspective, civilian-led evacuations subverted military authority and undermined the army's ability to retain enough soldiers to fight the war. It was a dangerous precedent.

The sanitary commissions undoubtedly improved soldiers' medical care by providing the army with additional hospital stores and other resources, but many officials had come to believe that the commissions were not helping military affairs. Instead, they were interfering.²⁶ According to one Ohio soldier, Sherman "cursed the Sanitary Commission as a body doing more harm in the rear, than the rebels did in the front." He responded accordingly, attempting to limit commission agents' access to soldiers under his command. When a USSC boat arrived in Memphis expecting to evacuate sick soldiers to Cincinnati, Sherman refused. Agents pointed out that soldiers were dying, but the general stood his ground: "There was plenty of room to bury them in Memphis."²⁷ Sherman, of course, was not the only commander annoyed by the USSC's growing expectation to have unrestricted access to the sick and wounded, though he might have been one of the few to express that frustration so openly. Responses like Sherman's only strengthened the popular perception that the military viewed soldiers as resources rather than as people and was willing to spend those resources liberally to defeat the Confederacy. Soldiers and their families did not feel the same.

To curb civilian interference, the US Army had to prove itself a good steward of soldiers' bodies, and responsibility for this fell largely to the officers of the medical corps. The challenge was twofold. First, medical officers had to become adept at collecting, treating, and caring for sick and wounded soldiers with limited civilian participation. Second, they had to execute these skills to the satisfaction of sanitary agents, journalists, politicians, soldiers, and their families. The goal, however, was not necessarily to eliminate the WSC and USSC's participation in the war effort. There was no doubt that civilian donations met tangible needs for food, clothing, blankets, and bandages. Rather, the medical corps's proficiency would simply relegate civilian relief organizations to an ancillary role in soldier health care.

Reform started at the top. By mid-April 1862, Clement Finley had been forced into retirement, and the US Army was looking for its next surgeon general. Traditionally, the office would have simply gone to the medical officer with the longest seniority, but Finley's resignation corresponded with a congressional act declaring that medical officers should be promoted on merit rather than by seniority.[28] Thus, William Alexander Hammond, an eleven-year veteran of the United States Medical Corps who had recently reenlisted at the start of the war, was appointed the new surgeon general on April 25. Despite his previous experience, Hammond's interest in science and research along with a desire to streamline operations and increase the medical corps's authority closely aligned with the USSC's calls for institutional reform. Subsequently, military officials were wary of the new surgeon general. Many considered Hammond the USSC's lackey and believed his appointment akin to infiltration. This included Secretary of War Edwin Stanton, who was eager to remind Hammond that the Medical Department was a subsidiary of the War Department and thus fell under the authority of the secretary of war. Hammond, however, was not easily intimidated. As the army's chief medical officer, he expected Stanton to defer to his judgment when it came to all medical matters. The result was a combative relationship between the secretary of war and the surgeon general that further embattled the Medical Department.[29]

With Hammond at the helm, the Medical Department slowly transitioned into an institution better suited to managing the complicated logistics of wartime medicine. One of Hammond's earliest triumphs was the appointment of Dr. Jonathan Letterman as the medical director of the Army of the Potomac. Letterman believed that to increase the efficiency and speed of the medical corps, he needed to shift the Medical Department's attention from regiments to divisions. Typically, a Civil War army corps was made of two to three divisions. Each division comprised two to four brigades, and each brigade contained anywhere from two to five regiments. At the start of the war, all medicine, equipment, and personnel were organized and distributed at the regimental level. The problem was that each regiment met different challenges during combat. Some regiments faced heavy fire, while others did not. Some regiments dropped back, while others advanced. Distributing resources at the regimental level created moments of shortage or surplus that were difficult to mitigate in the moment. Pooling resources at the division level, however, streamlined their use and allowed medical officers to focus their efforts on the patients who needed them most. In August 1862, the Army of the Potomac adopted a new ambulance corps based on Letterman's division model, implementing the strategy for the first time at Antietam. By December, Letterman had organized his field hospital service along division lines as well. In both instances, Letterman's efforts were embraced as positive changes, and other medical directors began to adopt the strategy.

While Letterman set about reorganizing the medical corps's field operations, Hammond was concerned with logistics and supplies. At the start of the war, medical officers were dependent on quartermasters and commissary agents to acquire materials, personnel, and transportation. This often led to paralysis within the system because quartermasters and commissary agents often regarded surgeons' requests as favors instead of commands.[30] In the spring of 1862, the War Department placed medical purveyors and bonded officers in charge of the selection and purchase of medical supplies.[31] The men in these positions provided aid for the sick and wounded, oversaw the transportation of medical supplies into the field, and had the authority to issue special requisitions when necessary. Perhaps most importantly, they served directly under the surgeon general. Shortly thereafter, Congress created the position of medical storekeeper, responsible for receiving, issuing, and accounting for medical and hospital supplies. Purveyors and storekeepers gave medical officers direct access to ambulances, tents, and other supplies. Ultimately, these reforms increased the medical corps's autonomy within the army as well as its authority over sick and wounded soldiers.

In many ways, Hammond's and Letterman's reforms presented universal solutions to universal problems. Supply distribution and patient management were a struggle, irrespective of location. Purveying depots, ambulance corps, and division hospitals offered tangible solutions to alleviate those challenges. However, sometimes medical officers faced problems unique to their location, and in these instances, solutions were unlikely to come from Washington. In the western theater, the region's geography—densely packed forests, muddy bayous, and unwieldly rivers—made the treatment and evacuation of sick and wounded soldiers even more difficult. As a result, hospitals ships were among the most important contributions made by the Medical Department's western administration.

Hospital boats were first employed in February 1862 when Brig. Gen. Ulysses S. Grant placed the *City of Memphis* under the direction of assistant surgeon W. D. Turner. Turner temporarily outfitted the steamer to care for the wounded at Forts Henry and Donelson, placing spring mattresses on the floor of the upper decks and the saloon, rearranging the staterooms to house wounded soldiers, and preparing for the storage of medicine and commissary items. The *City of Memphis* operated as a receiving hospital between February 7 and February 18, collecting large numbers of sick and wounded and transferring them to other ships for transport to Northern hospitals. It continued its service into April, where it again served as a receiving hospital during the battle at Shiloh. Convinced that hospital ships were integral to the quick management of western casualties, by the summer of 1862 the Medical Department bought two vessels to permanently outfit as hospital boats. The *D. A. January* was outfitted to serve as a transport ship and placed under the command of Dr. Alexander Hoff, while the interior machinery of the *Nashville* was stripped so that the steamer could serve as a receiving hospital.[32]

When viewed collectively, the reforms implemented by the Medical Department between April and December 1862 were sweeping. They overturned decades of outdated military procedures, particularly when it came to logistics and patient management. In fact, the Hammond/Letterman reforms have traditionally been heralded as the Civil War's primary contribution to military medicine.[33] But Hammond had even greater ambitions. While the Medical Department endeavored to streamline medical care, reduce suffering, and save lives, growing efficiency held important implications for medical professionalization and knowledge creation.

In the decades prior to the Civil War, the medical profession was characterized by a notable lack of regulation. The rise of proprietary medical schools, which privileged enrollment and matriculation fees over a standardized curriculum, meant that many newly minted physicians began their career woefully underprepared to practice medicine. And, remarkably, by the 1850s most states did not require any sort of licensure to demonstrate professional competency.[34] As a result, several irregular sects emerged to undermine the legitimacy of regular—or orthodox—physicians and challenge the efficacy of their treatments.[35] Thus, on the eve of the Civil War, the medical profession was a maelstrom of different practicing philosophies and educational backgrounds, and starting in April 1861 many of these practitioners began to enlist in the army under the title of "surgeon." At the time, there were no standard guidelines by which to measure prospective medical officers' qualifications.

John Newberry's description of the medical care administered at Fort Donelson was generous. In his account, operating surgeons and assistant surgeons seemed knowledgeable but lacked the resources to faithfully execute their job. This was not entirely accurate. While field hospitals undoubtedly struggled with supply issues, soldiers' medical care was also affected by a lack of training and knowledge among the medical corps. Newberry, however, sidestepped this issue. Afterall, the goal of his report was to justify the sanitary commissions' request for donations. In this regard, commenting on medical officers' expertise—or lack thereof—made little difference. But the inconsistent training and experience shared by the medical corps troubled Hammond, who encouraged a more stringent examination process that "scrutinized rigidly the moral habits, professional acquirements, and physical qualifications of" each candidate seeking appointment as a surgeon or assistant surgeon.[36] Under Hammond's guidance, the Medical Department adopted standardized examination boards, which acted as a type of licensure, defining competences that aligned with the surgeon general's standards. Included in the examination process were detailed questions relating to anatomy, pathology, and chemistry, subfields that closely aligned with orthodox practices. In addition to the examination boards, the Medical Department issued a standard supply table that restricted surgeons' access to specific medicines and defined standard treatments.

These reforms, however, were intended to do more than create rules and regulations for medical officers. Hammond's administration was also eager to embrace the scientific advancements developing elsewhere in the world. Reformers encouraged surgeons to shift from a systems-based medicine—a practice that employed theory to understand and treat ailments—to empirical medicine, which relies on observation and experimentation.[37] To accomplish this, reformers promoted the cultivation of a professional community capable of sustaining a national discourse. Their efforts were supported by the issuance of Circular No. 2, which was approved by and distributed from the surgeon general's office on May 21, 1862, and promoted the extensive collection and distribution of data gathered from the operating tables and hospital beds of thousands of soldiers. In keeping with the development of clinical medicine, the Medical Department was particularly interested in information on pathological anatomy and instructed surgeons to "diligently collect and forward to the office of the Surgeon General all specimens of morbid anatomy, surgical or medical, which may be regarded as valuable."[38] To this end, Hammond's initiatives were not simply about supporting the medical corps's work during the present war but were about transforming the future of the Medical Department. By creating stringent examination boards, establishing a standardized supply table, and encouraging the collection of new scientific information, the Medical Department might become the leading medical professional organization in the nation.[39] Hammond's efforts created an opportunity for cooperation as the USSC and Medical Department worked together to initiate and patrol such reforms.[40]

As ambitious as Hammond's efforts were, the quest for professional legitimacy was unimportant to most military officers. They were more concerned with winning the war, and most recognized that soldiers' bodies were a significant resource for attaining victory. More importantly, by the summer of 1862, a growing number of commanders were beginning to realize that soldiers' health and efficient medical care were important tools for prolonging the utility of those bodies. One only had to look to the Mississippi River to know that campaigns failed when soldiers' collective health collapsed.

On June 18, 1862, Union naval vessels under the command of Adm. David Farragut launched an assault against Vicksburg, Mississippi. After Farragut captured New Orleans on May 1 and secured Memphis on June 2, Vicksburg remained the last Confederate bastion protecting the Mississippi River. Its capture not only would secure river traffic for the Union but also would effectively sever the Confederacy. Operations began with a naval bombardment, which proved ineffective. Union guns could not elevate enough to reach the Confederate river batteries, and rebel artillerists struggled to sufficiently depress their guns to threaten the gunboats. In an effort to break the stalemate, 3,300 soldiers under the command of Brig. Gen. Thomas Williams were transported to De Soto Point, a peninsula on the west bank of the river. They, along with 100 enslaved laborers taken from nearby plantations, were tasked with digging a canal that, when flooded, might divert the Mississippi River around the Confederate stronghold. "If the cut succeeds," wrote Williams, "Vicksburg becomes an inland town with a mere creek in front of it. So the batteries will be made useless and Vicksburg will fall with the spade."[41] The canal was never completed.

Within weeks of their arrival, Union soldiers and sailors were suffering from protracted bouts of intermittent fever, diarrhea, dysentery, and scurvy. Disease decimated the ranks, leaving the force a fraction of its original fighting strength. By July 25, Williams reported only 800 men fit for duty. The other three-fourths of his command had either died or were in the hospital. The navy did not fare any better. "There is not a vessel in my squadron which is not rendered inefficient by sickness and vacancies," wrote Rear Adm. Charles Henry Davis. "In [the *Benton*] the number of sick and deficient is one in four; in the *Carondelet* it is one in two . . . ; in the *Louisville*, one in three." As the sick list grew, officers were faced with an important decision: stay and fight, or retreat. Assistant surgeon H. Beauchamp advised Davis to choose the latter. Beauchamp did not believe that the sickness would abate. Instead, he anticipated that it would evolve as the summer heat grew worse, "changing from the ordinary intermittent to the remittent congestion and typhoid fevers of this climate." If so, he warned Davis, "you can plainly determine to what extent the expedition may be crippled." Failure to act, Beauchamp feared, would have devastating consequences on the future health of his sailors and "eventuate in disabling our entire squadron." With little prospect of success, Union forces withdrew. "I regret to leave," wrote Williams, "but with an increasing sick list, which must soon, if it has not already, reduce me below the ability for effective service, I have no alternative but to go."[42] Union forces retreated to Memphis and New Orleans, where commanders studied Vicksburg from a distance.

Federal forces were not defeated by the Vicksburg garrison; rather, they were laid low by the city's natural defenses. Built on towering bluffs that extended nearly 200 feet above the river, Vicksburg was naturally fortified in a way that Memphis and New Orleans were not. But the city's natural defense system was not only topographic. The region's warm climate and marshy terrain created the perfect breeding ground for parasites, bacteria, and other microorganisms. Of course, neither Farragut nor Williams would have known about the microbes that invaded their men's bodies, but they could see the outcome. Their men got sick. Consequently, Union commanders recognized that the bombardment failed not only because of how they attacked but also because of when they attacked. The local terrain complicated the assault and slowed operations, but the climate made it deadly. "It seems to me that the only course now to be pursued is to yield to the climate and postpone any further action at Vicksburg till the fever season is over," Davis wrote.[43]

Vicksburg was not a city to attack during summer. Next time, they would wait until December.

By the end of 1862, Union presence along the Mississippi River was growing more extensive. Memphis in particular bustled with activity. The city had gone through a dramatic transformation since it came under Union control just six months before. When General Sherman entered the town on July 21, he had reported that "the people were all more or less in sympathy with our enemies, and there was a strong prospect that the whole civil population would become a dead weight on our hands." Seeking to relieve the growing tension between the Union army and the Confederate population, Sherman established strict lines between military and civil authority. He reinstated the mayor along with other municipal officials and encouraged the city to create and manage its own police force. Slowly but surely businesses began to reopen, as did schools, churches, even theaters.[44] As the city gradually returned to life, the military presence grew, and Memphis quickly became a vital staging area for the Union army in the western theater. Healthy, able-bodied soldiers prepared to move into the Confederate interior, while the sick and wounded were unloaded from boats and railway cars. Medical Inspector George T. Allen was at the nexus of it all. On December 17, Allen noted a rumor that nearly 25,000 soldiers had been ordered to accompany Sherman south. "This city is all excitement!" Allen wrote. "An immense fleet of transports has arrived to convey all disposable troops from this place to Vicksburg. . . . General Sherman expects a terrible fight."[45]

Unbeknownst to Allen, preparations for Sherman's departure had begun several weeks prior. By December 8, Grant, now major general, had sent word to Sherman informing him of plans to capture the River City. While Sherman, aided by Rear Adm. David Dixon Porter's fleet, moved his troops into position at Chickasaw Bayou, Grant planned to establish a supply line at Holly Springs and then push south through Oxford to draw Confederate troops under the command of Lt. Gen. John C. Pemberton away from Vicksburg.[46] For Grant, time was of the essence. Spurred by rumors that Union major general John A. McClernand intended to lead his own army against Vicksburg, Grant planned to get there first.[47] According to Porter, President Lincoln had famously declared Vicksburg "the key" to winning the war. If successful, Grant's plan to capture the city not only would secure that key for the Federal cause but also would give Grant the honor of atoning for the summer's embarrassing failure.

This new attack on Vicksburg offered the Medical Department an opportunity for redemption as well.[48] By December, William Hammond had been surgeon general for nearly eight months. Circular No. 2 had been published for seven months. The Medical Department had embraced the versatility of hospital boats and anticipated their use in western waters. And though Jonathan Letterman's new hospital system would not appear until December 11, his ambulance corps had already faced trial by fire at Antietam. Yet though these reform measures were in place, there was no guarantee that they would be successful. Sherman's assault across the Chickasaw Bayou was one of the first western engagements to occur after the 1862 reforms.

The Medical Department began preparations on December 18, when Allen wrote to R. C. Wood, assistant surgeon general in charge of the Department of the West, requesting the dispatch of several hospital steamers "without the least delay." Wood ordered three boats—the *City of Memphis*, the *City of Louisiana*, and the *Henry Von Phul*—outfitted as temporary floating hospitals and sent to Memphis. These three boats would prove invaluable as the supply base for Sherman's medical corps while at Chickasaw Bayou, making it unnecessary for surgeons to transport medical stores through the marshy bayous and swamps surrounding Vicksburg. They would also be the only semi-permanent structures suitable for use as field hospitals. Nevertheless, even with these improvements, the possibility of another medical disaster weighed heavily on Allen. He warned Wood that it was imperative for the steamers to arrive fully equipped with all the supplies and personnel needed to aid Sherman's army in the field so that "the disasters and confusion of Donelson and Shiloh may be avoided."[49]

To ensure the success of these floating hospitals, the Medical Department adopted strict regulations for the use of each vessel. No one, aside from the medical staff, the crew, and the patients, was allowed passage. Certainly, this eliminated the opportunity for deserters to sneak on board, but it also guaranteed the Medical Department's control over the hospital. Many surgeons in charge of hospital ships believed that the presence of soldiers, line officers, or even members of the sanitary commissions undermined discipline and the hospital crew's authority.[50] Over the next eight months, these floating hospitals would become a medical and administrative success. Capitalizing on the intricate waterways of the western theater, hospital steamers were responsible for the quick transportation of casualties as well as medical goods and supplies. They also became centralized locations where patient information was collected, making it possible to track wounded or sick soldiers who had been evacuated from their regiments.

If procuring reliable hospital transportation was easy for Allen, there were other headaches. As of December 1862, the Medical Department did not have enough medical personnel to meet the needs of an expanding army. This shortage contributed to growing disagreements between the Medical Department and the military over where surgeons' skills were most beneficial. Soldiers usually came into contact with surgeons in either the field hospital or the general hospital. Each location presented different responsibilities and challenges for the practicing surgeon. Field surgeons were responsible for triaging combat casualties, performing emergency operations, and stabilizing the seriously wounded for transportation. While the number of casualties routinely made these tasks overwhelming, the need for field surgery and combat care was episodic. It increased during and immediately after a battle and decreased while in camp or on campaign. Of course, field surgeons used the reprieve to worry about diet, hygiene, sanitation, and disease. Surgeons assigned to general hospitals, conversely, were not subject to the ebb and flow of combat. Because they cared for their patients over a longer period of time, it was more noticeable when general hospitals were understaffed and undersupplied. At times, the work seemed relentless.

Patient care, whether in the field or the general hospital, had the same objective. But the distance between field and hospital bred tension, a clash of priorities. In Memphis, Allen's primary concern was the efficiency of the expanding general hospital system, while Sherman prioritized the health of his troops in the field. Although there had been great improvement in the hospitals around Memphis, Allen still saw problems. Concerned that the manager of hospitals, Dr. Holsten, was already overworked, Allen recommended the appointment of a chief medical officer to handle the administrative responsibilities. He selected surgeon Charles McMillan, who had accompanied Sherman's army when he took over the city in July. However, Sherman also valued McMillan. "General Sherman declared that his command now extends down the river to Vicksburg," Allen complained, "and that he shall take the Doctor with him."[51] Sherman's primary concern was securing the best medical care for his men during the upcoming march, but Allen feared that McMillan's removal toward Vicksburg would weaken the general hospitals in Memphis. Thus, McMillan was being asked to serve two masters. In the end, Sherman, of course, won.

After weeks of preparation, Sherman's army left Memphis just five days before Christmas. For many soldiers, like Reuben Scott, the following weeks would be a hard introduction to the realities of war. At first, many of the soldiers seemed captivated by the display of military prowess. Frank Mason called the departure a "magnificent spectacle" that glistened in the bright morning sun. "As the long line of boats, covered with troops and guards with flags and streamers, swept down the broad and winding river, to the music of bands and the battle-songs of regiments, the scene was one of superb color and spirit."[52] Soon, however, soldiers realized that river transportation was anything but exciting. Instead, it was a slow, miserable experience. At first Samuel Black, a member of the 1st Iowa Artillery, thought that the steamboat was preferable to marching but soon decided otherwise: "The officers occupied the boat's cabin [leaving] the soldiers being crowded on deck . . . like hogs in a car for shipment with no place to sleep in comfort." Still, artillerymen had it easier than the infantrymen, since they could "get under the gun and caisson carriage and on top of the ammunition chests so as not to be trampled on." To make matters worse, the cramped conditions denied soldiers the simplest of conveniences. They were not permitted to go onshore, and there was no place to cook. Black and his comrades subsisted on hardtack, raw bacon, and coffee made from hot water taken from the ship's boiler.[53] The transports arrived just above the mouth of the Yazoo River sometime around Christmas Eve. Not long after daybreak, Sherman ordered Brig. Gen. A. J. Smith to have a detachment of troops disembark at Milliken's Bend to sever the Vicksburg, Shreveport & Texas Railroad. The rest of the convoy docked at Young's Point, where they spent Christmas. The following morning the transports turned up the Yazoo.[54]

For many Union soldiers, particularly those hailing from the flat Midwestern plains, Vicksburg was an imposing sight. Schuler Coe of the 1st Illinois Light Artillery wrote that "Vicksburg is situated on a high bluff and a range of hills behind it, at the bottom of which is low ground about a quarter of a mile and then comes a deep bayou from four to eight rods wide filled with water which runs all the way round on the side we were."[55] Coe was describing the Chickasaw Bayou, which Sherman's troops would be forced to cross for an assault against the Walnut Hills surrounding Vicksburg. It was along these hills where the Confederate lines were strongest.

The men disembarked on the morning of December 27. Almost immediately, the challenges of fighting in the dense forest and thick undergrowth presented themselves. "It was impossible to advance through the swamp from this side," remembered John Buegel, a corporal in the 3rd Missouri. "As we took position, we sank in the swamp over the shoe tops, and could not get our feet out again."[56] For one Illinois soldier, it was not the mud but the vegetation that proved problematic. His division was sent "tramping through a huge growth of cockleburs" to reach the forest, only to find it "wild with

Map of Chickasaw Bayou by Louis-Philippe-Albert d'Orléans, comte de Paris.
Histoire de la guerre civile en Amérique Atlas (Paris: Michel Lévy, 1890),
pl. 17. Library of Congress, Geography and Map Division.

the luxuriance of semi-tropical vegetation, through which the column slowly pushed its way."[57] Despite the fact that Confederates became aware of the Union convoy on December 26, they did not immediately attack the fleet. Instead, they waited.

Upon landing, Brig. Gen. George W. Morgan ordered Col. John DeCourcy to lead a detachment along the road running east to a plantation, where it crossed the Chickasaw Bayou.[58] Assistant Surgeon Henry C. Davisson of the 54th Indiana was among Morgan's men who now stood on "the memorable banks of the Yazoo." He recalled that "we had not gone more than half mile when we heard firing in the distance. Soon we came up to the contest. Our gun boats ran up and shelled them and soon dispersed them." As a result of the skirmish, Davisson and a fellow surgeon were compelled to "take entire charge of the wounded in the field." They were largely unprepared for the endeavor. "We have no bandages," he wrote, "and are quite busy."[59] By nightfall Davisson and his regiment had returned to their boats, where they slept, dining on navy beans to sustain them after the day's fight. The following morning a heavy fog had settled into the low-lying areas of the Yazoo River valley. Much of the day was spent preparing a frontal assault along the Confederate center.

As Sherman's troops reconnoitered through the marshy woods of the Chickasaw Bayou, the medical corps made its own arrangements. Prior to disembarkation, Medical Director Charles McMillan issued orders outlining medical officers' responsibilities while under fire. Hospitals, supplies, and personnel would be organized and distributed at the division level rather than at the regimental. This would reduce the possibility that wounded soldiers would be evacuated to the wrong hospital, where treatment could be delayed. The senior surgeon of each division was to select a suitable location for a field hospital approximately 200 yards from the line of battle. Three principal "operators" were appointed, and each operator was assigned an assistant. Two additional assistant surgeons were employed as a recordkeeper and a cook, respectively. In the midst of a battle, medical officers would be engaged in the recovery, treatment, and evacuation of the wounded. Each regiment was accompanied onto the field by an assistant surgeon and a hospital steward. Stationing themselves in the rear, they would tend to the immediate needs of the wounded and then send the soldier to the field hospital for treatment. Members of the ambulance corps were furnished by each regiment and reported directly to the division surgeon. They were to wear strips of white bandages around their arms for easier identification. No other soldiers were permitted to break rank to rescue their comrades, eliminating the convenient opportunity for able-bodied men to flee the battlefield.[60]

Early on the morning of December 29, 1862, members of Brig. Gen. Frederick Steele's Fourth Division stood in the overgrown woods of the Mississippi swamps, staring out across the water. They were to lead a frontal assault against the tall bluffs bordering the southeastern edge of the Chickasaw Bayou. Their goal was to take the high ground, clearing it of the Confederate troops and gaining Sherman's army direct access into Vicksburg. The challenge must have seemed daunting, for even the land seemed to cast its favor upon their foes. "The bayou in our front . . . ," recalled Brig. Gen. Frank P. Blair, "was deep and the bottom of it nothing but a treacherous quicksand[.] . . . The bed was perhaps 100 yards in width, covered with water for a distance of 15 feet." Upon emerging from the dense timber, Blair's forces would have to descend a steep bank, eight to ten feet in height. Once at the bottom, they would encounter

Wartime sketch depicting the land surrounding Chickasaw Bayou.
Battles and Leaders of the Civil War, Being for the Most Part Contributions by Union and Confederate Officers, Based upon "The Century War Series," edited by R. U. Johnson and C. C. Bue (New York: Century, 1887), 3:462. British Library.

a thick growth of cottonwoods that had been cut down by the Confederate forces. The tops of the trees were scattered among the stumps, forming a "perfect net to entangle the feet of the assaulting party." Only then would troops reach the water's edge. Here, they would wade across the "deep" and "miry" bayous. Finally, they would climb out the other side of the embankment, which stood "at least 10 feet high" and was "covered with a strong abatis and crowned with rifle-pits from end to end." Having reached the other side of the bayou, Blair's men would then encounter a plateau, sloping gently toward the foothills of the bluff.[61] Despite his belief that "the formidable works . . . would seem to require almost superhuman efforts to affect their capture," Blair issued his orders. Standing in arms with his comrades, Buegel described the breathless moment before the charge as "still as a cemetery."[62]

The battlefield soon turned chaotic. Soldiers watched as the hills before them became a sheet of flames. Amid the thunder of muskets and cannon, Federal soldiers threw themselves into the bayou, floundering through water and mud that came up past their knees. Then, clawing their way up the muddy banks, they disappeared into the smoke.[63] For some, the experience defied comparison. "Officers who have been in several battles say they never saw anything equal the fire we received," wrote Capt. Douglas Ritchie Bushnell.

"We were in open ground and were [fired] upon by a dozin [sic] batteries of artillery on both sides of our flank and on our front."[64] Sometime during the fighting a violent rainstorm set in, pouring nearly two feet of water into the swamp and exacerbating the already treacherous conditions. "Since now those, who were still alive in Blair's brigade, could neither advance nor retreat, they stuck in the mud, and so they were simply shot down or perished wretchedly."[65] Preparing to push in behind Blair's men, Buegel and the rest of the 3rd Missouri watched in horror.

As the battlefield dissolved into pandemonium, surgeons struggled to impose order at the field hospital. Compared to the chaos of Manassas, Fort Donelson, and Shiloh, the medical service at Chickasaw Bayou was better disciplined. Edmund Andrews, one of the operating surgeons for the Second Division, reported that the retrieval and evacuation of wounded soldiers occurred "without confusion" and that "the injured of each day were safely lodged on the hospital boats the same night."[66] Meticulous records were kept. Wounded soldiers first appeared in the division hospital's record book from which Charles McMillan later compiled a master list of all the casualties. In addition to patients' name, rank, and regiment, these rosters also listed details about the injury, treatment, and the operating surgeon.[67] Patients also appeared in the logbooks for the hospital steamers that transported them upriver. Upon their arrival, these records were amended to include the receiving hospital and the patients' date of admission.[68]

These detailed records maintained the army's control over wounded soldiers. They not only prevented deserters from stowing away on hospital transports but also allowed commanding officers to easily locate debilitated subordinates within the expanding system of Northern hospitals. They also benefited the medical profession. Months after the assault, Andrews wrote *Complete Record of the Surgery of the Battles Fought near Vicksburg*. Taking advantage of the systematic routine of recovery, operation, and evacuation, Andrews gained access to an unprecedented amount of information. Using the extensive records of the field registrar kept by assistant surgeon L. C. Brown of the 113th Illinois, Andrews was able to compile medical histories for every patient he treated at the bayou. These histories followed the patients twenty days after the injury was received, allowing field surgeons an opportunity to learn from the cases' outcomes.

Andrews's work was the first of its kind. The medical records at Fort Donelson and Shiloh were either lost or so fragmentary that no continuous case history could be compiled from either of those engagements, rendering the "vast and costly experience of so much blood and death . . . worthless for the settlement of the many difficult questions in practical surgery."[69] From Andrews's perspective, the tragedy of Donelson and Shiloh was not simply that soldiers suffered and died but that they did so in vain. Medical officers, unable to track the long-term prognosis of soldiers whose medical treatment began in the field, learned nothing from their patients. Thus, they were liable to make the same decisions with the same results, not knowing what those results actually were. The medical corps's organization at Chickasaw Bayou, however, offered to change all of that. The speed with which its members could collect, treat, and evacuate battlefield casualties largely depended on the corps's order and efficiency, two characteristics needed to create and properly maintain the records necessary to track patient progress.

In this regard, Sherman's assault across Chickasaw Bayou was a medical victory. Hospital ships, supply distribution, the field hospital system, and records management were successfully employed in ways to maximize medical officers' battlefield performance and ensure that casualties received the best care possible given the region's geographic challenges. Of course, the system was not flawless. When preparing to leave, patients were not distributed evenly across the three hospital ships. This led to overcrowding on some of the transports and contributed to devastating outbreaks of erysipelas and gangrene.[70] Still hindered by their limited understanding of pathological anatomy and microorganisms, surgeons were helpless to curb the infection. Even so, there was a dramatic difference between patient care at the bayou versus Shiloh, Donelson, and Manassas. There was no civilian interference and no frantic evacuation through the bayou's murky waters. Through the fighting, medical officers retained control of their patients, and that control ultimately produced valuable data.

And yet, despite these achievements, Chickasaw Bayou was a military failure. The assault was repelled and survivors' retreat across the bayou was anything but orderly. In the midst of the confusion, the 13th Illinois broke apart. Blocked from the view of the rest of the battlefield, Bushnell and other members of Company C were unaware of their comrades' retreat until it was too late. Upon realizing their mistake, the remaining members of the 13th Illinois fled the battlefield, dodging Confederate fire until they rejoined their unit, but not before they were mistakenly recorded as killed in action.[71] Others were not so lucky. The retreat had left 332 Union soldiers abandoned across the battlefield.[72]

After the assault, Sherman's men stayed long enough to bury the dead, care for the wounded, and reconnoiter the surrounding areas, searching for another path to Vicksburg. None was feasible. On January 2, what was left of Sherman's army was en route to Milliken's Bend, where Sherman would turn over his command to John A. McClernand. McClernand, who was already frustrated over Grant's taking charge of the Vicksburg expedition in his absence, wasted no time writing to Secretary of War Stanton, outlining the reasons for Sherman's disastrous assault. Not only had Sherman not obtained enough troops, but he was too slow to attack the bluffs. Because of these failures, the Vicksburg garrison was being reinforced in preparation for another assault.[73]

McClernand was not alone in blaming Sherman for Chickasaw Bayou. Word of the Federal defeat spread across the North, spurred by reporters in the field. A correspondent with the *New York Times* declared it "one of the greatest and most disgraceful defeats of the war."[74] The fault, he argued, lay with Sherman, whose "insane ambition" had been to gain "immortality in his attack upon Vicksburg."[75] Such sentiments were echoed in the *Chicago Tribune*, which headlined the "Strange conduct of General Sherman."[76] In the aftermath of his defeat, Sherman became popularly characterized as a tyrant who "suppressed all intelligence ... of his bungling disaster." For readers, proof of his cruelty lay in the carnage: "There are over 1,300 sick and wounded on board of these boats here, the *Von Phul, Louisiana,* and *City of Memphis.* The poor men are suffering for want of proper attendance. The climate is fatal to their wounds. They are in the language of the doctor in a fair way to die, all of them, from hospital gangrene. Yet, they cannot be sent north, General Sherman has ordered it so. Is not this murder?"[77] If the members of the medical corps could point to improvements in their services at Chickasaw Bayou, no one seemed interested.

In the two years since the firing on Fort Sumter, the United States Medical Department had undergone a transformation. Straining under accusations of inefficiency and incompetency, the medical system appeared unable to endure the chaos of battle. Soldiers were abandoned to suffer alone on the battlefield. Others were overlooked amid frenzied evacuations. Surgeons were consistently understaffed and undersupplied. Many struggled to make sense of the mangled bodies brought before them. In light of these failures, the Medical Department drew the ire of both the general population and military commanders, but by the time Sherman launched his assault against Chickasaw Bayou, the Medical Department was making progress. By early summer of 1862, the sanitary commissions' effort to reform soldiers' health care using the latest "teachings of Sanitary Science" was gaining ground, thanks to the newly appointed surgeon general. By embracing reform, Hammond's Medical Department took charge of the effort to improve the efficiency and quality of soldiers' medical care and, in doing so, sought to create opportunities for civilian organizations such as the WSC and USSC to participate in soldier health care without undermining officers' authority over their command. Countless problems remained, but the systematic and methodical process of rescuing, treating, and evacuating patients showed promise. Although the battlefield continued to be a place of disorder where bodies were contorted into unnatural forms, the field hospital emerged as a space of systematic response. And if soldiers failed to appreciate the significance of these changes, their commanding officers would not. The Medical Department's ability to provide timely and effective health care would become invaluable to Grant's campaign.

As 1862 passed into 1863, Vicksburg still stood as a Confederate sentinel, silently watching over the river. Sherman's failure at Chickasaw Bayou marked the second thwarted assault against the town and destroyed all hope for easily breaking the Confederate stronghold. Instead, military operations would require a prolonged presence in the Lower Mississippi River Valley. Popular theories regarding disease suggested such a campaign would not be easy. Exposure to the miasma and climate of the surrounding bayous would prove deadly. Failure to take Vicksburg before spring would result in another campaign threatened by malaria and yellow fever. None of this, of course, was the primary concern of Sherman's troops as they returned to their transports after burying their comrades. What mattered to them was the present, and that present was torturous. On January 1, the *Henry von Phul* pulled off from the banks of the Yazoo River, carrying 370 sick and wounded soldiers to the Overton Hospital in Memphis. Among the staff was assistant surgeon Henry Davisson, who wrote to his wife. "I am quite sick today and feel lonesome. To hear the groans of the wounded is terrible."[78]

2

The Golgotha of America

Henry Clemons had the shits. He wrote his wife in February 1863, informing her of his deteriorating health: "I am alive, but not very well. . . . I have not been very well for five weeks." The diagnosis was simple. "It is the shits and no mistake, but I am getting better."[1] Still, if Clemons survived this ordeal, it would be a miracle. His regiment, the 23rd Wisconsin, had been stationed at Young's Point in eastern Louisiana for less than a month, and in that time nearly everyone had suffered to some extent. In fact, the men of the regiment were so sick that they could barely maintain guard duty. Entire companies were left without commissioned officers fit for the field.[2] One of Clemons's comrades, John Jones, reported that his company had numbered over 100 when it left Camp Randall. "Now we number only 64, privates and all."[3] By the middle of February, the regiment could muster only 250 men.[4] "This is a hard country," Clemons wrote. "There is a great many sick and a great many dieing every day."[5]

And yet, while it was undeniable that the men's health was devastated by the regiment's new post, there was disagreement over the exact cause of soldiers' sickness and what, if anything, the army should do to alleviate their suffering. Clemons was convinced that he and his comrades suffered because of the location of their camp. "We are in a cursed swamp," he complained, "with nothing but the wet ground to sleep on."[6] However, the regiment's surgeon, John Angell, believed that there were other factors to blame such as overcrowding, poor rations, and contaminated drinking water. Most damning of all, however, was the fact that most soldiers were raw recruits who were "not yet inured to the hardships of a soldier's life."[7] Angell's conclusions were echoed by General Sherman, who believed that the vulnerable constitution of new enlistees was enough to undermine the efforts of even the most well-prepared medical department. As a result, he was unconcerned by the growing sick list. "In war we must expect sickness and death," he counseled, but his conscience was clean knowing that "all has been done and will continue to be done which skill, science, and foresight can accomplish."[8]

Because Sherman thought that the growing sick list was reasonable given the circumstances, and because he believed the Medical Department had done everything in its power to alleviate the suffering, there was nothing else to do but stay the course. Clemons, however, interpreted the commanders' inaction as a direct threat to his life. "They can't keep us here much longer," he insisted. "If they do there won't [be] enough of us left to swear by." Clemons eventually got his wish. On March 9 the 23rd Wisconsin was moved twenty miles upstream to Milliken's Bend, but by then, the private had lost all his fervor for soldiering. "I wish I was home with you and the children again and the war . . . and government might all go to the dead together."[9] Henry Clemons died aboard the *City of Louisiana* on April 8, 1863. His cause of death was listed as chronic diarrhea.[10]

Whatever changes the medical reforms of 1862 might have brought to the Medical Department and, by extension, to soldiers' health care, progress was not linear. While the reforms undoubtedly improved the department's ability to harness the necessary resources to care for sick and wounded soldiers, they did not eliminate the factors that threatened soldiers' health to begin with. Furthermore, the reforms did not automatically instill confidence in the army's ability to care for soldiers' bodies, nor did they quell fears that soldiers' lives might be squandered in the quest for a hopeless victory. Despite the Medical Department's best efforts, soldiers still suffered. Of course, suffering was expected. As Sherman pointed out, it is a natural product of war. Tensions rose, however, as Americans struggled to determine what suffering was reasonable and what was gratuitous.

Just like Chickasaw Bayou the previous month, the marshy landscape of eastern Louisiana thwarted Union efforts to capture Confederate-held

Vicksburg. Charged with building a canal that would bypass the city, troops were constantly exposed to rising floodwaters and chilling winter rains. They fell ill by the thousands, and those who retained their health feared for their lives. Indeed, by early spring of 1863, the Army of the Tennessee seemed to have yet another controversy on its hands. Unfortunately, the situation was not easily rectified. The environmental factors that undermined troop health created discord between soldiers, civilians, medical officers, and commanders as each group attempted to assign blame for the army's deterioration. While many identified the climate and weather as prominent factors, others pointed to a lack of resources. To some, soldiers' laziness and inexperience made them complicit in their own sickness, while officers were characterized as heartless and cruel for their refusal to send soldiers upriver.[11]

Ultimately, the central disagreement among those involved with the canal project revolved around the question of necessary suffering. For soldiers and civilians, the growing sick list and alarming death rate was not adequately justified by the strategic value of the completed canal. Commanders, however, believed that the canal was extremely important, particularly if it meant no direct assault against Vicksburg. Less interested in military objectives but nonetheless bound by their orders, medical officers endeavored to eliminate suffering where they could. As a result, the Army of the Tennessee's ordeal in Louisiana reveals the limits of authority within the military camp. Commanding officers set military objectives and issued orders that their subordinates had to follow. Medical officers' perceived inability—or unwillingness—to advocate for troops' health reinforced soldiers' greatest fear: that they were an expendable asset. If given the choice between military strategy and soldiers' well-being, military strategy would always prevail. As soldiers railed against the impossibility of obtaining leave, newspapers questioned the efficacy of General Grant's canal project, and civilians wrote letters to Congress, demanding that someone intervene. Once more, the army's ability to care for sick and wounded soldiers was called into question. This time, however, Union officials would not yield.

If Chickasaw Bayou had proven anything, it was that a direct assault against the Vicksburg bluffs would be too costly in terms of lives and resources. Unfortunately, the same terrain that deterred an overland attack also made Vicksburg's capture essential. From their station high above the waterways, the Vicksburg batteries were a formidable threat against enemy ships. If the Union was to maintain control of the Mississippi River, those guns had to be nullified. Aware that Union morale was sagging, Grant was hesitant to retreat to Memphis and wait for spring. "It was my judgement at the time," he later recalled, "that to make a backward movement . . . would be interpreted . . . as a defeat. . . . There was nothing left to be done but to go *forward to a decisive victory.*"[12] On January 20, 1863, Grant proposed a new plan, one that would ultimately make Vicksburg's capture unnecessary. Grant wanted to return to the canal project first begun the previous summer under the direction of Brig. Gen. Thomas Williams, with some modifications. His new plans called for the canal to cut across De Soto Point and enter the river below the Vicksburg bluffs in order to "give our gunboats a fair chance against any fortification that may be placed to opposed them."[13] This new strategy offered a tactical advantage. By shifting the channel of the Mississippi River, Union boats could travel the distance from Memphis to New Orleans virtually unopposed.

Not everyone was convinced it was a good idea. Privately, Sherman declared the venture a "pure waste of human labor."[14] The canal might offer a strategic advantage, but it would do nothing to eliminate the environmental threat to Union forces in the region. Of course, Civil War soldiers often found themselves in hostile and unforgiving environments. They endured snow and rain, marched in the scorching sun, and suffered through droughts, all while navigating dense forests, marshy swamps, jagged terrain, and turbulent rivers. Sherman's men were no exception. Having spent a month slogging through backswamps, charging hills, and attacking Confederate trenches, the soldiers of the XV Army Corps had endured their share of trials. But to them, the waterlogged landscape of the Lower Mississippi River Valley was more than a logistical challenge. As men who believed that their physical and mental health was influenced by their immediate environment, the region's foul smells, damp air, and muddy water was deadly.[15] What might otherwise be a tactical victory could easily become a medical disaster. Nevertheless, despite his personal opinion of Grant's plan, Sherman followed orders. His men left for Young's Point, Louisiana, on January 18 and were accompanied by soldiers from Maj. Gen. John A. McClernand's XIII Army Corps.[16]

Upon their arrival, the first challenge was to find suitable ground to establish a healthy camp. This was easier said than done, for dry land was limited. The land on the west bank of the Mississippi River resembled the swamps and bayous through which Sherman's men had waded the previous December. The earth was etched in intricate patterns, a consequence of the annual spring floods. As the river rose, it passed along the tightly packed bank, carrying any loose silt or sand to the water's edge. Year after year, these deposits created winding trails of natural levees, ten to fifteen feet in height and extending

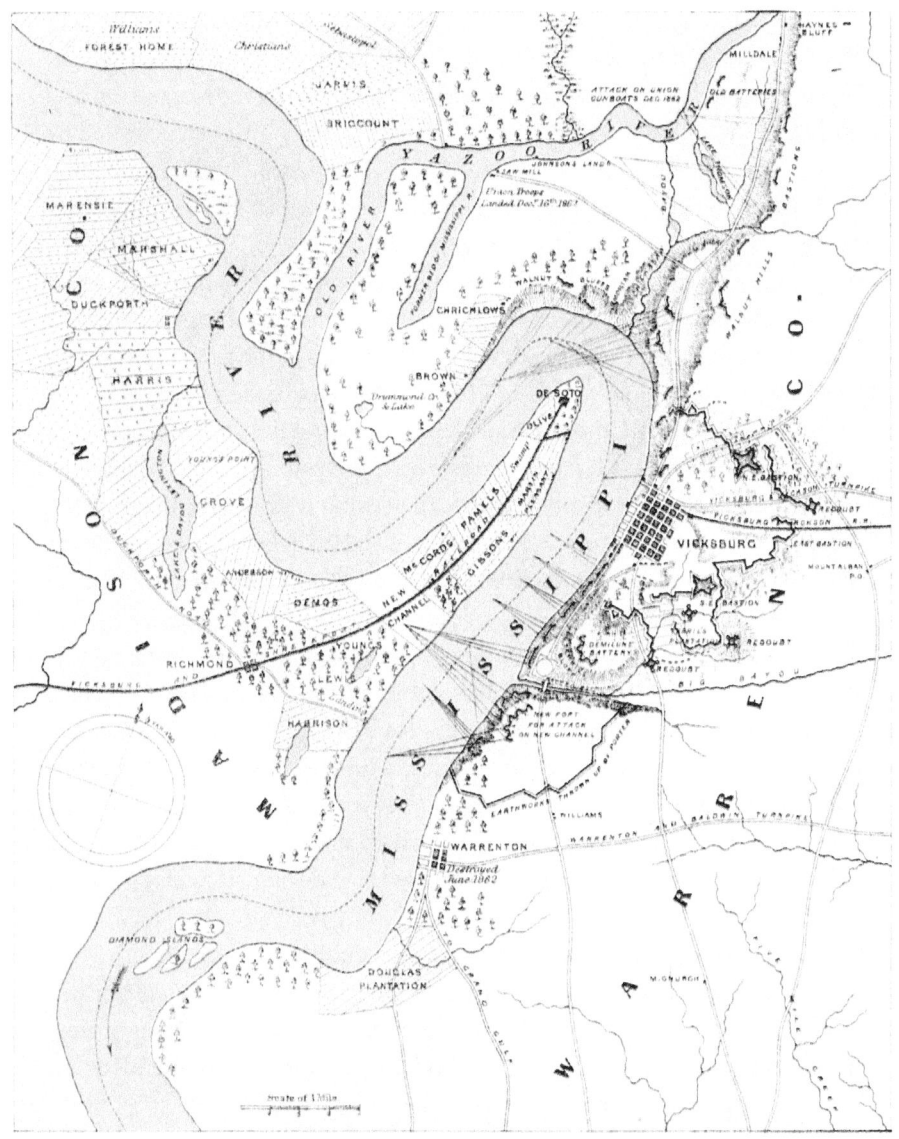

This map shows the proposed channel for Grant's canal, its proximity to Vicksburg, and the railroad bed, as well as local plantations.
Charles Scholl, *Vicksburg and Its Defences* (New York: s.n, 1877).
Library of Congress, Geography and Map Division.

anywhere from 100 yards to several miles in width.[17] This was the only land that stayed dry throughout the year. By 1863, plantations dotted the levee tops, making use of the elaborate network of bayous carved by the river's changing course. It was an impressive scene, these neatly kept houses surrounded by cabins, stables, and outbuildings. Iowa surgeon Seneca Thrall recalled that each plantation gave the impression of a small village but admitted the order of the plantation contrasted sharply with its surroundings. "The flat low country extends back for miles," he wrote, "thickly covered by timber and brush resembling cane brush, looking as miserable and uninviting as any land."[18] For disembarking soldiers, the untamed wilderness of the Louisiana bayous was just as hostile as the Confederate batteries that guarded the river.

By the start of 1863, the Medical Department and the United States Sanitary Commission had set clear guidelines to help soldiers and officers establish and maintain a sanitary camp. According to the literature, healthy camps had dry soil and fresh water. They were also sheltered from the winds and well ventilated. Of the many environmental factors nineteenth-century Americans monitored, air was one of the most important. In general, "good" air was crisp, circulating air. It was odorless, while "bad" air or "miasma" was stagnant and foul.[19] Rotting organic matter, either vegetable or animal in origin, was considered a principal source for bad air.[20] Soldiers and medical officers alike believed that the feral, organic world of the swamps and bayous expelled a dangerous poison that clung to everything from water to skin.[21] This meant that officers should not establish camps near swamps, bayous, or other bodies of stagnant or slow-moving water. Additionally, camps should not be overcrowded, and confined spaces should offer 108 cubic feet of fresh air per soldier. If ventilation did not occur naturally, medical officers were encouraged to cut squares into tents, to open windows, and to introduce flues to facilitate airflow. Finally, because all camps were eventually poisoned by the miasma produced by soldiers' bodies, the USSC recommended that campsites move every thirty days, regardless of soldiers' health.[22]

The problem with these recommendations is that they were often impractical. Military commanders rarely established their camps in locations ideally suited to promote soldiers' health but instead chose locations that were strategically significant for the military objective. Consequently, none of the land around De Soto Point met the conditions for a healthy camp. The winter rains and rising floodwaters put dry land at a premium, making it nearly impossible for soldiers to escape the miasma. Neither was it possible for soldiers to move their camps to a more desirable location, since the logistical value near the De Soto Point canal outweighed the potential health threat. Left with little choice but to adapt, soldiers followed the locals' example. They pitched their tents along the dry mounds of the levees and on the bed of the Vicksburg, Shreveport & Texas Railroad. The men from Sherman's XV Corps occupied the land immediately surrounding the canal. Soldiers in Brig. Gen. David Stuart's Second Division occupied the rise along the edge of the canal, while Brig. Gen. John McArthur's Sixth Division camped at the entrance.[23] Of the three brigades in Brig. Gen. Frederick Steele's First Division, two camped along the levee at the canal's exit, and the third brigade remained in reserve.[24] These arrangements left room for the XIII Corps to occupy the levees running along the Mississippi River from Young's Point to the canal's entrance. To the men of the 48th Ohio, this camp in particular was "dark and gloomy," for it was trapped between the rising waters of the Mississippi River to the north and stagnant swamps located west and south of the railroad line.[25] If given the option, most soldiers would have set their camp somewhere else. By staying where they were, they were putting their lives at risk.

While soldiers settled themselves along the gently sloping gradient of the levees, surgeons struggled to obtain desirable land for their patients. Unfortunately, acceptable accommodations proved difficult to secure. Upon arriving at Young's Point, Thrall attempted to explain to his wife, Mollie, the challenges of his new assignment. He was in the process of moving the sick from the boats to the shore but had "no decent place to put them." One of the hospital tents leaked, and he could find no firm, dry ground on which his patients could lie. He confessed that the entire situation had given him "the blues." Luckily for Thrall, he soon came across an "old negro cabin" that had been "partially destroyed." According to him, it was a "dirty, filthy cabin" and would otherwise hardly meet sanitary guidelines. But it had a roof, a floor, and two large fireplaces. For these features alone, "the sick were *glad* to get in it."[26] Thrall's patients were fortunate. Not all regimental surgeons had access to permanent shelter. Instead, they often had to make do with the drafty, leaking tents.

Although regimental surgeons struggled to acquire proper housing for their sick, surgeons serving at the division or corps level had an easier time of it. Like the complex hospital system that stretched from rural battlefields to urban general hospitals, the XIII and XV Army Corps established a series of facilities to treat a range of patients. While regimental surgeons such as Seneca Thrall were responsible for procuring suitable locations to treat basic complaints, a general hospital would treat soldiers too sick to remain with their regiment, soldiers deemed incurable, or soldiers designated for transfer north. On January 23, McClernand issued orders to establish such a hospital.

Wartime photograph of the hospital the USS *Nashville*.
Library of Congress, Prints and Photographs Division.

The new hospital was placed under the charge of surgeon Edward C. Franklin, who was instructed to request whatever "number of medical officers, attendants, books, and nurses, as may be necessary." Located on Ballard's Farm, the general hospital at Young's Point was divided into several wards, each located in the slave dwellings behind the house. Yet even that area was threatened by rising floodwaters. On March 1, the hospital was broken up and transferred to the USS *Nashville*, a hospital steamer that had been acquired by the Medical Department the previous spring. With all machinery removed from the interior to make more room for patients, the *Nashville* was immobile but, like other hospital ships, made effective use of the region's most dominant geographic feature.[27]

Establishing camp was only the first struggle. In fact, the longer that troops remained in the area, the more conditions seemed to deteriorate. For the next three months, soldiers' lives revolved around three ever-changing features: the river, the rain, and the threat of potential flooding. Men lived in a perpetual state of uncertainty, performing their assignments while prepared for a quick evacuation. Seth Wells nervously watched as the river rose a little each day.

"It is on a level with our camp," he wrote on January 25. The following day he noted that it was still rising.[28] As the water rose, Sherman ordered his men out of its path. Brig. Gen. John Thayer's and General Blair's brigades relocated their camps to Mrs. Lake's Plantation, where Brig. Gen. Charles Hovey's brigade was already established, and Brig. Gen. Hugh Ewing's brigade was pushed to the far edge of a nearby swamp.[29] "We were slowly developing into semi-amphibians," complained one soldier from the 55th Illinois.[30]

Forced to evacuate their camp to escape rising floodwaters, the men of the regiment pitched their tents along the steep slope of a nearby levee. With dry ground already scarce, Grant revoked a previous request for additional troops from Helena but asked that the post send extra transports so that it might be possible to "take on board all the troops, artillery, and public property in case of the rise in the river driving us out."[31] It was a discouraging possibility, for as miserable as the levees were, the boats were even worse. Having previously boarded the tightly packed and improperly ventilated vessels, both soldiers and surgeons worried about the long-term effects on troop health.[32] As Ohio soldier Joseph Thatcher Woods described it, "Our privation on steamers and in cypress swamps had well fitted us as victims to the noxious vapors and miasma of this charnel-house."[33] Now, soldiers despaired at the prospect of having to return.[34]

Weakening levees only worsened the flooding.[35] Within days of the troops' arrival, the manmade embankments began to fail. By January 26, there were at least five crevasses, two upstream from Young's Point and three to the south, between Brown's and Johnson's Plantations and around New Carthage.[36] Wells, visiting the canal shortly after the breech, recorded in his diary, "The boys encamped [at the canal] say the water has risen one foot today. It is now five feet deep and has a rapid current. It averages over twenty feet wide upon the surface."[37] Since it was impossible to labor in a flooded ditch, construction stopped until the levees were repaired. The constant threat of inundation required Grant to divide his labor force between excavating the canal, maintaining roads, and reconstructing levees, but technology helped. On February 19, troops turned to a steam pump to help keep the canal's entrance free of water, and dredging units were brought in to accelerate construction. When a sixth dam collapsed on March 6, a discouraged Grant confessed that the dredging units were the only reason the project continued. Without them, work on the canal would have had to cease pending a three-foot fall in the river.[38]

Given the circumstances, soldiers managed the best they could, but they suffered especially from insufficient shelter. With few trees or buildings to protect against the winds, soldiers' tents regularly collapsed during the region's strong winter storms.[39] Surgeon Henry Strong endured one such occurrence during an exceptionally severe rainstorm in late March. Already feeling poorly, Strong had just turned in for a few hours' rest when water began leaking through his tent "at a rapid rate." "The wind and rain increased until I saw that I must get up or be covered by the downfall of my habitation." While trying to pack his things so that they could be stored safely in the apothecary wagon, a strong gust of wind dismantled the tent, leaving him searching for a dry place to spend the rest of the night. He soon discovered that "most of the tents in camp were flat and the few remaining ones were only kept standing by the efforts of ... sundry men holding on." With no dry place to lie down, Strong spent the rest of the evening huddled in a large overcoat, sitting on a bucket next to a painstakingly kept fire.[40] Thrall had a similar experience when heavy rains caused the ridge pole of his tent to snap in half: "We had to plunge out in the storm to find a rail to prop it up or have our tent down." Upon setting the tent back up, he discovered that the canvas was leaking. Trying vainly to move his cot to a dry spot, Thrall eventually gave up and went to bed. He fell asleep to the patter of rain dripping against the soaked bedding.[41]

Exposure to the elements further weakened the army's health. Perpetually wet, blankets molded and rations rotted.[42] Damp clothing made the winter winds more biting, and these conditions increased the risk of hypothermia. Characterized by slurred speech, clumsiness, drowsiness, and confusion—not to mention the shivers—hypothermia occurs when the body loses heat so rapidly that its core temperature drops below 95°F/35°C. This drop can be the result of radiated heat escaping through unprotected areas of the body's surface. More significantly for Grant's men, the body's temperature also drops when in contact with objects that are significantly colder. This includes water as well as the ground. And then, of course, there is the wind, which sweeps away the warm air clinging to the skin's surface, thereby removing the body's natural barrier against the cold. Healthy bodies, while still vulnerable to hypothermia if given enough time, are more capable of maintaining their core temperature for a longer period. However, bodies that are exhausted or malnourished—an apt description that applies to soldiers laboring day and night to dig a canal in the dead of winter while subsisting off army rations—are more vulnerable to the elements.[43] And all of this—the hypothermia, exhaustion, and limited rations—worked together to suppress soldiers' immune systems.

Soldiers who had managed to stay healthy aboard the transports began to fall ill, and those already sick, worsened. William Wiley spent January 15 aboard a steamer waiting to depart for Young's Point. That night caused lingering health problems that would plague Wiley for months. "The rain and snow blew in on us and wet our blankets and clothing and a great many of us caught terable colds. I could not speak above a whisper for several days and from the effects of the fever and enclosure I became so still and sore that I could hardly walk about and remained in that condition for the next three or four months."[44] Wiley's pain was typical. Seneca Thrall saw a similar pattern among his men. Prior to their arrival at Young's Point, there had not been a death in the 13th Iowa in over four months. After fourteen days at their new location, though, there were already nine soldiers in the hospital, four of which Thrall considered to be "very sick." Indeed, his regiment was as unhealthy as it had ever been.[45]

In the face of such travails, soldiers employed a variety of self-care techniques in an effort to make conditions more tolerable.[46] Several regiments picked up the spade to keep themselves dry. Stationed at Young's Point, within clear range of Confederate artillery, Thomas Barton, a hospital steward with the 4th West Virginia, did not even have a tent. He and the other hospital attendants originally slept outside on the dry levee ground but were forced to modify their arrangement once the rain began. To stay dry, they dug holes into the levees and covered the openings with blankets to form a makeshift shelter.[47] Conversely, the men of the 77th Illinois had tents but were camped in a marshland that flooded with each rainstorm. They spent an entire afternoon devising a way to drain their camp. "We had to dig a deep ditch on each side of our rows of tents and between each tent to drain the water away," recalled Wiley. Then, they used the excess dirt to elevate their lodgings. Once they were convinced that they were above the water line, they set about gathering corn stalks, weeds, and brush, which they slept on to provide an additional barrier against the mud.[48]

Soldiers, however, were more committed to some techniques than to others. Unsurprisingly, they tended to embrace projects that would increase their physical comfort and tried to avoid tasks that were otherwise unpleasant. And they made these decisions without considering the effect on their overall health. But while soldiers routinely privileged comfort over wellness, their commanding and medical officers were often more concerned with behaviors that prolonged soldiers' health. Hygiene was a common source of conflict. Unwashed bodies—and particularly unwashed hands—could easily facilitate the transmission of viruses and bacteria from person to person, increasing the risk of infections such as pneumonia or gastrointestinal ailments such as diarrhea. Additionally, soldiers' tendency to forgo regular bathing and laundry rituals often led to lice infestations or scabies outbreaks, which carried their own risk of infection.[49] As days turned into weeks and weeks turned into months, some officers began to grumble about the camps' deteriorating hygiene. Surgeon Eugene Sanger believed that the lack of personal hygiene severely weakened his men's constitution. He explained: "Men lay down in clothing saturated with effete animal matter and were compelled to breathe constantly the poisonous exhalations of the human body. Reabsorption necessarily followed."[50] While Sanger was worried about the effect of poor hygiene on soldiers' physical health, Capt. Jacob Ritner was worried about the damage to their mental health. He complained to his wife that "most company commanders allow their men to lay round in their tents, in dirt and filth till they nearly rot." Ritner attributed the behavior to laziness and compelled his men to keep clean. As a result, he believed his men had more "snap" and "git-up" than any other company.[51]

Though Ritner believed that laziness was the reason for soldiers' declining personal hygiene, there are other reasons that men might avoid bathing, particularly in the colder months. Typically, swimming in nearby eddies, creeks, and lakes was a favorite pastime that relieved the monotony of camp life and decreased stress.[52] Florison Pitts became so fond of "bathing in the bayou" that by the beginning of May he was swimming almost daily.[53] But the experience was entirely different in January and February. For soldiers who were constantly wet and chilled by the wind, bathing was not a physical or mental reprieve from camp life. It was difficult, unpleasant, and exacerbated the very conditions that already made them miserable. And laundry was just as unappealing. By February, many soldiers had entered what Andrew Sperry referred to as "one of the last stages of poverty": They had only one shirt, and washing meant wearing nothing until it was dry again.[54] When given the choice between being clean and being warm, men chose to be warm.

The growing scarcity of dry land and the dearth of reliable shelters also resulted in strife between commanders and medical officers. Struggling to obtain suitable accommodations for the soldiers under their care, they often disagreed on how to best use the limited resources they had. Should the army designate the most desirable land to preserve the health of well soldiers, or should the land help restore the health of the sick? By the end of January, tensions had come to a head between the commanding officers of the 54th Indiana and nearby medical staff over this very issue. Upon their arrival, soldiers in the Indiana regiment established their camp in a series of huts located along the riverbank. However, with permanent structures at a premium, the medical director insisted that the huts be used to house the sick and requested that the 54th Indiana relocate. The regiment's colonel initially refused, prompting the medical director to appeal to General McClernand to settle the dispute.

This wartime sketch shows canal operations on the west bank of the Mississippi River. Henri Lovie, *The Head of the Canal, Opposite Vicksburg, Miss., Now Being Cut by Order of General Grant*, published in *Frank Leslie's Illustrated Newspaper*, March 28, 1863, 8–9. Library of Congress, Prints and Photographs Division.

McClernand acceded to the medical director's request but insinuated that it was a frivolous demand made by a covetous surgeon.[55] Not wanting to appear under the thumb of the Medical Department, McClernand contended that it was still necessary to occupy the land around the huts. Shortly thereafter, the surgeon submitted another complaint regarding the 54th Indiana's proximity to the hospital, suggesting that the shelters had been tampered with.[56] In retaliation, the regiment's colonel charged the surgeon with insolence, claiming that his men had "voluntarily cared for the sick, who had been brought out and left on the ground uncared for."[57] Although the reasons for the surgeon's objections are unclear, it seems likely that regimental officers were undermining the authority of the medical staff by interfering with their patients' treatments and accommodations.[58]

McClernand was left to mediate the dispute. While his natural sympathies might have been with the colonel, he also had a responsibility to uphold the medical director's authority.[59] "Officers can discharge their own duties without impertinence to others charged with other equally important duties," he wrote, adding that he hoped "patriotism [would] so far animate the feelings of all as to bear with inconvenience."[60] It did not. Five days later, word of the dispute had reached Grant, who ordered the 54th Indiana moved outside of hospital boundaries and a guard stationed near the hospital.[61] For McClernand, who believed that it fell within his authority to handle the dispute himself, Grant's interference was outrageous.

The dispute over the 54th Indiana's camp location is attributable to many factors, and overinflated egos is certainly one of them. But the extent to which the army competed with itself for access to limited resources is also important. Despite the fact that they were committed to uphold the same military objective, commanders and medical officers held different responsibilities within that objective. Commanders were invested in the health and well-being of their subordinates, hoping to reduce suffering where possible and preserve soldiers' bodies for work. Medical officers, by contrast, labored over bodies that were already sick, wounded, or dying. They fought for accommodations that would give their patients an opportunity to heal. Both sets of officers, then, advocated for soldiers' health, knowing that the group driven off of the land was likely to deteriorate. And they were right. The 54th Indiana's relocation held devastating consequences for the unit's health.

After the men were ordered to turn over their huts, B. B. Brashear, medical director of the XIII Army Corps, received several reports regarding the unsatisfactory conditions of the regiment's new camp. Assistant surgeon B. S. Chase of the 16th Ohio inspected the site and found the rumors to be true. The camp was on low ground with improper drainage, causing an abundance of filth and decaying organic matter. However, the condition of the men's bodies was even more alarming. Having gone without bathing or washing their clothes, the soldiers, both sick and well, were "covered with vermin and dirt." Like his colleagues, Chase blamed a combination of inexperience and laziness. He noted that though some of the men were unable to care for their personal hygiene, several were new recruits who simply did not try. Consequently, the regiment's health declined rapidly. Of the 481 soldiers present, 168 were sick in camp and 20 had already died, weakening the regiment by a little less than 40 percent.[62]

All things considered; it is unsurprising that soldiers fell ill in droves. Army camps were like large, hastily constructed cities and subject to similar sanitary and hygienic challenges.[63] Days after the army's initial arrival, the austere and rural lands surrounding the canal struggled to sustain 45,000 lives.[64] Soldiers lived on top of one another, clamoring for space on dry land. There were few permanent shelters and limited means of dealing with human waste, and there was no way to guarantee access to clean drinking water. In the wake of these environmental—and microbial—threats, soldiers' health collapsed. And as the command deteriorated, soldiers, medical officers, and other low-ranking officers quickly found that they had limited authority to cope with the pending crisis. Regrettably, what little authority they did have threw them into conflict as each attempted to leverage his own power to protect soldiers' lives.

The ailments that beset the 54th Indiana typified the diseases that prevailed throughout the Army of the Tennessee. Chase reported that most soldiers suffered from "Typhoid, Pneumonia, Common Continued Fever, and Chronic Diarrhea."[65] The prevalence of these ailments is indicative of the camps' deteriorating sanitation. Common continued fever and pneumonia were inextricably linked with one another. With little understanding of how microorganisms altered the body, nineteenth-century diagnoses were often just descriptions of patients' external symptoms.[66] Fever, for example, was not a disease. It was a symptom. But physicians' inability to understand what caused the symptom resulted in an imprecise classification system for symptomatic fevers based on persistence (remittent fevers fluctuated during a twenty-four-hour cycle, while intermittent fevers disappeared entirely) and occurrence (quotidian fevers appeared every twenty-four hours, while tertian fevers spiked every forty-eight).[67] Thus, a common continued fever would be any ordinary fever that did not fluctuate at all. Since pneumonia rarely presented with fluctuating fevers, it was often reported as "common continued fever" instead of pneumonia. In fact, pneumonia was not part of the classification system used by the Medical Department, and there are no records for diagnosed cases of pneumonia found on the sickness and mortality graphs published in *The Medical and Surgical History of the War of the Rebellion*.[68] Instead, it was classified under several different categories, including common continued fever, bronchitis, and catarrh. Increased diagnoses of these conditions could easily indicate an outbreak of acute respiratory distress syndrome, a condition caused by a buildup of fluid within the lung's air sacs, often the result of pneumonia. Researchers have long established a connection between military camps and acute respiratory distress syndrome outbreaks, particularly during the winter when respiratory infections are exacerbated by the cold, wet weather and overcrowded living conditions.[69]

The presence of typhoid and chronic diarrhea also indicates that camp sanitation was collapsing. Thomas Barton was particularly concerned about typhoid, which he declared to be one of the most prevalent illnesses plaguing the Army of the Tennessee. He explained that the problems arose because soldiers were forced to use "surface water, which was contaminated with human excrement in a partially putrefied condition, thus making the drinking water a fit nidus for the germs of this disease."[70] Barton's assessment was reasonable and fairly accurate. Typhoid victims fall ill after contracting a bacterium called *Salmonella typhi*, which invades their digestive tract causing chills, headaches, stomach pain, a rash, and, most significantly, diarrhea. As the bacteria multiply within the patient's body, some is expelled through loose, watery stools, where the bacteria spread to nearby water sources, clothing, and even skin.[71] Chronic diarrhea when caused by bacterial or parasitic infections such as amebiasis is contracted and spread much the same way.[72]

Certainly, nineteenth-century Americans appreciated the importance of clean drinking water. There were multiple regulations in place to ensure that the water was not contaminated by feces. John Ordronaux's *Hints on Health in Armies*, for example, recommended that regimental sinks be "encircled by bushes, and every evening a portion of the earth dug out of them should be thrown in. A *special privy should be allotted to the dejections coming from hospital patients*; and this should, when much sickness prevails, be daily disinfected."[73] But typhoid and chronic diarrhea had as much to do with soldiers' hygiene as it did their drinking water. In an environment where diarrhea was so prevalent that sick soldiers could not make it to the latrines—or did not even try—maintaining a clean camp was increasingly difficult. A complaint sent to McClernand on February 25 reported that the patients at the Ballard's Farm hospital "constantly and apparently universally, use the top of the ground west of the hospital for evacuation of the bowels."[74] Add to this the soldiers' tendency to avoid bathing and laundry and their general inattention to washing their hands, and the result was potentially ruinous, particularly in light of the fact that some typhoid survivors can become chronic carriers, excreting the bacteria in their stools long after their symptoms have abated.[75]

Be it the result of inadequate hygiene or contaminated water, disease fell upon the Army of the Tennessee like a scourge that, according to Corp. Reuben Scott, turned the entire camp into a "veritable hospital for the sick and dying."[76] Such circumstances not only burdened soldiers' bodies but also weakened their spirits. Soldiers and their officers became alarmed over their comrades' growing melancholy. McClernand wrote to Grant asking whether anything could be done to lessen his men's hardship. "These extraordinary drafts are bearing heavily upon the strengths and spirits of the men. Prevalent sickness and exposure to rain and mud are telling with fearful effect."[77] Charles Willison of the 76th Ohio described his time in Louisiana as "demoralizing, and dispiriting, and pathetic." He especially worried about the new recruits "doubtless aggravated by homesickness; they seemed to succumb so easily and quickly when sickness seized them."[78] Willison was not the only one to draw a connection between soldiers' deteriorating physical health and their failing spirits. For Iowa soldier Alonzo Abernethy, the relationship between the sick body and growing depression represented a vicious cycle: "Sometimes sickness, which was not readily cured, brought first discontent, and then despondency; a conviction that they would not recover without better treatment and better care, followed by the longing for the comforts of home. This too often settled in a despair that greatly lessened the untimely grave. But if some lives were lost by despondency and homesickness, many, many more were saved by 'clear grit.'"[79] It was not a revelation, this connection between the body and the mind. Soldiers were simply acknowledging what medical literature had long recognized—that strong emotions such as anger, fear, and grief played a role in aggravating or even producing sickness.[80] Soldiers, however, were more trenchant when describing their circumstances, drawing parallels between their environment, mental health, and physical well-being.[81]

Keenly aware of their helplessness, the men grew angry and bitter toward the command structure that kept them along the canal. At least part of soldiers' frustration lay in their inability to make the most basic decisions regarding their physical well-being. As conditions deteriorated along the Mississippi River, it became increasingly obvious that soldiers held little autonomy over their own bodies. This was one of the hard-learned lessons of soldiering: the moment they enlisted, soldiers relinquished much of their personal autonomy to the United States Army. The army clothed their bodies, fed their bodies, and trained their bodies. As a result, choices regularly available to civilians were glaringly absent from military life. Soldiers had limited authority to make the most basic decisions about their health.[82]

Most obvious was the soldiers' inability to leave a visibly diseased environment. Although camps were continually relocating to dry ground, the change in location was not enough to affect soldiers' health. To do that, they would need to leave the region, but it was not that simple. James Newton, a sergeant in the 14th Wisconsin, had a difficult time explaining to his mother why his sick brother could not simply return home. "You seem to take it for granted that he could either come home discharged, or on furlough if he only wanted to." Many soldiers looked for an escape but found it nearly impossible to obtain a discharge or furlough. Newton admitted as much to his mother. "I want you to recollect that there never was so hard a time to get out of the service since the war commences as now."[83] Certainly the vast majority of these men were not malingering. They genuinely believed that their deteriorating health prevented them from faithfully executing their duties. The problem was that they could not convince their commanding officers of the same.[84] "There is no doubt but what Edward ought to go home a while to recruit his health," Newton wrote. Indeed, he believed that a number of men in his company should be discharged, but the "head men *will not*" permit it unless the soldier had been wounded or was otherwise "entirely useless."[85] Many soldiers like Newton felt trapped. After willingly enlisting, they could not freely leave.

Because decisions on furloughs or discharges often fell to their commanding officers, some soldiers became resentful of their superiors.[86] Sherman's reputation, for example, suffered dramatically. Many already questioned his generalship after the disastrous attack against Chickasaw Bayou. "[We were] at a loss to account for the curious generalship of the attack," admitted Ohioan Frank Mason, and "suspected that he might be insane. This was not the opinion of enlisted men merely, but of their officers as well."[87] Now, only a month later, Sherman's men were subject to more questionable orders, and the end goal did not seem to warrant the sacrifice. Soldiers complained about Sherman's priorities, arguing that he valued military success over the health and safety of his own men. "He was a great fighter, but very far from being a great soldier. . . . [And] not a safe leader," recalled T. B. Marshall.[88] Their faith in Sherman faltered. Men came to fear that they were little more than an expendable resource. "It is rumored," wrote Samuel Black, "that General Sherman said it was easier to dig a hole for a man than make out furlough papers."[89] Convinced that their officers cared little about their lives, desperate men were willing to sacrifice soldierly honor to ensure their survival. Surgeon Henry Ankeny grew increasingly concerned that his men would attempt to desert.[90]

Medical officers did not necessarily support the army's restrictive furlough policy. Surgeon Thomas Reece declared that it was "necessary for the sake of humanity, and the efficiency of service, that every man laboring under any physical infirmity . . . should be promptly discharged from the service by his commanding officer."[91] Opinions aside, few medical officers had the power to sway military policy, for they, too, were bound to orders regarding the appropriate nature of leaves of absence. A circular issued on February 21, 1863, announced the creation of a board of medical examiners appointed to investigate the resignation of four officers from the 120th Ohio and the "circumstances under which the surgeon's certificate of disability had been given in those several cases and of other resignations of officers in the same regiment upon similar grounds."[92] The investigation was a forceful reminder that, though surgeons had the authority to recommend patients for furlough or discharge, that authority was easily checked. Anyone who issued a suspicious number of certificates of disability was subject to investigation.

In the wake of growing frustration among both soldiers and medical officers, Assistant Surgeon General R. C. Wood attempted to sway Grant into a more lenient position. In a letter dated March 14, Wood reminded Grant that "additional hospital accommodations have been prepared for the sick at St. Louis.... Five hospitals boats are also available near Vicksburg."[93] He urged Grant to use the resources, but Grant remained resolute. When at all possible, his men would remain with him in the field. The canal's success depended on the army's ability to harness—and maintain—manpower in the region, and each furlough, discharge, or evacuation drained the supply of men fit for physical labor. Men sent north were not quickly returning. As a result, Grant insisted that any furlough or leave of absence should be granted only in the most necessary of circumstances and, even then, for no longer than twenty days.[94]

For Grant, the suffering that soldiers endured along the levees was necessary in order to complete the objective and nullify Vicksburg, but his subordinates disagreed. "I'm getting tired of soldiering, as well as the rest of the boys," griped one Wisconsin soldier, "I mean for this reason: What are we fighting for?"[95] Soldiers grew more desperate to leave, convinced that if they stayed, they would join their comrades buried in the mud. Death, after all, did not seem hard to imagine. Even soldiers considered well were not healthy. Iowa soldier Charles Musser told his father that the men already looked "like corpses ... pale and thin from the living [conditions] and confinement."[96]

Perhaps it was the unceremonious way that the living became the dead that made the specter of death all the more disturbing. Upon waking one morning, William Royal Oak observed several cots behind the regimental hospital, each "with a blanket thrown over them, covering the forms of soldiers that had died during the night."[97] Such sights were becoming more common. "These were the worst times the 15th Army Corps ever saw," wrote Joseph Grecian, "for the sickness was general and the soldiers continued to die off by the hundreds."[98] A sense of weariness and hopelessness settled throughout the camp. "Nothing was left us but to look ... into a future, cheerless as the grave to which we were hastening as scurvy, erysipelas, typhoid fever, and pneumonia seemed to stand as ghastly sentinels in every tent," recalled Joseph Woods.[99] During an afternoon walk of three-quarters of a mile down to the canal, Capt. Douglas Ritchie Bushnell counted as many as eight freshly dug graves, waiting patiently to be filled. "Walk upon the levee in either direction at any time," he wrote, "and you will meet burial parties. The interior slope of the levee is almost completely filled with graves."[100] In fact, the levee's surface was dotted with little mounds for miles in either direction. It was as if the entire camp had succumbed to an epidemic.[101]

Caring for the corpses became a routine part of camp life. Empty caskets were sent down the river by the shipload. Oak, standing at the steamboat landing when the *St. Louis* docked one afternoon, recalled that "besides her cargo of supplies for the army, every available place on her was loaded with caskets." "There was a grim suggestiveness about that particular craft," wrote Frank Mason shortly before the clash at Chickasaw Bayou, "but we had seen to[o] many dead men buried without coffins to be much disturbed by that careful provision for the inevitable." The coffins were simple, pine but stained to resemble walnut. They were unloaded at Milliken's Bend from a supplier in St. Louis, and soldiers camped along the levees at Young's Point were regularly detailed to Milliken's Bend with instructions to bring back enough coffins to bury the dead. For some soldiers, the regularity of such a trip undermined its solemnity. On one such trip, Charles Willison recalled that a comrade suggested they load an extra one for a fellow soldier who was sick but not yet dead. Disturbed by the suggestion that they plan a man's burial on the mere assumption that he was going to die, Willison refused. "Gol darn it," replied his comrade, "he'll be dead by the time we get back there." Sure enough, upon their return to Young's Point, the sick man had indeed died, and the convoy had to make another trip to Milliken's Bend.[102]

It all seemed pointless, this digging and waiting and wasting away. On the levees men passed from life into death without a meaningful glance. It was a far cry from how most nineteenth-century Americans thought they would die. Prior to the war, men and women alike anticipated a comfortable passing at an old age, an *ars moriendi*—a "good death." Surrounded by loved ones, they would bestow comforting last words and an assurance of salvation. Then, they would pass into an eternal slumber and be mourned.[103] The war deprived hundreds of thousands of soldiers of an *ars moriendi*. But though a good death remained unattainable, some military deaths were preferable to others. "The men could and were perfectly willing to march and fight even unto death," Willison wrote, "but this helpless waiting and digging ditches and disease and ignoble way of dying were very hard to endure with patience."[104] Death upon the battlefield, away from the comforts of home and the care of loved ones, disrupted important mourning rituals, but it was an honorable sacrifice. There was no honor in dying of dysentery along the bayous of eastern Louisiana. It was even worse when no one was there to mourn. For some men, there was a makeshift funeral, attended by a handful of the deceased's friends. But other interments were attended only by members of the burial detail. Attendants attempted to infuse their comrades' burial with rituals befitting their sacrifice, but these rituals quickly became routine, uniform, and emotionless. "Our dead, as a rule, were buried without religious rite or ceremony," recalled Willison. "The coffin was lowered, and a volley fired over the grave. Then, with drums unmuffled... the burial party, at quick step, returned to quarters." Years later, Willison remained haunted by the sound of the drums and fife playing the regiment's funeral march.[105] Such funerals were a far cry from the green churchyard ceremony so many had anticipated in civilian life. Instead, they merely reaffirmed the loneliness of present circumstances.

Graves of the dead became a constant reminder of the potential fate waiting for everyone. William Wiley, suffering from malaria and rheumatism so painful he could hardly bear to move, could not help but imagine himself in one of those sodden graves: "I shudder at the thought of being buried in such a dreary and forbidding spot."[106] There was no escaping them. The living and the dead existed in close proximity to another, occupying at times the same land. With limited access to dry ground, soldiers resorted to burying their comrades in the levees. "Our cemetery consisted of an old railroad grade and the levee, which were soon filled with the bones of the dead," recalled Samuel Black.[107] This, in turn, was the same ground where regiments relocated after their camps flooded, and adapting the levees to the needs of the living required soldiers to desecrate the graves they had so carefully dug and marked. When the men of the 55th Illinois were forced to move their tents to the slopes of a nearby levee, they had to remove the headboards and to level graves in order to create a thoroughfare for troops and wagons to pass along the ridge.[108] Even without the visual cues of wooden markers and small mounds, it was impossible to ignore the dead. Soldiers could smell them.[109] Ultimately, living among the levees pockmarked with the decaying bones of dead men further added to the camp's bleakness. "The whole atmosphere of the place was gloomy and depressing," wrote Willison, "aggravated ... at night by the piping and creaking and croaking of all sorts of creatures in the woods and swamps."[110]

Taken together, soldiers' letters and diaries along with military reports and medical inspections suggest that conditions around Young's Point and De Soto Point were objectively awful. Nevertheless, soldiers and commanding officers disagreed over whether or not the canal project should continue. Most enlisted men, for example, did not believe that the canal was so valuable that it warranted so many lives. Conversely, many officers were convinced that the project was a military necessity. To them, the Union army's health was vulnerable to the same environmental adversary that protected Vicksburg's guns along the Mississippi River. Defeating their environmental opponent meant completing the canal. The command could do nothing else to improve troop health. As a result, neither Sherman nor Grant believed—or at least they refused to acknowledge—that mounting sickness was the result of reckless neglect.

One problem that commanders could identify was a growing shortage of medical officers in the field. Brashear estimated that the Ninth Division had a third fewer surgeons than the full allowance and that they were unequally distributed throughout the division. For example, the healthiest regiment in the division was the 16th Ohio, which averaged 24 patients per surgeon. Conversely, the 114th Ohio had one surgeon struggling to care for 307 men.[111] The shortage and unequal distribution of medical personnel stemmed from several causes. Some regiments arrived without the proper number of medical staff to care for their men. Many surgeons who did reach Young's Point fell ill themselves. A. A. Johnson, assistant surgeon of the 48th Ohio, was remembered fondly by his comrades. He labored devotedly among his patients until he was "scarcely able to stand and neglected himself while attending to the duties of the hospital." Unable to perform his job, Johnson was left with no choice but to resign.[112]

There was some disagreement over who had the authority to rectify the personnel shortage. McClernand complained that surgeons were being detained elsewhere, thus preventing them from serving in the field.[113] Grant was inclined to agree and asked Maj. Gen. Stephen Hurlbut to detach all the surgeons and assistant surgeons who could be spared from the regiments stationed around Memphis. He also requested that any competent surgeons not needed in the Memphis general hospitals be assigned to field service.[114]

Naturally, Grant and his officers emphasized supporting the army in the field, but his interference with medical personnel was not welcomed by Assistant Surgeon General R. C. Wood. In a sharply worded letter, Wood reminded Grant that he had other options than simply uprooting surgeons from their posts. There were at least four volunteer surgeons who had been assigned to Grant's command but had not left Memphis. One had been there for three weeks. "I am thus particular General that you may have the necessary orders given for their prompt execution, as some of them will tarry." Wood also suggested that Grant could make better use of the Medical Department's resources if he would only evacuate sick soldiers up the river and stop burdening his field staff. Ultimately, Wood acknowledged that whatever Grant decided to do with the sick men was the general's decision to make. Wood could not compel Grant to release the patients upriver. However, surgeons and assistant surgeons fell under the authority of the office of the surgeon general. They were stationed where they were most needed, be that in the field or in the hospital. Wood concluded his letter by reminding Grant that they were fighting the same war and that the orders issued from the surgeon general's office were intended to be helpful, not a hindrance.[115]

By the end of February, the canal project was becoming a public embarrassment. Newspapers quickly spread word of the suffering, reigniting citizens' doubt in the Medical Department's competence and reliability. "Monstrous Medical Abuses!" proclaimed a headline in the *Milwaukee Daily Sentinel*. "There is a great lack of medical stores in the army, whole brigades being without an ounce of quinine." The article went on to describe the prevalence of unfit surgeons, "some drunk, and others becoming hardened and indifferent to suffering."[116] Other papers claimed to reprint soldiers' letters for general readership. They contained "darkly colored descriptions of hardships endured by the soldiers, discouraging accounts of the sanitary conditions of the army, or complaints of its inaction, and even slanderous suggestions of inefficiency or worse in the commander," observed one Illinois soldier. He and his comrades doubted the authenticity of such letters, not because they were inaccurate but because the soldiers questioned the newspapers' source.[117]

The public outcry that surrounded health conditions in the Army of the Tennessee put both Grant's command and the integrity of the Medical Department in jeopardy. Grant asserted that the press had exaggerated the entire situation, while Sherman discounted popular concern as ignorance about the cost of war.[118] "In all armies there must be wide difference of opinion and partial causes of disaffection—*want of pay*—, bad clothing, dismal camps, crowded transports, hospitals rudely formed and all the incidents of war." From Sherman's perspective, the deteriorating health conditions along Young's Point were an unfortunate but expected result of the environmental conditions to which the soldiers were exposed. However, the only way to alleviate those conditions would be to leave the region, and as the army could not leave until Vicksburg was secure, there was nothing more to do. By printing stories about such conditions and attributing them to the "negligence of commanders" instead of to the realities of war, Sherman believed the Northern press not only sowed disillusionment among its readership but also undermined the war effort.[119]

Frustrated soldiers took matters into their own hands, blurring the lines of authority in their attempt to circumvent their officers' obstinate assertions and advocate for the command's health and safety in their stead. Soldiers wrote home about the atrocious conditions and illnesses that killed their comrades. In a letter to a family friend, Thomas Townsend declared that the men of the 23rd Wisconsin were nearly destroyed by their time near Vicksburg. Stationed at Young's Point, their camp was "in a nasty low swamp without our tents and while there it came a drenching rain wetting us very nicely in consequence of which our Regt is nearly half sick."[120] Townsend's comrade John Jones wrote to his parents admitting that there were only about twenty-five men fit for duty in his entire camp.[121]

Alarmed at news of their loved ones' suffering, some citizens endeavored to intervene. Upon receiving letters from his son describing the high mortality, poor sanitation, and drunken surgeons, James Wright of Des Moines, Iowa, wrote to Senator James Harlan, pleading for help. Wright characterized his son's comrades as vulnerable and innocent men held captive by the very people who were supposed to care for them. "From every source we hear complaints of drunken officers and surgeons," he wrote. "Cannot our governors be allowed to take better care of our brave soldiers! We have tried and failed. We have been expelled by Drunken Bloats, with shoulder straps, who should have a ball and chain instead." If the army would not care for its soldiers, other measures should be taken. Wright asked Harlan to consult with the president and secretary of war and "see if we can be allowed to save our beloved sons, brothers, and fathers from the fearful pestilence."[122]

Wright was not the only concerned civilian to appeal to powerful allies. In another instance, a correspondent for the *Cincinnati Daily and Weekly Commercial* wrote to editor Murat Halstead from the front: "There never was a more thoroughly disgusted, disheartened, demoralized army than this, all because it is under such men as Grant and Sherman.... Disease is decimating its ranks, and while hundreds of poor fellows are dying from small-pox and every other conceivable malady, the Medical Department is afflicted with delirium tremens.... How is it that Grant, who was behind at Fort Henry, drunk at Donelson, surprised and whipped at Shiloh, and driven back from Oxford, Miss., is still in command?"[123] Halstead promptly forwarded the missive to Secretary of the Treasury Salmon P. Chase, adding his own question: "Will you wake up one of these days and find we have no Army of the Mississippi?"[124] Twenty years after the war, Halstead's interference still infuriated Sherman:

Mr. Lincoln wanted success, and had more sense than a thousand . . . Halsteds [sic] . . . who from their safe places in the rear knew how to fight battles, and to hold the General's responsible for high water, crowded camps, and the consequent pestilence which we tried to hide from the country, and even from the men—I well remember when the high water of the Mississippi drove us to the Levees which were also the only burial places, when the living and dead lay with but a foot of damp earth between, when Grant and his army demonstrated the largest measure of patience and courage, and perseverance, whilst Halsted in Cincinati [sic] . . . was trying to create panic, mistrust, and failure.[125]

The letters from the front, written by soldiers and battlefield correspondents, stirred the public to action, and politicians attempted to intervene. On February 17, Ohio representative and Peace Democrat George H. Pendleton requested an investigation into the efficiency of Grant's Medical Department.[126] Pendleton would later admit to Wood that he was inspired by letters published in the *Cincinnati Times*, several copies of which had been sent directly to him.[127]

On March 7, Medical Inspector E. P. Vollum received orders to report to Grant's headquarters. He was instructed to investigate the administration and condition of the Medical Department of the Army of the Tennessee as well as the "medical administration in the west."[128] Wood was exasperated by the news. If the reports were accurate, it was because army officials were withholding information. "I have had several interviews with General Grant at Corinth, and more recently at Memphis and heard no complaints. . . . The official reports received by me are satisfactory that the Western Armies are well provided."[129] Nevertheless, he wrote directly to Grant to ascertain the true nature of the situation. "Complaints of a grave character through official and other sources have reached me, respecting the inefficiency of the Medical Staff connected with the Army now operating before Vicksburg. . . . I have the honor to inquire whether these allegations are founded on facts." Once more, Wood recounted all of the resources available to Grant's command and added his own plea. "Any additional suggestions are asked for, and all available means will be provided by the Medical Department to improve the sanitary condition."[130] It was the department's job, after all, to support soldiers' health while in the field. Unfortunately, as Wood undoubtedly realized, if the Medical Department could not make immediate gains to remedy soldiers' health, the Louisiana canals would be yet another blemish against the department's reputation.

Grant, for his part, dismissed the charges of negligence as idle gossip. Instead, he praised the Medical Department's dedication: "Really, our troops are more healthy than could possibly have been expected with all their trials," he asserted.[131] True, there had been a shortage of surgeons, but Grant considered that problem now remedied. In fact, he even claimed that the Medical Department had done everything in its power to ensure the continued health of his troops, declaring that "no army ever went into the field better supplied with Medical Stores or Medical Attendants than is furnished the army now before Vicksburg." If sickness continued to prevail, the problem stemmed from environmental conditions outside of the surgeons' control. Crowded transports, camping on the low ground, and terrible weather were responsible for the illnesses, he argued. By mid-March, Grant claimed that those conditions were steadily improving and, with them, the army's health.[132] And there was truth to that. Records indicate that sickness had peaked by March and was slowly on the decline by the start of April.

Grant's response to Wood's inquiry was measured and diplomatic. He acknowledged irrefutable facts: Sickness did prevail; there was a shortage of surgeons; the environmental conditions were terrible. But he conceded little else. Still, Grant's insight offers perspective. Unlike civilians who were increasingly alarmed over the casualty count and soldiers who despaired at their inability to obtain leave, Grant was not concerned. As a commander and a veteran, Grant was familiar with the demands of war and the burden that it placed on men's bodies. Suffering was necessary for victory. The canals, he believed, warranted the sacrifice.

Unlike the USSC's work that contributed to the reforms adopted by the Medical Department the previous year, the public outcry that resulted from Grant's canal expedition resulted in no discernible change. Ultimately, both Vollum and Wood corroborated Grant's claims. After a careful investigation, Wood concluded that "all the reports of the great prevalence of sickness, want of supplies, and inefficiency of the medical staff were exaggerated and, in many instances, false." He agreed with Grant that "military necessity" required troops to be stationed in an unhealthy location.[133] In other words, the Medical Department had, to the best of its ability, provided the supplies necessary in order to support soldiers' health while in the field. However, the medical corps did not have the capability to override environmental factors that contributed to soldiers' failing health, nor did it have the authority to override military strategy and demand Grant remove his troops to a healthier

Table 2.1. Disease in the Department of the Tennessee, winter 1862–1863

	December 1862	January 1863	February 1863	March 1863	April 1863
Typhoid fever	416	656	666	716	405
Typho-malarial fever	278	409	493	371	358
Intermittent fevers	4,642	4,771	4,566	5,076	4,695
Diarrhea (chronic and acute)	7,370	13,140	9,519	9,437	8,349
Dysentery (chronic and acute)	1,388	1,869	1,782	1,523	1,508
TOTAL	14,094	20,845	17,026	17,123	15,315

Source: United States Surgeon General's Office, Medical and Surgical History, 1:240–54.
Note: The drop in numbers from January to April suggests that Grant's assertions were correct and that health conditions among his troops were improving by April.

location. Vollum and Wood's inspection called into question the very reports declaring that the Army of the Tennessee was rife with sickness and death. There was not nearly as much disease, they claimed, as the public feared. "Newspaper correspondents have placed the mortality [in Grant's army] as high as one hundred a day," reported the *Medical and Surgical Reporter* of Philadelphia. "We are glad to learn, however, that the amount of disease has been overstated. Medical Inspector Vollum, U.S.A., has, by order of the Surgeon-General, gone to examine into the sanitary condition of General Grant's army, and the Western Sanitary Commission is doing much to provide necessaries and comforts for the sick."[134]

Obviously, Vollum and Wood's conclusions contradicted soldiers' accounts, but it is not clear why. Perhaps Grant was right. Perhaps by March things had improved to the point that there was no need to interfere with the general's operations. Vollum and Wood possibly felt that conditions could be managed with additional resources, thus allowing the canal project to continue. After all, the two medical officers had to have recognized the impact a negative inspection might have had on the public's opinion of the war. Morale was already faltering, and an unfavorable report would not only undermine Grant's authority but also call into question the Medical Department's ability to care for sick and wounded soldiers. Since state governments and civilian organizations had already set a precedent for interfering with military affairs at Shiloh, any further interference was to be avoided at all costs. In order to do that, the army and the Medical Department had to work in unison, consolidating the authority each had over soldiers' bodies and restricting information to the public.

Of course, it is also likely that by the time of the inspection, it was already clear that the canal project was a failure. The dam break on March 6 left soldiers scrambling for protection from the rising waters. A few days later, steamboats carried McClernand's men north to Milliken's Bend as Sherman's troops moved to the Young's Point levees. The men of the XIII Corps celebrated their change in location. Those previously depressed by their circumstances began to write with more hope about improving conditions. William Shurtleff of the 23rd Wisconsin noted how "good camp, good water, and kindness of friends at home" were bringing back health and spirits since the regiment had moved. "We are at least out of sight if not beyond the influence of the river of death."[135] All efforts to suppress the canal's flooding failed, and by March 27 the dredging units were targets for Confederate artillerists. Grant finally surrendered: "The canal may be useful in passing boats through at night, to be used below, but nothing further."[136]

Between January 21 and March 31, the Army of the Tennessee encountered few human combatants, and yet the war continued. Just as it had the previous December, the region's terrain and climate created formidable obstacles that undermined Federal strategy. Stranded on the levees to dig a canal, soldiers endured chilling winds, harsh rains, and rising floodwaters. These factors created logistical challenges as both soldiers and medical officers struggled to find dry ground to establish camps and hospitals. But they also created a breeding ground for the unseen organisms that ravaged soldiers' bodies. When combined, these natural elements created a formidable foe that the army could not defeat. Efforts to do so threatened the mental and physical strength of Grant's command. Soldiers became increasingly aware of their newfound vulnerability. They railed against the army that endangered their lives and the commanding officers who did not seem to care. Even the Medical Department seemed like a passive bystander willing to sacrifice soldiers for a military necessity. Whether the health crisis endured by the Army of the Tennessee was avoidable or a product of negligence, it is difficult to say. What is clear, however, is that it reignited public fear that the United States Army and its Medical Department were not reliable guardians of soldiers' health. Consequently, soldiers' efforts to advocate for their own well-being simply revealed what little power they had.

In the coming months, Grant's army would begin the final campaign for Vicksburg. Soldiers would march countless miles, fight several battles, and besiege a city. With each day, the suffering experienced on the Louisiana levees would fade. But just because the army moved does not mean it left nothing behind. Young's Point, like any land on which the army came and fought, bore the physical reminders of troops' presence. Grant's men left behind thousands of their comrades, forever interred among the stagnant swamps and noxious fumes. Their bones filled the levees "like the layers of stones in a work of masonry," remembered Lurton Ingersoll. It was a sacred site, he declared. It was "the Golgotha of America."[137]

3

The Killing March

On March 29, 1863, Maj. Gen. John A. McClernand received orders to transfer his men from Milliken's Bend to New Carthage, Louisiana. In response, McClernand sent a small detachment to scout a route that would best facilitate the army's relocation. The reports were not favorable. "The whole country is a water waste," declared one Iowa soldier.[1] The roads were muddy and narrow, sometimes completely impassable. Portions of the land were still flooding, requiring soldiers to cross by boat. Yet, in a few days those floodwaters would recede and the boats would be rendered useless. Even then, though, the land would not be dry enough for marching. Wary of the original route, McClernand proposed another path that would move the army west of the Mississippi flood zone and establish a base at Perkins' Plantation. According to Grant, this new plan increased the march from twenty-seven to forty miles and required the army to build around 2,000 feet of bridging in order to cross the bayous.[2] Still, he believed that McClernand's route was viable, and on April 20 Grant issued orders to move south.

Although McClernand's proposed route was feasible, not everyone thought it practical. In fact, of all Grant's commanders, McClernand was the only one with confidence in the venture. Sherman certainly had no qualms about expressing his doubts: "60,000 men will thus be on a single road, narrow, crooked, and liable to become a quagmire on the occurrence of a single rain."[3] His prediction ultimately came true. It rained almost constantly throughout the eight-day march, turning the land into a mixture of water, mud, and slush. Soldiers, so eager to leave their flooded camp at the Young's Point canal, quickly realized that their new situation was not an improvement. In fact, the floodplain around New Carthage looked remarkably similar to that around Young's Point. George Crooke of the 21st Iowa remembered that "the rivers and bayous were all very high, the levees in some places were breached, and the whole embankment of the Mississippi was neglected and weak." Because of this, Crooke and his comrades were worried that the levees would fail, and "the whole country should be inundated, and the carefully prepared campaign frustrated or delayed by an enemy more formidable than man."[4] It was an astute observation. Ultimately, the campaign's success would depend on the army's immediate environment. At this point, the Confederates seemed like an afterthought.

In many ways, the XIII Army Corps's expedition through Louisiana was a valuable precursor to the Mississippi operations.[5] While the specific environmental threats transitioned with the seasons and the change in geography, the logistical challenges first encountered in Louisiana remained as the army crossed the river into Mississippi. Commanders were tasked with moving large numbers of men, animals, supplies, and wagons over insufficient and unreliable roads. To accomplish this, they stripped their army to only the essentials. Soldiers would not be consistently supplied with rations from the rear, nor could they rely on reinforcements should they encounter enemy troops. And because wagons were limited by the conditions of the roads, soldiers could bring only what they could carry. They were dependent on the land for the rest. But while the land could contribute to the army's provision, the natural world also created problems. As the spring sun grew more fierce, overheated and exhausted soldiers struggled to negotiate a balance between officers' expectations and their own autonomy.

To be sure, these experiences were not unique to the Army of the Tennessee. Rising temperatures, persistent thirst, and inconsistent rations plagued all Civil War armies to some extent. Military campaigns were exhausting. Men marched for hours on uneven terrain or through thick mud, often in extreme weather. Their daily routine was regulated by their commanding officers, who determined when they ate and how often they rested. And because officers were not primarily concerned with soldiers' comfort, troops were frequently hungry and tired. In light of these circumstances, soldiers employed a number of informal self-care practices that challenged the boundaries of military discipline. For example, they regularly supplemented inadequate rations by foraging. They constructed shelters to protect themselves from the sun or rain. And when pushed to the limit, they straggled.[6] Many of these practices were adopted by soldiers during the Vicksburg Campaign. What is notable, however, is the extent to which commanders sanctioned these strategies in an effort to transform the environment from enemy to ally.

During the canal projects, military authority over soldiers' bodies had remained rigid. Soldiers were permitted to manipulate their immediate surroundings but were otherwise kept on the levees despite worsening conditions. Ailing soldiers remained in camp until their condition worsened enough to justify their removal to the hospital at Milliken's Bend. Even then, commanders were hesitant to send sick soldiers out of the region, preferring instead to keep them with the command. That way, soldiers could return to their regiment as soon as their health permitted.

Having abandoned the barren Louisiana bayous, Union commanders recognized that Mississippi's fields and forests held the potential to sustain life, particularly in light of the coming spring. Consequently, military authority became more flexible, allowing soldiers autonomy to care for themselves. This autonomy did not threaten the authority afforded commanding officers and medical officers because it worked in tandem with the tactical objective. Unable to obtain consistent rations, soldiers were encouraged to procure their food from lush fields and well-stocked smokehouses. Such freedom had a positive impact on soldiers' physical and mental health. The influx of fresh fruits, vegetables, and protein provided important nutrients, not to mention calories, that kept campaigning men on their feet. Soldiers relished the freedom to provide for themselves and embraced an active role in caring for their bodies. In doing so, they created opportunities to indulge in luxuries that were otherwise absent from army life.

This, of course, is not to suggest that the Vicksburg Campaign was not physically demanding or that troops did not suffer. They did. However, soldiers began to draw distinctions between different types of suffering. In doing so, they often interpreted their experiences in relation to their own personal autonomy, opportunities for self-care, and the rigorous expectations placed on them by commanding officers. Thus, they distinguished between honorable sacrifice and superfluous misery and responded accordingly with either endurance or resistance, just as they had done at the canal. The only difference was that in Mississippi, there was no recourse. Limited

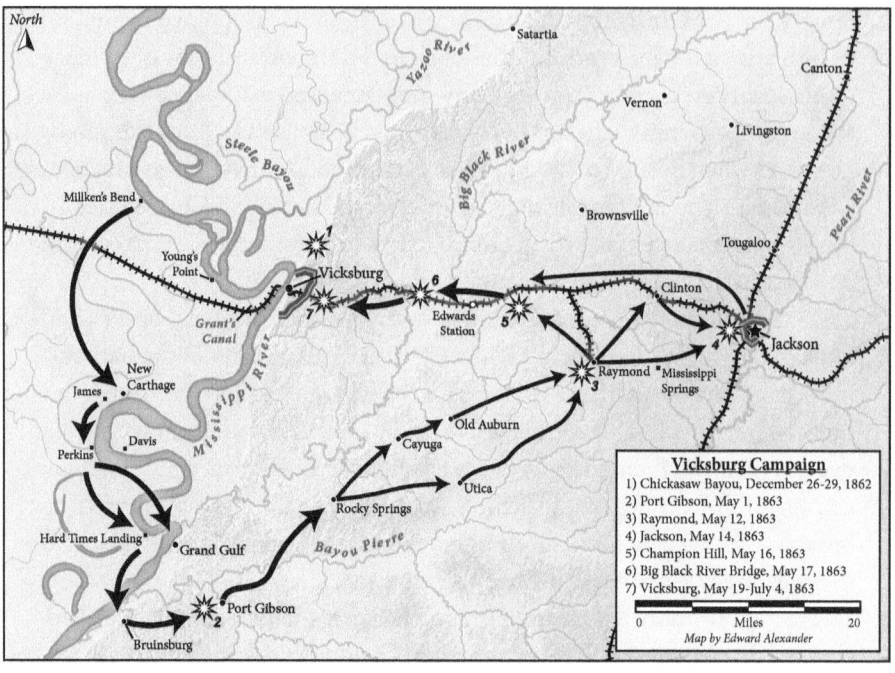

Union military operations against Vicksburg from December 26, 1862, to July 4, 1863.

communication with the outside world meant fewer opportunities for interference from the civilian organizations that had scrutinized the army's health since Shiloh.

In short, isolation dominated Union military operations in April and May of 1863, forcing commanders and medical officers to negotiate a variety of strategies to account for limited transportation, a lack of supplies, and deficient evacuation procedures. As a result, the army's fighting strength was almost entirely dependent on soldiers' self-care and the medical corps's ability to keep men in fighting condition. While the region's isolation, climate, and biota impacted soldiers' bodies in both positive and negative ways, growing autonomy and the ability to define the meaning of their suffering were, in the end, valuable to soldiers' physical and emotional endurance.[7]

It would take the Army of the Tennessee only eight days to make the journey from Milliken's Bend to Perkins' Plantation. In that time, however, the army would be almost entirely separate from supplies and reinforcements. The road's abysmal condition made it almost impossible to supply the army with food and munitions. To account for this, Grant detached his army from its supply base at Milliken's Bend. Soldiers were issued three days' worth of cooked rations and sixty rounds of ammunition prior to their departure. Regimental teams were to carry enough rations and ordnance to complete the trip. The only other accoutrements permitted were a tin cup and a coat or blanket. Everything else, including tents, was left behind with the brigade quartermaster.[8] In the meantime, Rear Adm. David Dixon Porter ran six steamers and twelve barges loaded with rations and equipment past the Vicksburg batteries. Those supplies awaited soldiers' arrival at Perkins' Plantation. Until then, soldiers had to scavenge from the land or do without.[9]

The army's pending isolation produced another problem, however: how to provide for sick and wounded soldiers. This detail, in particular, vexed Grant. "We are necessarily very destitute of all preparations for taking care of wounded men," he confessed to Sherman. "The line from here to Milliken's Bend is a long one for the transportation of supplies and . . . an impossible one for the transportation of wounded men."[10] The army's isolation and threatening environment were only part of the problem. Grant's desire to retain control over sick and convalescing soldiers further complicated matters. Ultimately, Grant needed a medical director with the administrative skills and professional expertise necessary to manage the army's health without compromising Grant's strategy. On March 22, Grant announced that surgeon Madison Mills would replace Henry S. Hewitt as medical director for the Army of the Tennessee.[11]

A regular army surgeon with nearly thirty years of experience, Mills straddled the lines between medical professional and military officer in a way that Hewitt, a volunteer in the service, did not. Though a skilled surgeon and administrator, Hewitt had gained a reputation for being rude and discourteous to his subordinates. Mills, on the other hand, was used to operating within the hierarchy of military command. In the coming months, Grant would grow to admire Mills's administrative skills and professional expertise, noting after the campaign that "Surgeon Mills has filled the position of Medical Director as it has never before been filled in this Department."[12] Grant's regard grew from the complex nature of the campaign itself. Together, Mills and Grant implemented and enforced a policy to ensure that sick and disabled men received the requisite medical care while remaining under the jurisdiction of the Army of the Tennessee. Under Mills's leadership, the medical corps moved to strengthen its efficiency in the weeks prior to the Mississippi invasion by formally adopting Jonathan Letterman's ambulance corps and division hospital system on March 30 and April 8 respectively.[13] Additionally, Grant ordered a series of general hospitals established between Duckport and Milliken's Bend, where "all sick and disabled soldiers will be left."[14]

These orders placed authority within Mills's medical corps to control, maintain, and distribute its own resources. Van Buren Hospital, for example, was established at Marshall's Plantation on March 11. It could accommodate 1,500 patients with the ability to increase to 2,500 if necessary. Furthermore, everything on the plantation—the buildings, cisterns, ovens, cooking utensils, and even shrubbery—was designated for hospital use. Grant's orders specifically prohibited "all persons," including other military personnel, from "removing them, or any portion of them from ... the property."[15] By restricting nonmedical personnel from tampering with or removing hospital resources, Grant's orders reinforced medical officers' place within the military hierarchy. Hence, from the very beginning of the campaign, Grant recognized that the medical corps would provide vital support in executing his strategy.

While the Army of the Tennessee granted surgeons authority over the resources in their hospitals, their authority over soldiers' bodies was not absolute. Military hierarchy was complicated. Medical officers were responsible for patients under their care, but it still fell to commanding officers to ensure that soldiers "earn their pay and do military duty to the extent of their abilities." Sherman was adamant that just "because men are unable to march or because they are under medical treatment, there is no reason why they should not remain in camp and be prepared to handle their muskets when the lives and safety of all require it." For this very reason, each division was permitted to appoint one "disabled" officer to stay behind and command the troops.[16] Keeping convalescent soldiers in Louisiana ensured that men could return to service as soon as their health permitted. This reduced the impact that sickness and minor injuries had on the army's manpower. Once these men were fit for duty, they were employed as guards, protecting the line running between Milliken's Bend and Duckport. They also performed guard duty at nearby hospitals and, along with local Black refugees, furnished all the labor for loading and unloading supply boats.[17]

But leaving convalescent soldiers behind also created problems. It meant that the army had to divide its resources between the soldiers at the hospital and those in the field. This included food, medicine, and personnel. From the very beginning, there were concerns that the hospitals were undersupplied. Hundreds, if not thousands, of soldiers were left behind when the army moved south at the end of April. Charles Foster was detailed to help consolidate one of those convalescent camps. When he arrived, he found "545 invalids in all stages of health" and declared it "hard work to organize a camp of cripples."[18]

Dr. Henry Warriner, an agent with the United States Sanitary Commission, reported that by late May the convalescents "numbered nearly five thousand. About ten per cent are under medical treatment." These men, Warriner worried, were not getting enough food. On May 4 he reported, "There is a universal scarcity of milk and butter here. . . . Eggs would be immensely serviceable." Additionally, he requested that the USSC forward a shipment of concentrated beef, soda crackers, green tea, codfish, crushed sugar, and a variety of dried and canned fruit.[19]

While the hospitals around Milliken's Bend benefited from the tents, blankets, utensils, and other materials abandoned by the army, they were burdened by a shortage of manpower.[20] Ichabod Frisbie, a hospital steward left in charge of a ward at Milliken's Bend, was completely overwhelmed. His frustration was palpable: "You know when the regiment left how they took away everything able for duty leaving only the sick and those unfit to march to take care of them. Our help has been so scarce during the past few days that I have been doing the work of steward, ward master, nurse, cook, &c. And to add to our misfortunates the baker of whom we had been getting our bread was ordered to the rear of Vicksburg and left me with eighteen men to feed without an oven or stove." Frisbie eventually solved this problem with the help of a patient who had been a former cook, noting that "[he] contributed the knowhow and I . . . contributed the strength." Proud of his newfound skill, Frisbie bragged to his wife. "You would have smiled to see me humbling a large lump of bread (unbaked) about our table—I think you women call the process kneeding." In fact, Frisbie was so pleased, he even considered writing a treatise on bread making, if he could find the time.[21]

Overworked hospital staff frequently relied on convalescing patients to do the extra work. Hezekiah Baughman, who had been fighting a case of bilious fever on the same day that his regiment left Milliken's Bend, had been transferred to the hospital ship *Nashville* for treatment. "The doctors at this place seemed very attentive," Baughman wrote. "They gave me some medicine right away." Three days later his fever had broken, and Baughman expressed interest in returning to the front. "I am getting pretty stout again and would be glad if I was with the Regiment." The surgeon would not release him. Baughman tried various ways to sneak away from the hospital, including joining the crew of a nearby ship destined to run the gauntlet. None of them worked. In the end, he was placed in charge of a group of infirm soldiers being treated on the *Nashville*. "[The surgeon] says he has not got well men enough to take care of the sick," Baughman reported. Several days later, he noted that he had "been on duty here 30 hours with little or no relief."[22]

While hospitals established around Milliken's Bend cared for the soldiers who had been left behind, they became inaccessible once the campaign began. Soldiers who were injured or took sick in the field had to stay with the army. Eventually, another hospital was established to care for these soldiers at James' Plantation, an adjacent property just north of Perkins' Plantation. But supplying this location proved even more challenging than Milliken's Bend. On April 24, Grant reported that all the medical supplies intended for the hospital had been placed on the *Tigress*, which was the only ship to sink while running the batteries. Thus, the army was furnished only with the materials that surgeons carried with them, and even that was limited. Anxious that this shortage be rectified, Grant questioned whether more supplies could be easily brought overland.[23]

But Grant's men were more vulnerable than he realized. That same day, McClernand received word from John Holston, the medical director of the XIII Corps, informing him that several surgeons had left their supplies and tents at Milliken's Bend for "want of transportation." Exasperated, Holston declared that "it is of the highest importance in view of probable events . . . that they should have those things always on hand, and as medical men, without their supplies [they] would be comparatively useless." Holston asked McClernand to have all division commanders order medical provisions and tents at once.[24]

In addition to a shortage of supplies, the James' Plantation hospital was subject to a serious administrative error. On April 30, McClernand received a missive from Asst. Adj. Gen. Walter Scates alerting him that there were no surgeons stationed at the hospital to care for the men. There were also no medical supplies on the premises, and "one of the wounded had died and another was still living but allowed to become full of maggots." After a brief investigation, Scates discovered that the surgeon whom McClernand had put in charge of the hospital had "left there without having prepared anything or attending the wounded. He says he was ordered away."[25]

While the debacle among the XIII Corps's medical officers could be attributed to an honest miscommunication or to surgeons' laziness, this was not the first time that McClernand rushed his men to the front without making proper accommodations for his sick and wounded, nor would it be the last. A political general who was keenly interested in furthering his own reputation, McClernand tended to privilege the fame and glory of battle over his more mundane administrative responsibilities such as establishing hospitals and ordering medical supplies. On April 16, an annoyed Grant informed McClernand that "in leaving here you left one thousand men sick and straggling without any provisions either of tents or Medical attendance," adding that "great difficulty has been experienced in providing for them." Nevertheless, McClernand insisted that accommodations had been made. Instead, he charged that the complaint had been made in bad faith. He accused medical director Madison Mills of holding a grudge and declared that the grievance was "made because I had expressed indignation at his refusal to receive the sick of my command until forty-eight hours' notice had been given." McClernand also admitted that the decision to leave his medical dispensary wagons and ambulances behind was deliberate, citing Grant's order that "wagons be prohibited from being brought over ... on boats." Regardless of his rationale, McClernand's inability—or unwillingness—to interpret Grant's orders in a way that distinguished the difference between dispensary wagons and ambulances from wagons used for general transportation was imprudent and reckless.[26]

Scates corrected the problems at James' Plantation as best he could by ordering additional staff to the hospital. He was satisfied that after a hearty reprimand the surgeon would "lose no time in fixing up the place for the reception of the sick and wounded."[27] Then, he instructed surgeon James Hunter to conduct a detailed examination of all sick and wounded soldiers remaining at Perkins' Plantation. Hunter was to mimic the procedure that had occurred at Milliken's Bend a few weeks prior by sending sick and invalid patients to the hospital and returning able-bodied soldiers to their posts. Apart from Hunter and his assistant surgeon, Alexander Whitehall, all other medical staff were to join their regiments in the field.[28] The following day, McClernand's men led the invasion into Mississippi.

It is unlikely that the march from Milliken's Bend to Perkins' Plantation had any lasting effect on troop health. After all, sick and convalescing soldiers were left behind, and those who marched south with McClernand were the healthiest in the army. Though it was a hard march, conducted with limited rations in miserable circumstances, these hardships were temporary inconveniences. The march does, however, demonstrate important differences in how commanding officers approached soldiers' health and the importance they place on medical care as an ancillary service to the campaign. While Grant created close ties with his medical director, ensuring that the medical corps had the resources necessary to support soldiers' recovery and return to the field, McClernand remained relatively unconcerned. Instead, he focused on the coming invasion. The ramifications of these approaches are not particularly pronounced during the brief march to Perkins' Plantation, but the campaign through Mississippi was more than twice as long as that through Louisiana. As a result, soldiers' health was more vulnerable to the conditions created by the local environment as well as to the army's response to those conditions. From Grant's perspective, the campaign's success depended on speed. But that speed put undue pressure on soldiers' bodies. In reality, it was not speed but the delicate balance between strategic demands and soldiers' physical needs that ultimately won the campaign.

Grant's initial plan was for the Army of the Tennessee to cross the Mississippi River at Grand Gulf, but the Confederate position proved too strong for Porter's fleet, and soldiers of the XIII Corps landed at Bruinsburg, about ten miles to the south. By the end of the day on April 30, 22,000 soldiers of the XIII Corps were sitting on the east bank of the Mississippi River.[29] In order to exploit the army's surprise crossing, it was essential to send McClernand's men north along the Rodney Road, where they intended to seize the bridge crossing at Bayou Pierre before it could be destroyed.[30] But there were already problems. The march was delayed by nearly four hours because soldiers had not been issued their customary three days' rations prior to their departure, causing them to arrive in Mississippi tired and hungry.[31] The distribution of rations took place hurriedly and haphazardly. "There was such haste," recalled one soldier, "that many companies were obliged to roll their provisions along as they marched."[32]

At first, the land over which the army moved was low and flat but dry, a pleasant change from the soggy levees of eastern Louisiana. S. C. Jones, a lieutenant with the 22nd Iowa, recalled that "the whole army could be seen for miles, worming its way over the vast flat country with bayonets gleaming in the sunshine.... It was picturesque and beautiful to behold."[33] Soon, the land became broken and jagged, and soldiers grew concerned at the prospect of fighting on hostile ground.[34] They became even more alarmed as the sun began to set. One officer recalled how "everyman was looking into the darkness ahead, with ears alert and nerves strung to the utmost tension.... What was before him in the darkness he knew not:—what pitfall, what ambush, what masked battery, what yawning pit, or engine of death or mutilation." As darkness fell, the army slowed to a crawl, often stopping completely. It was during these moments of quiet that bodies succumbed to the adrenaline and exertion of the past forty-eight hours. The men fell asleep during these interludes, much to the frustration of their commanding officers who, like Isaac Elliot, found that "it was no little trouble to rouse them and move on again."[35]

Shortly after midnight, a patrol of six companies came across a Confederate outpost protecting the Rodney Road at Magnolia Church. A brief skirmish ensued, after which Federal soldiers retreated until daybreak.[36] The Battle of Port Gibson commenced the following morning. If the terrain had challenged soldiers' stamina while marching, it made their battlefield maneuvers almost unmanageable. "The country in this part of Mississippi stands on edge," recalled Grant. "There are no clearings, the sides of the hills are covered with a very heavy growth of timber, and with undergrowth[,] and the ravines are filled with vines and canebrake, almost impenetrable."[37] The land was so broken that soldiers struggled to fall into line.[38] Israel Ritter's regiment made up the right flank. "We . . . went down into a deep ravine and up a steep hill on the other side where our line extended across from the road through the ravines and over the hill." These hills, Ritter found, were nearly impossible to climb. They were so steep that soldiers had to pull themselves along using the cane.[39] Conversely, members of the 43rd Iowa found themselves racing—bayonets fixed—blindly into the canebrake, where Confederates remained concealed. Eventually, they drove the Confederates into an open field, where they were defeated.[40]

For nearly twelve hours, Union troops pressed steadily against the Confederate lines, ultimately forcing a Confederate retreat to Grand Gulf. They did not pursue. Instead, as the sun began to set, Federal soldiers made camp and surrendered to their exhaustion. "I think this was the hardest days work for me that I ever experienced in my life," wrote William Eddington; "when darkness came I felt more dead than alive." McClernand's men had not rested for nearly twenty-four hours. Neither had they eaten. Their supper of hardtack and coffee must have felt like a feast.[41] These hardships, though, only made the victory more satisfying. McClernand, always quick to point out the superiority of his troops, believed that their hardships elevated the soldiers' accomplishment. "Our men were, literally, warriors tripped for the conflict," he reported. "For the first time, so far as I have seen or read, our efforts came up to the highest examples of military energy." And they did it all with no sleep or food, wagons, or ambulances. They had nothing except uncooked rations and ammunition.[42]

After securing a foothold at Port Gibson, Grant wasted no time in establishing his base on the east bank of the Mississippi River. Fortunately, Confederate forces had abandoned their post at Grand Gulf, making it easier to transfer goods and equipment from Hard Times Plantation across the river. On May 4, Charles Dana reported that "one hundred and twenty wagons loaded with Hard Bread, coffee, sugar, and salt" were expected from Milliken's Bend, with another "four hundred thousand rations similarly constituted . . . to run the Vicksburg Batteries."[43] But Grant did not want to wait. Anxious that Confederates would quickly strengthen their hold on Vicksburg, Grant intended to march his men to Jackson and neutralize the state's capital before turning west. In all, the Army of the Tennessee would march nearly 180 miles, and it needed to reach Vicksburg as quickly as possible.

The corps commanders, however, worried that Grant's plan was unrealistic. McClernand warned that "without necessary provisions and ammunition . . . I cannot answer for results," while Sherman saw no other alternative than to stop the campaign and wait for rations. He advised Grant to "act as quickly as possible . . . for this road will be jammed as sure as life if you attempt to supply 50,000 men by one single road."[44] But Grant was determined. Unwilling to halt his advance, even for food, Grant resolved to manage as best he could. "I do not calculate upon the possibility of supplying the army with full rations from Grand Gulf," he wrote to Sherman. "I know it will be impossible without constructing additional roads. What I do expect, however, is to get up what rations of hard bread, coffee, and salt we can, and make the country furnish the balance."[45] It was not that Grant did not care about his army's health. He just anticipated that casualties were a part of any campaign, and when considering the consequences of waiting for rations versus forging ahead, it seemed more dangerous to wait.

The landscape around Port Gibson was an early indicator of how physically demanding the Vicksburg Campaign would be. Rolling hills, dense flora, and oppressive heat overwhelmed soldiers' already weary bodies, driving some to the brink of collapse.[46] Certainly, extreme physical exertion was expected; campaigns were arduous. But in addition to the monotony, demanding pace, and physical exhaustion, Grant's men faced a host of environmental factors peculiar to the season and location of their march.[47] It was the factors unique to the Lower Mississippi River Valley that were so threatening to Union soldiers. In fact, many Confederates believed that the environment would provide a natural defense for the region. After all, Southern physicians had long argued that the South's unique climate, geography, and racial makeup made the region medically distinct from other parts of the country.[48] "The men, coming from a northern climate, endure a heat which even an acclimated person avoids," fretted one Ohioan.[49] They were right to be concerned.

The region's hot, humid summers and stagnant waterways created a breeding ground for *Aedes aegypti* and *Anopheles* mosquitoes, which transmit yellow fever and malaria, respectively. Both diseases were endemic to the South and, coupled with the unruly Southern wilderness, gave the South a reputation for being diseased.[50] Visitors to the Lower Mississippi River Valley, then, were thought to be especially vulnerable to the South's diseased environment.

Indeed, Gen. Robert E. Lee was so convinced that the Deep South's diseased climate would thwart Grant's campaign that he declined to send troops to reinforce the Vicksburg garrison. On May 10, 1863, Lee wrote to Confederate secretary of war James Seddon to explain that reinforcements "could not reach [Pemberton] until the last of this month. If anything is done in that quarter, it will be over by that time, as the climate in June will force the enemy to retire."[51] Instead, Lee proposed an invasion to the north.

Lee had cause for confidence. Disease had played a large role in Adm. David Farragut's failure to take Vicksburg the previous July, and as far as Lee was concerned, there was no indication that Grant's campaign would end any differently. But in the preceding months, Grant had made his own observations about the environment's ability to function as both enemy and ally. Together, the low marshy swamps and high towering bluffs merged to create a landscape that was easily defended but difficult to assault. Similarly, the cold winter rains and rising floodwaters contrasted with hot and humid summers to forge a disease environment that would threaten the life of any soldier who lingered in the region. In short, the contrast between two extremes made the environment a natural defender of the Confederate position. In order to mitigate these two threats, the Union strategy had to strike a balance between the winter floods and summer droughts.[52]

To accommodate both extremes, Grant launched the invasion into Mississippi nearly two months earlier than Farragut's ill-fated bombardment. In all respects, May was the perfect month to conduct a campaign. It was the end of the rainy season, so the roads were mostly dry and easily navigable. It was also before the height of summer, when the sick season began. With any luck, Vicksburg would be in Federal control by the start of June. But that would not be the case if the army stalled at the river, building roads and waiting for supplies.[53] Unwilling to waste time, Grant stripped his army of all but the essentials. In doing so, he took a gamble: that a moderate spring could sustain his men with both nourishment and health. Thus, when the army departed Grand Gulf on May 6, it left behind over 15,000 rations of meat and another 10,000 of hard bread. When rations gave out just days into the campaign, soldiers were instructed to live off the land.[54]

Foraging was a universal experience during the Civil War. Regardless of their location in the East or West or their loyalty to the Union or Confederacy, soldiers regularly supplemented their diet with foods foraged from the countryside.[55] Still, the extent to which foraging was sanctioned by the military command often changed. The Union policy toward Southern civilians was initially conciliatory, meaning that civilian property was technically protected from destruction, confiscation, and forage. While some soldiers still took from the civilians they encountered, their actions ran contrary to official orders. Conciliation, however, proved unsuccessful, and Union policy began to shift by the summer of 1862. Over time, the army began to target property held by civilians directly engaged in helping the Confederate war effort, and by 1864 this strategy was solidified into a "hard war" policy intended to crush Confederate morale.[56] As the Union military policy changed, it legitimized soldiers' foraging. Although soldiers most often used foraging as a self-care technique to supplement dietary deficiencies, their actions had political consequences, especially if their forage was originally Southern property. By moving away from conciliation and toward hard-war tactics, Union policy shifted soldiers' foraging from an act of insubordination to one of obedience.

Grant's decision to have his army live off the land for the duration of the Vicksburg Campaign anticipated the Union army's formal adoption of hard-war strategy a year later, but it also met a practical need.[57] By moving quickly to Jackson and then Vicksburg, Grant hoped to undermine any effort to strengthen the Vicksburg garrison. Still, the decision had plenty of other benefits. While the quantity of forage was not always consistent, the quality was substantially better than most army rations. During the campaign, soldiers' diet consisted of an unusual amount of fresh fruits, vegetables, and meat, which helped to replenish vital nutrients and energy. Furthermore, foraging provided an important escape from the regimentation of army life, which also helped to improve soldiers' health and spirits.[58]

Foraging orders changed soldiers' relationship with their natural environment. No longer were they to simply move among the local flora and fauna; they were expected to thrive upon it. Like their commanding officers, some soldiers doubted that the plan would work. William Bentley thought that the army had simply traded one undesirable landscape for another. "We were now operating in a rough and rugged country," he wrote, "[having] left the low, flat and swamp lands of Louisiana far behind us."[59] But as the army marched east, away from the river, the terrain began to shift. The jagged river bluffs fell away, replaced with gently rolling hills that traced a route from Port Gibson to Raymond and beyond to Jackson. The bulk of the inland campaign would take place within this geographic region of Mississippi known as the Pine Hills.[60] Many soldiers, enamored with the change of scenery, pushed the bayous from their minds as they looked around with appreciative eyes. "You don't know what beautiful flower gardens there are here," enthused Charles Dana. "I never saw such roses; and the other day I found a lily as big as a tiger lily, only it was magnificent red."[61] Touched by the bountiful hand of spring, this land seemed more than capable of supplying the army's needs.

At least part of this discrepancy resulted from soldiers' evolving perceptions of the land. While there were still elements of the untamed wilderness, soldiers began to identify familiar characteristics of a tamed and cultivated landscape. "The plantation mansions are grand, and the grounds and outbuildings are fitting up in fine style," wrote Seth Wells, noting that "each plantation has a splendid steam gin, and some have steam cane-mills as well." Wells found these mills particularly impressive because of the wealth they represented. He estimated that they "must have cost between ten and twenty, possibly thirty, thousand dollars."[62] These structures, in all their grandeur, proved that the land could provide. Consequently, soldiers gravitated toward these farmsteads and plantation homes when searching for forage. Just a few months prior, locals had planted their fields and gardens, much of which was ripening by early May. Sherman was pleased. "The planters never dreamed of our coming," he wrote home. "They had planted vast fields of corn and vegetables."[63] Wells estimated that the corn was "nearly two feet in height."[64] Sometimes soldiers took the food right off the table, as was the case for John Myers, whose regiment surprised a local family: "I told them they neat not be scart for we was only yankey soldiers and never nowen to harm laides but was hungry and wanted some thing to eat. [W]e took posesion of the table and eat a harty dinner."[65] In other instances, soldiers gathered corn and hauled it to nearby plantations where they used horse-mills to make meal for corn bread.[66]

Meat was also plentiful, a fact that dismayed Sherman. "I tell you, tis all nonsense about the South being exhausted," he confessed to his brother, adding that "we saw everywhere cattle, hogs, sheep, [and] poultry."[67] Sometimes the army seized whole herds for easy distribution. While camped at Rocky Springs, T. B. Marshall heard that his brigade had captured a flock of sheep. "We were told, if we wanted one, to go and get it. I think it was John Beard went with me, and we made one into mutton in very short order."[68] Even if soldiers failed to find livestock to slaughter, they had their pick of all the smoked meats they could imagine. "Every southerner regards his home incomplete without a large and well filled smoke-house," wrote Charles Johnson, who declared that "the southerner has no equal" when it came to preparing and curing ham. Even empty smokehouses did not concern him, for there was usually a supply of meat hidden nearby. "Often the meat was buried or put in some retired spot in the woods, but through a darky or some such means its hiding-place was in nearly all instances sought out by the persistent Northerners."[69] Hungry men would always find their food.

Foraging orders were not a perfect solution to the army's supply problems, nor were they intended to be. They required soldiers to invest more effort to procure food, made men more vulnerable to shortages, and sometimes required creative substitutions. While foodstuff was initially abundant, the army's presence strained local resources. Shortages developed. As the campaign progressed, foraging parties had to travel farther and farther away from the army's designated path in an effort to find food. According to one Ohio soldier, these parties, commonly known as bummers, rarely wore their uniforms. Instead, they dressed "in such clothes as suited their fancy—the Union blue, the rebel gray and butternut, with a considerable number in citizens' attire"—in order to travel beyond the lines to procure their food.[70] Other soldiers made substitutions when possible. When their coffee ran short, soldiers in the 83rd Ohio collected sassafras to make a substitute. T. B. Marshall thought the drink disgusting but "considered it as one of the things to endure and said nothing."[71] Many soldiers considered such hardships as little more than an inconvenience.

After spending the winter digging a failed canal, many soldiers were willing to suffer hunger pangs as a noble sacrifice for the sake of the Union. After all, they felt like soldiers again. But even so, the hope of the next forage bolstered their endurance. William Eddington often acknowledged how food helped to "prolong [his] existence." "We had gotten no rations and were getting pretty close on the end of endurance, but I got a handful of blackberries," he rejoiced. On other occasions he wrote about eating the bark from slippery elm trees and stealing corn from the army horses.[72] By the end of the campaign, the promise of good food drove soldiers' success on the battlefield. Ephraim Blake never forgot the celebration that took place after receiving word that Jackson, the state's capital, had been captured by Sherman's men. "No one not with us in that memorable campaign could ever appreciate what such cheering reports meant to us.... It meant good hard-tack and juicy sow belly to hungry stomachs now receiving but an occasional nubbin of green corn, or dry parched corn and a few green peaches as a daily allowance." To Blake and his comrades, the food captured at Vicksburg was only about temporarily alleviating their hunger pains. It also promised "success to our arms in the next battle, and Vicksburg's investment."[73] In this way, full bellies were bound up with soldiers' duty.

Access to local farmsteads offered an important respite from the hardships of campaigning. Of course, plenty of Federal troops used Confederate property to unleash their frustrations, as well. Trapped in the field, isolated from loved ones, and without fresh clothes, water, or food, soldiers often struggled with a sense of powerlessness. The ability to confiscate or destroy Confederate property proved cathartic. After John Myers and his comrades feasted at the table of Confederate sympathizers, they ambled about the house taking whatever else they pleased. If Myers's conscience bothered him, he did not admit it. Instead, he gleefully reflected on how they had "left the ladies to reflect over the lost dinner and the aprotch of the yankee soldiers."[74] William Bentley believed that soldiers' wrath was understandable, a natural result of the army's dwindling food supply: "An advancing and victorious army is not very conscientious, and it is but reasonable to suppose that some depredations were committed, especially as we were on short rations."[75]

While Union soldiers often did interact with Confederate property in violent or destructive ways, many simply saw Southern homes as yet another resource to provide for their comfort and prolong their endurance.[76] That, after all, was the purpose of foraging. As a self-care strategy, soldiers foraged to sustain their health and nourish their bodies. But forage was not restricted to food. They also foraged for comfort. When the 13th Illinois discovered a plantation owned by a local doctor, they spent the afternoon indulging in luxuries far removed from army life. "A grand piano, in one of the front parlors . . . gave forth more patriotic strains than had been evolved therefrom for some years; and dance music rippled from under the ivory keys for those who desired to trip 'the light fantastic toe,'" recalled Asa Munn. For his part, Munn spent the evening "reclined on a richly upholstered sofa-lounge, on the front gallery of the house, [where he] absorbed more luxury in one night . . . that he ever knew before or since."[77] Likewise, John Jackson Kellogg was elated when he found quarters in a deserted homestead. Not only did they get supper and fresh coffee, but they also "slept on a bedstead." It was a simple act but a luxury that satisfied Kellogg's desire for refinement.[78]

During the campaign, sleep and shelter were readily sacrificed in favor of a rapid march. Because soldiers did not have the stamina to carry extra supplies and the wagons were strictly for transporting ammunition and medicine, soldiers never reclaimed their baggage once they arrived at Port Gibson. "If we ever see it again it will be a mystery," despaired surgeon Henry Strong. And Strong was fortunate. He traveled with two blankets attached to his saddle. Even so, he admitted that "I shiver some and sleep some. The nights are quite cold."[79] While blankets and overcoats would have been a welcome protection against the cold, soldiers especially missed their tents. On clear days it did not matter so much. When it rained, however, men struggled to find a place to keep them dry. Some crawled under houses and other raised structures, while other ripped boards and siding off nearby buildings.[80] After one particularly brutal day marching through the rain, William Eddington and three of his comrades were determined to have a good night's rest. They raided a warehouse where cotton bales were stored and cut them in half, and each took one for his bed. "It was no use to sleep in the mud, even if cotton was one dollar per pound," Eddington insisted. They next morning, he and his comrades rose "feeling fresh and find [sic] and of course we thought that this feeling was caused by sleeping in such a high-priced bed."[81] No doubt, the memory of Eddington's good night's sleep sustained him in body and spirit for the next several days.

While soldiers relished the opportunity to indulge in small luxuries, extend their comfort, and improve their sleep, these occasions were the exception. In more cases, the opportunity for restorative rest was limited, and its absence threatened soldiers' health even as the land promised to nourish their bodies. This was readily acknowledged by contemporary physicians. Writing in 1863, Dr. John Ordronaux declared that sleep was "such an imperative necessity with the young that to rob them of it is to strike the most cruel blow at their physical vigor." Indeed, he believed that it had a more devastating effect on soldiers' health than hunger or long marches. Without sleep, soldiers became more vulnerable to colds, fevers, and gastrointestinal ailments. These conditions, Ordronaux explained, "debilitated" the troops and made them "unfitted for the successful performance of their duties in the field." But Ordronaux was not only worried about how much soldiers slept. He was also worried about where they slept. Like most of the enlisted men, Ordronaux feared that the troops' immediate environment was too wet, too cold, and filled with dangerous miasma. He and Surgeon General William Alexander Hammond both warned against sleeping on damp ground, given the risk of absorbing decaying organic matter through skin and clothes. Hammond was especially anxious that the men not sleep in their shoes, stockings, and "outer clothing except when absolutely impracticable."[82] The thing was, such orders always seemed impracticable, especially during a fast-moving campaign.

While soldiers' sleep habits weakened their immune system and made them vulnerable to a number of physical ailments, there were other physiological and psychological effects that contemporary physicians did not highlight. While minimum sleep requirements vary according to the individual, loss of sleep can contribute to a growing "sleep debt" that might take days to recover. Unfortunately, most Civil War soldiers were rarely granted the opportunity for such restorative rest. As a result, many of the physical, mental, and emotional struggles that soldiers endured as a result of combat fatigue were likely exacerbated from lack of sleep, including symptoms like tunnel vision, impaired hearing, indecisiveness, mood changes, and lack of motivation or energy.[83] And when they did sleep, soldiers often fell into fitful slumber where dreams reigned and sometimes morphed into nightmares. Many years after the war, Frederick Grant, Ulysses S. Grant's eldest son, recalled the sleepless night he spent after the battle at Port Gibson. Having gone to the field without his father's permission, the young Grant was unfortunate enough to have all "the horrors of a battlefield ... brought vividly before me." He spent time with a burial party and later wandered through a field hospital, giving up both posts when the sights and sounds became too much. He was quickly rescued by an orderly who collected him and made him a place to sleep for the night. "This I did," Grant wrote, "but my sleep was broken by dreams of the horrors I had witnessed."[84]

Like any other campaign, the Army of the Tennessee's march through Mississippi was strenuous, and General Grant's decision to privilege speed over supply lines only added to the strain. Footsore soldiers suffered from sleep deprivation and hunger. But increased access to the land and its resources helped to mitigate at least some of the burden. For soldiers, the ability to forage for both nourishment and comfort contributed to a sense of freedom and gave them the autonomy to manage the stress produced by hunger and sleeplessness. Even when the forage was meager or the opportunities few, soldiers indulged in small comforts: a handful of fresh blackberries, a longing gaze upon a colorful rose, a dry place to sleep. Through these luxuries, they nurtured a sense of cheerful, willing sacrifice, which became essential to maintaining their physical and emotional endurance.[85] In this way, they transformed the environment into an ally.

Although the Union army's foraging policy made effective use of the spring bounty, there were other ways in which the environment threatened Federal success. The sickness that Lee anticipated to rack Grant's army never took hold, but as May progressed, temperatures soared. By May 14, Sherman's and Maj. Gen. McPherson's troops had effectively pushed the remnants of the Confederate army from Jackson, and the Army of the Tennessee shifted course to the West. As Union forces converged on Vicksburg, they fell victim to an oppressive heat that threatened to upend the equilibrium necessary for troop health. Soldiers suffered from exertion, sunstroke, and dehydration. And unlike hunger or fatigue, which seemed necessary to the campaign, this suffering did not seem noble or warranted.[86]

For the soldiers who had served at Young's Point, the climbing temperatures were initially a welcome reprieve. It was an invigorating promise that the previous trials were behind them and that winter was fading into spring. And for William Wiley, an Illinois soldier, who spent the miserable winter exposed to cold snow and freezing mud, spring brought hope. "The weather [is] becoming warm and pleasant and [I'm] having a better chance to take care of myself," he wrote on April 16. Unfortunately, Wiley's hope was short-lived. One month later, as his regiment arrived at Champion Hill, the weather had become too warm, and Wiley admitted that he and his comrades were "badly exhausted and suffered for want of water."[87]

Whether Union or Confederate, soldiers in Mississippi were held captive by the heat. It dominated every aspect of their lives. Men wrote about it constantly, noting how it "boiled," "scorched," and "raged," as if searching for the perfect word to describe what they felt.[88] As the heat grew worse, soldiers became more vulnerable to illness. Such was the case for the men in Brig. Gen. Nathan Kimball's Provisional Division, which advanced from Satartia, Mississippi, to Snyder's Mill, just ten miles north of Vicksburg, at the start of June. There were few opportunities to rest, and surgeon James Whitehill, Kimball's medical director, noticed that his men struggled in the extreme heat, with a large number falling out of line and lying by the road. "I immediately told [the general] of this and said to him if he continued the march under the circumstances, we would [lose] five hundred men from sunstroke to which he replied, it would be better to lose five hundred from the heat, than fifteen hundred from a fruitless fight." Kimball informed Whitehill that they could not risk slowing their pace—they were needed in Vicksburg to reinforce Grant's army—and that "I should do the best I could." In response, Whitehill made arrangements for an ambulance to follow each regiment to pick up "the men as they fell out." Several hours later, Whitehill received another dispatch from a brigade surgeon in the division's rear, informing him that "the men were falling rapidly and he was at a loss to know what to do." Eventually the situation rectified itself. Overheated soldiers rode in the ambulance until they had regained their strength, and by the end of the day they were "all up"—all, that is, except for Whitehill. "I was so overcome with the heat, and suffered to such extent from a violent headache, was so exhausted they had to lift me from my horse," he wrote. The next morning, he arose "weak and feeble" but resumed his duties until the division reached its destination. At that time, "I was taken from my horse in a semiconscious condition and remained so for several days."[89]

The suffering endured by Kimball's division highlights the two most common ailments that plagued soldiers during the Vicksburg Campaign: dehydration and heat exhaustion. Physiologically, dehydration and heat exhaustion are two separate ailments arising from two separate complaints. Dehydration occurs when the body has lost so much fluid that it struggles to maintain normal function. As fluid leeches from the blood, red blood cells shrink to become more concentrated. Blood pressure drops as the amount of oxygen in the bloodstream decreases. Organs, notably the brain, begin to swell. Those in early stages of dehydration report severe headaches, parched mouths, and swollen tongues. If left unresolved, symptoms progress to muscle fatigue, dizziness, and possible seizures.[90] While dehydration is certainly caused by heat, other factors including humidity, distance between water sources, excessive sweating or bleeding, vomiting or diarrhea, and physical exhaustion can also deplete the body's fluids. And while any one of these factors might challenge individuals' health and undermine their endurance, soldiers usually suffered from a combination.

Heat exhaustion, by contrast, results from the body's inability to control its own temperature. As the body's internal temperature begins to rise, cramps, headaches, dizziness, and nausea occur. If left unchecked, victims could succumb to heatstroke, which at the time was more commonly referred to as sunstroke. This leads to organ failure, loss of consciousness, and eventually death. Of course, while different, dehydration, heat exhaustion, and sunstroke were closely related to one another, with one condition often leading to the others.

Both medical officers and their patients recognized that the heat posed a growing danger, not only to soldiers' bodies but to the entire campaign. However, they had a limited understanding of how exactly it weakened the body. Mid-nineteenth-century medical theory was largely dominated by the drive to maintain a balanced body. The emphasis on balance was originally rooted in the concept of the four humors. This was the belief that the human body consisted of four elements—blood, phlegm, black bile, and yellow bile—and that healthfulness meant a perfect balance among all four. While humoral theory had faded out of practice by the 1860s, the correlation between sickness and an imbalanced body remained.[91] Most Americans held that the internal balance of the body was intimately tied to the external balance of the natural world. As a result, Americans closely monitored both their bodies and their surroundings for dangerous disparities so that they could make corrections. Unfortunately, such adjustments, however small, were far more challenging when faced with the rigors and demands of army discipline.

Ultimately the problem, just as it had been the previous winter, was excess. Instead of striking the ideal balance between cold and hot in which the body might remain healthy, the temperature swung from one extreme to the other. Grant's men were painfully aware that they were surrounded by an imbalanced environment and, if left uncorrected, this would have disastrous consequences on their health.[92] Anxious men carefully monitored their bodies and those of their friends for signs of heat-related illnesses. After a long march, Minnesota private Isaac Vanderwarker fretted about intense cramping in his feet and legs, while surgeon Robert Jameson feared that his pounding headache was the result of something more sinister. Both were relieved when their symptoms subsided and they were able to resume their normal duties.[93] Not everyone was so fortunate. After Philip Roesch's regiment landed at Haynes Bluff, several of his comrades suffered sunstroke and died on the march to Vicksburg. In fact, the march was so grueling that even the colonel's horse died from the heat.[94] "The rest of us got through but were so overheated that it made many of us sick." Upon reaching their destination, the men of Roesch's regiment had the opportunity to rest. But it still must have weighed heavily on the survivors' minds that they endured while their comrades had perished. After all, it was impossible to identify the distinguishing factor between those who lived and those who died.

While soldiers monitored their bodies for signs of imbalance, surgeons made their own observations. Considering how easily campaigning soldiers might overheat, John Ordronaux noted that "the excess of heat at the surface generated by prolonged exercise, finds no ready means of escape through [soldiers'] thick clothing. The weight of the knapsack and the constriction of the chest caused by its cross-belt, greatly impeded the function of respiration, and give rise to acute disorder of its organs."[95] Ordronaux was not wrong. Soldiers' uniforms hindered the body's ability to regulate its temperature. Though soldiers might sweat, and sweat heavily, the mixture of cotton and wool made it difficult for perspiration to evaporate.

Surgeons and commanders employed a number of strategies to counter the excess heat building in soldiers' bodies. Ordronaux recommended that marching soldiers be allowed to unbutton their coats and turn down their collars and that the space between ranks be widened to twice the usual distance to facilitate airflow.[96] To help mitigate the growing threat at Vicksburg, Sherman ordered his men to march in the mornings and evenings but rest in the afternoons.[97] "The weather is becoming hot here, and soon marching will be attended with the risk of sunstroke and fever," he wrote in April, acknowledging that "the enemy counts on our exhausting ourselves without their taking the trouble to shoot us."[98] Sherman's orders recognized that the heat remained an important component of the Confederate defense, but it was an enemy to overcome just like any other.

Still, it was far easier to prevent soldiers from overheating than it was to cool their bodies after they reached the point of heat exhaustion. Just as too much heat was bad for the body, so it was with too much cold. Medical officers in particular worried that soldiers' bodies would cool too much or too quickly and upset the balance in the other direction.[99] And because of this, water became a fiercely contested resource. Civil War canteens held about three pints of water, and Ordronaux recommended that this amount suffice for an entire day's worth of marching.[100] He worried that, in an effort to quench their thirst and cool their bodies, soldiers would make matters worse. In reality, Ordronaux's recommendations meant that, even on their best days, soldiers were likely not procuring or consuming enough water to replenish the fluids lost while marching.[101]

Nevertheless, medical officers lamented soldiers' lack of self-control to deny their thirst and limit their water intake. "Experience teaches the old soldiers that the less he drinks when on the march, the better," wrote Surgeon General William Hammond. "He suffers less in the end by controlling the desire to drink, however urgent."[102] To do otherwise not only demonstrated an individual's lack of discipline but also endangered his life. Hammond hoped that by learning to control their thirst, soldiers might become more discerning about the quality of water they consumed and its effect on the body.[103] Hammond's advice fell on deaf ears, however, and this became a point of frustration within the Medical Department. "The men fill their canteens before moving in the morning; which is all right as the water at the camp is generally good, but before they had made one fourth of the day's march it is all consumed," surgeon Charles Tripler complained. Then, "at every stream [soldiers] meet with, or pool of water, they will, if unrestrained, break their rank, rush to the water, fill their stomachs, and refill their canteens."[104] Because of soldiers' refusal to deny their thirst, surgeons perceived their patients as impulsive and careless, unable to make the sacrifices necessary to preserve their health. Soldiers, by contrast, found themselves bound by expectations that they continue in their misery even when comfort was easily obtained.

Just like at the canals, soldiers, commanders, and medical officers disagreed over the necessity of soldiers' suffering and the extent to which their bodies might be pushed in order to achieve a military objective. By encouraging soldiers to open their coats, loosen ranks, and rest during the day, officers and surgeons attempted to mitigate the worst effects of the heat, but they could not eliminate it. Treating victims of heat exhaustion, dehydration, and sunstroke requires taking intentional steps to reduce the body's internal temperature, and that meant rest, shade, and plenty of water—three luxuries that surgeons could rarely prescribe.

While foraging orders created flexibility leading to greater autonomy in soldiers' ability to acquire food and shelter, their freedom was not universal. It did not, for example, extend to their ability to fall back, take rest, or ride in a wagon unless explicitly permitted to do so. For his part, Sherman was adamant that while "thirst and fatigue are to be expected … the safety and success of all will make all good soldiers bear cheerfully the deprivation of rest and water."[105] It was wishful thinking. Soldiers were rarely cheerful about their thirst and seldom pushed their bodies to the extremes that their commanding officers expected. Instead, they employed straggling as a strategy to manage the heat's most deleterious effects.[106]

Sometimes soldiers used straggling to forge a compromise between military orders and their physical needs.[107] There were several wagons with Kimball's division on its march from Satartia, but they were either ambulances or dispensary carts. That meant that, while transportation was available, it was under the restriction of the Medical Department and reserved for medical purposes only. At first, commanders and surgeons were lenient with these permissions, allowing weary and fatigued soldiers to ride in any available wagon, but this practice quickly became impractical.[108] Eventually, men claiming disability had to be examined in order to receive permission to ride in a wagon. This meant that surgeons, not soldiers, bore the responsibility for distinguishing between legitimate illness and malingering. Such responsibility often put surgeons at odds with their patients, who, failing to receive the treatment or care they anticipated, declared their medical officers apathetic to the regiment's needless suffering.

In other instances, straggling soldiers temporarily rejected military authority altogether. Chauncey Cooke of the 25th Wisconsin was forced to resort to straggling during Kimball's march to Snyder's Mill. "It was a killing march," Cooke wrote to his sister, conducted in the "hottest sun I ever felt. … Hundreds lay down in the corn rows, under the trees, and on the banks of the creeks, many of them in the faint of a sunstroke, others fanning themselves or cursing those in command." Unable to keep up with his regiment, Cooke fell back until he was marching with a group of Indiana soldiers with whom he shared the last of his water. "I was just about fainting with the heat when one of the Indiana boys said, 'My boy you better lay down, your face is awful red.'" Heeding the advice, Cooke broke rank. "We were on the bank of a muddy creek. I walked away from the road up among the trees and after taking a drink from the creek I lay down in the shade of a tree with no one in sight and fell asleep."[109] He slept for five hours.

Though not always malicious, straggling introduced a level of insubordination into the ranks.[110] McClernand wrote a sharply worded rebuke against the practice, reminding his soldiers that such behavior was "strictly forbidden," while Sherman declared it "as much as a crime as rebellion."[111] But while commanding officers saw straggling as a disciplinary problem, most soldiers considered it a necessity. It was the only way to care for their bodies when they could not access formal avenues of rest and recovery. Cooke was not the only soldier to break rank on that march, but the keen seventeen-year-old was nevertheless ashamed. He woke from his prolonged rest embarrassed to rejoin his regiment, believing that his inability to endure the physical demands of soldiering was proof of his weakness. He wandered back to the road where he fell in line with a group of stragglers. Suddenly, Cooke felt a hand on his shoulder and turned to find his captain smiling back at him. "The Captain had never looked so good to me. He had lain down by the road like me, overcome by heat, and he was anxious to find the company. Until I found Captain Dorwin I was ashamed to think that maybe I was the only one lost from the company. The Captain is a great big strong man and nice looking. And when I found the heat had played him out just as it had me, I took courage." After extensive searching, the men rejoined their company and suffered no disciplinary action. But Cooke harbored a growing resentment toward his officers: "If there is a just God he will punish the man that ordered that awful march."[112]

The Vicksburg Campaign was a grueling and physically demanding march. It began in the temperate days of spring when April showers meant flooded bayous and muddy roads, and it ended on the cusp of summer when the sun burned its brightest. From mid-April until the end of May, soldiers in the Army of the Tennessee moved through the countryside as quickly as possible. With limited access to the rear and carrying everything on their backs, soldiers endured hunger, sleeplessness, thirst, and exhaustion. They lived off the land, but they did not necessarily thrive. One soldier in the 28th Iowa quipped that his "eyes were sunken into his head so far, he could roll them down and see his own gizzard and it was empty."[113] Jokes aside, many men connected their suffering to notions of duty and honor. T. B. Marshall of the 83rd Ohio explained it this way: "There was a general feeling that every man was expected to do his full duty. . . . Personal danger, personal discomfort, or personal hardship, hunger, thirst, weariness were never thought of for a moment, or, thought of only to endure."[114] Still, there were limits to what men might endure *cheerfully*. Those limits closely aligned with soldiers' freedom to tend to their physical and mental needs. While troops who were hungry or tired had greater autonomy to procure nourishment or comfort, overheated and dehydrated soldiers remained at the mercy of their superiors.

And yet, the campaign's success would not rest on mere endurance. Grant's decision to not wait for supply lines before pursuing Vicksburg was an immense risk. By isolating his army, Grant chanced a disruption to the delicate equilibrium of soldiers' health and fighting effectiveness. If his army's health failed, the entire campaign might have collapsed, or worse—the Army of the Tennessee might have reached the outskirts of Vicksburg with a force incapable of assaulting the Confederate stronghold. To this end, the defining moment came on May 12, 1863, when Federal troops under the command of General McPherson appeared along the banks of Fourteen Mile Creek, prepared to fight their way into Raymond, Mississippi. As the first encounter between Union and Confederate forces in nearly two weeks, the clash at Raymond was the first opportunity to show whether Grant's strategy would succeed. As weary, thirsty, and underfed as Union soldiers were, their performance on the battlefield would expose any physical weaknesses within the fighting force. But the Union army won the Battle of Raymond, and over the next week, Grant's army became an unstoppable force, winning a total of four engagements over the course of six days. And on May 19, they arrived at Vicksburg.

4

The Surgeon's War

Surgeon Henry Strong of the 11th Wisconsin was delighted when the Army of the Tennessee abandoned the canal project around Young's Point. As far as he was concerned, the entire venture had been destined for failure, a feat of engineering hubris implemented in one of the most hostile environments he had yet to encounter. "In some ways there has been more stupidity manifested in these enterprises than I supposed possible for this age," he wrote.[1] Strong was tired of waiting. He was ready to march, and he soon got his wish. A month later, he found himself in a firelit camp somewhere between Black Rock and Utica, Mississippi. "It seems hardly possible in the quiet of an evening that we are in the enemy's country and shooting each other in self-protection," he marveled to loved ones at home. The campaign was challenging—more so, perhaps, than the canals—but Strong found this work satisfying. "We are enduring sacrifices and hardships in earnest now, but little to eat, nothing to cook with and no tents, but it is all right as we are accomplishing something." In many ways, Henry Strong was like any other member of the Army of the Tennessee. He endured the same physical hardships—thirst, hunger, dehydration—as his comrades. But Strong's position within the medical corps also meant that he had a unique experience of the campaign, which added to his sense of accomplishment. After all, campaigning meant fighting, and fighting meant casualties. While Union soldiers reveled in their victory over Confederate forces at Port Gibson, Strong basked in that triumph and more: "[General] Grant told [General] Carr ... that he had never known the Medical Department so well conducted as in our division during the late battle," he bragged.[2]

There is no doubt that soldiers' self-care played an important role in the Army of the Tennessee's ability to conduct the Vicksburg Campaign and threaten Confederates on the battlefield, but it was only one factor that made the campaign successful. When considering the challenges posed by the Mississippi interior, historians often emphasize how Grant's decision to reduce dependency on his supply lines affected soldiers' participation during the campaign.[3] More commonly overlooked is how those same environmental elements undermined the medical corps's ability to deliver reliable and sustainable medical care. Certainly, the army's isolation provided some benefit when it came to officers' ability to retain authority over soldiers' bodies. Limited engagement with the rear meant there was little opportunity for civilians to interact directly with those on the march. Few letters made their way out of Mississippi and were posted upriver before the campaign was over, and those that did were not heavily circulated with enough time to generate public concern. Reformers, politicians, and loved ones could not be enraged by the condition of soldiers' health if they did not know what those conditions were. But there were also disadvantages to the isolation. Just as the limited supply lines affected soldiers' rations, so too did they affect medical officers' access to hospitals, supplies, and personnel. The sanitary commissions were not there to scrutinize the medical corps's performance, but neither were their relief boxes that contained extra bedding, bandages, and other goods. In short, the medical corps was entirely reliant on its own resources, knowledge, and procedures to sustain soldiers through the campaign.

Thus, for the medical corps of the Army of the Tennessee, the geographic isolation and rugged terrain that characterized the Vicksburg Campaign introduced a host of new threats. Limited transportation routes challenged medical officers' supply management strategies and crippled evacuation procedures, making it more difficult to provide extended care to patients as the campaign advanced. These dangers alone could have sunk operations, particularly after May 12, when the army engaged Confederates in a series of battles as it made its way toward Vicksburg. Each engagement generated hundreds of new patients whose treatment was contingent on their unique injuries. There was no such thing as a standard combat wound. Instead, surgeons relied on their professional skill to make quick decisions. However, the unrelenting nature of field medical care challenged not only medical officers' professional knowledge but also their physical and emotional resilience. There was a potential for the medical corps to dissolve into chaos as it had done at Manassas and Shiloh. If the campaign were to become paralyzed by shortage and needless suffering, it would hold devastating consequences for soldiers' mental and physical endurance. But this did not happen. Instead, the army's isolation created an opportunity for members of the medical corps to sharpen their skills and prove themselves capable of caring for their patients. The Medical Department's regulations and procedures lay the framework by which medical officers could adapt to their present circumstances and communicate patients' needs throughout the corps. As the campaign progressed, they adjusted to their environment, leveraging local resources to overcome deficiencies and maximize their effectiveness. It was through this process that medical providers shed their past selves as civilian physicians, became seasoned veterans of the medical corps, and grappled with the physical and emotional demands of their profession. In the end, surgeons, assistant surgeons, and other medical providers were both professionally and personally transformed by their experiences during the Vicksburg Campaign.

The medical corps's ability to provide care capable of sustaining the campaign and ensuring that enough able-bodied soldiers arrived on the outskirts of Vicksburg to fight their way into the city was not a foregone conclusion. In fact, the early days of the campaign were plagued by the same administrative inefficiency that had characterized the XIII Corps's march south from Milliken's Bend. Just as Maj. Gen. John A. McClernand's medical staff had arrived at Perkins' Plantation with no ambulances and limited supplies, so too did they arrive at the battlefield in Port Gibson without full access to their medical resources. Brig. Gen. Alvin P. Hovey observed that his division was not accompanied by medical wagons or ambulances but that his medical officers carried their supplies to the battle on foot and cared for their patients on the field. Unconcerned that his soldiers' medical care might have been hindered because medical officers were limited to the supplies they could carry on their backs, Hovey instead saw the episode as a noteworthy example of the medical corps's dedication. It was a sentiment shared by Brig. Gen. Eugene A. Carr, who lauded his surgeons' dedication to their patients, proclaiming that "rarely have troops in battle the good fortune to be provided with such an abundance of professional skill, administrative ability, patient care, and industry."[4]

As it turned out, medical officers arrived at the battle without dispensary wagons and ambulances because they were instructed by some commanding officers to leave them behind in order to privilege the transportation of ammunition. This discovery infuriated William S. Forbes, the corps's medical director, who declared the orders an "almost criminal interference," noting that "except for chloroform, instruments in cases, and the stimulants carried on the persons of the regimental medical officers, there would have been no medical supplies in the 13th Army Corps." Upon discovering the shortage, Forbes immediately wrote to Grant pleading for supplies. Grant, in turn, instructed the Commissary Department to send all the army's stimulants to Forbes until the medical officers were more adequately supplied. But while this rectified the shortage, the episode reveals one of the central challenges of the campaign: that the medical corps remained subordinate to the decisions made by commanding officers. Therefore, while medical care during the campaign could break down as the result of the faults and inefficiencies of the medical corps, it was also vulnerable to disinterest and neglect on the part of commanding officers. When officers decided that medical care was not a priority in their command, surgeons were forced to perform their duties without adequate support.[5]

The various reports that emerged from the Port Gibson debacle are significant because they highlight how military commanders and medical officers measured success. For commanders, success meant victory on the battlefield and everything else was ancillary, functioning in support of the main goal. Even Grant, who had a reputation for supporting his medical officers' needs, would limit that support if it interfered with military operations.[6] Hence, Hovey and Carr could praise their medical staff's performance at Port Gibson with little concern for the supply shortage or the struggles it produced. Forbes, by contrast, was greatly concerned that the shortage had contributed to unnecessary suffering, noting that "some wounded men perished from shock who otherwise would have recovered from this state."[7] But Forbes's frustration was not simply about the waste of human resources. As a medical officer, William Forbes was bound to two masters: He was a soldier, but he was also a physician, and this meant that while he served the United States Army, he also served his profession. For members of the medical corps, the war was not simply about defeating Confederates. It was a fight to minimize suffering and death.

The Battle of Port Gibson marked the start of the Vicksburg Campaign. Given this, it is arguable that rendering medical care in the wake of the battle was easier than it would be for the rest of the march. Traditionally, the key to efficient medical care was a reliable evacuation route that conveyed wounded soldiers from the field as quickly as possible. But on the eve of crossing the Mississippi River, the possibility of having a sustained evacuation route seemed doubtful. Hospitals were established at James' and Hard Times Plantations in Louisiana, but neither site was particularly well supplied.[8] After the crossing, they were separated from Grant's army by the river, and the road to Milliken's Bend remained unpredictable. This changed on May 3, when Grant's army moved north from Port Gibson and took possession of Grand Gulf. Not only was the river town better fortified than the army's original landing at Bruinsburg, but it was also ten miles closer to Vicksburg, almost directly across the river from Hard Times. After securing a base at Grand Gulf, Grant determined to shorten his supply route, ordering Brig. Gen. Jeremiah Sullivan to construct a new road starting across the river from Young's Point and running to a landing just south of the Warrenton batteries.[9] Once there, supplies could be loaded onto steamers and transported to Grand Gulf.

While Grant was rerouting his supply line to Grand Gulf, medical officers were struggling to find an accessible and secure location to care for soldiers unable to continue with the campaign. By May 2, most of the casualties from Port Gibson had received medical care, and surgeons began consolidating the field hospitals.[10] At first, casualties were relocated to the Yates hospital in Port Gibson, where they waited transfer to the Grant hospital located near Bruinsburg.[11] But there was growing concern that these field hospitals were vulnerable to attack from Confederate raiders. On May 5, five ambulances were reportedly captured near the battlefield. The following day, nineteen ambulances loaded with wounded men appeared at McClernand's camp just outside of Grand Gulf, having evacuated Port Gibson for fear of being captured. Consequently, McClernand became increasingly concerned for the security of the Port Gibson hospitals. "The Medical Director for the department will know whether any [wounded] still remain at Port Gibson," he wrote to Grant, adding that "if so; ought they not to be rescued from the danger of capture?"[12] In the end, casualties from Port Gibson were transferred to Grand Gulf, where a large hospital was established under the supervision of surgeon John Holston. Holston described the location as "delightful, cool and free from malaria." "I have several small buildings and increasing numbers of hospital tents erected," he informed Henry Hewitt, who was serving as acting medical director in the field while Madison Mills made the journey from Milliken's Bend. Holston declared his new hospital "just the place for severe wounded of whom we can now accommodate 1 to 200. Lighter cases can with ease be shipped from here to James Point or any other place you made direct."[13] Yet, while the hospital at Grand Gulf was initially capable of managing convalescent soldiers and overseeing their evacuation, it was not a long-term solution.

As the army moved farther away from the Mississippi River, medical officers' ability to transport wounded soldiers to Grand Gulf became impossible. The medical corps, after all, could only make use of the army's transportation lines. It did not have the authority to establish—or guard—lines itself. And by May 6, Grant had already decided to cut ties with the rear. The Army of the Tennessee was not building or maintaining roads capable of comfortably transporting wounded soldiers back to the river. Since the goal of the campaign was to secure Vicksburg, there was little effort to occupy and protect the lands through which the army had already passed.

After their victory at Port Gibson, the Army of the Tennessee advanced through the Mississippi countryside unopposed for eleven days. The next encounter with Confederate forces came on May 12, when Federal troops met a rebel detachment along the banks of Fourteen Mile Creek. By nightfall they had won a second battle, forcing the Confederates to retreat through the hamlet of Raymond. Four divisions from the XV and XVII Corps pursued the rebels all the way to Jackson, where they effectively neutralized the Confederate military presence in the capital city. Intent on stopping Grant at the Big Black River, Lt. Gen. John C. Pemberton, commanding the Vicksburg garrison, moved his army near Edwards Station. There, on the morning of May 16, the two armies met once more, fighting along a crest known as Champion Hill. Unable to hold his position, Pemberton fell back to the Big Black River, where he attempted one last stand. Failing that, he withdrew into the proven safety of the Vicksburg fortifications. Grant's army pursued, but after two failed assaults on May 19 and 22, Vicksburg remained undefeated.[14]

Because the battles fought between May 12 and May 22 occurred in a short time frame, the outcome of each fight held important implications for the next. Union morale increased with each victory, while the Confederate army fell into a state of panic and confusion. Of course, the outcome of these battles was not merely psychological. Each clash put hundreds of men in desperate need of medical care, burial, or both. In fact, 8,064 Union soldiers would be killed or wounded that May. Nearly 90 percent of them would fall in a ten-day span, and it was the medical corps's responsibility to care for these men

Table 4.1. Casualties treated by Union surgeons

	Union killed	Union wounded	Confederate prisoners
Port Gibson	131	719	—
Raymond	66	339	—
Jackson	42	251	—
Champion Hill	410	1,844	—
Big Black River Bridge	39	237	—
May 19 assault	157	777	—
May 22 assault	502	2,550	—
TOTAL	1,347	6,717	~ 6,000

Sources: OR 24 (2): 167; OR 24 (1): 37.

Note: While not all the Confederate missing required medical care, the Union army was burdened by a large number of Confederate wounded, particularly after the fights at Port Gibson, Raymond, and Champion Hill.

as quickly as possible. After all, incapacitated soldiers, in the words of one medical reporter, were a "vexatious hindrance" to the army's progress. Surgeons shouldered a heavy burden to take "proper care of these unfortunates without a real or apparent weakening of the available force."[15] The Army of the Tennessee's isolation, however, made things even more challenging. Although Grant maintained a connection to his base at Grand Gulf, that base continued to offer limited support. There would be no reinforcements—of either soldiers or surgeons—until the army established a stronger connection with the Mississippi River. Until then, wounded soldiers either moved forward with the army or were left behind. Beginning with the Battle of Raymond on May 12, Union casualties were consolidated into local field hospitals, where they were left with rations, supplies, and personnel until further arrangements could be made at the end of the campaign.[16]

The medical corps's isolation at Vicksburg is noteworthy when compared to other battles and campaigns during the war. For the most part, medical officers relied on a network of roads, railroads, or rivers to help facilitate soldiers' removal from the battlefield. Surgeons worked quickly to treat everyone in their care and either return them to their command or facilitate their transfer to Northern general hospitals. The goal was to consolidate and dismantle the field hospitals as quickly as possible. In the aftermath of the Union victory at Gettysburg, medical officers in the Army of the Potomac consolidated their patients into a central facility known as Camp Letterman. Located near the York Road and Gettysburg Railroad, the hospital's location was meant for easy evacuation to facilities near Philadelphia. It also, however, meant that medical providers had consistent access to fresh supplies.[17] This was essential.

Evacuation could not always happen quickly, but field hospitals needed access to supplies, personnel, transportation, and even knowledge if they were to stand independent from the advancing army. During the Chickamauga Campaign, the Army of the Cumberland employed a backhaul evacuation method to remove sick and wounded soldiers from the front. As supply wagons arrived from the rear, they were loaded with patients on their outbound journey. These men were then dropped off at a central hospital, which was supplied with provisions from Nashville. From there, they awaited further evacuation via the railroad.[18] This strategy, of course, was only successful if field hospitals were established between the advancing army and its supply base. At Vicksburg, they were not.

Consequently, each battle during the Vicksburg Campaign represented a dramatic drain on the army's medical resources, not only because of the materials consumed during combat but also because of the resources left behind. Fortunately, the medical corps was remarkably well supplied thanks to the army's medical director, Madison Mills. Mills's appointment in late March corresponded with Grant's realization that the canal project would not work, and thus Mills arrived at Milliken's Bend just as the army was preparing to move south toward Perkins' Plantation. Mills's extensive military experience was undoubtedly an asset as the medical director arranged to streamline the medical corps's performance and eliminate administrative deficiencies, and through these efforts, Mills unintentionally overprepared his officers for the isolation ahead.[19]

Mills's complaint had to do with the way his surgeons were requesting medical supplies. Standards protocol handed down by the Medical Department required that the medical directors for each army corps submit a requisition for supplies at the start of every month. However, Mills's predecessor did not enforce this procedure. Instead, officers requested supplies whenever they ran out. Mills, intent on rectifying this lapse, ordered his corps medical directors to submit a supply requisition on April 1. However, only one of the three corps complied. Unable to verify what supplies his medical directors had and what they were missing, Mills determined to supply them with everything—whether they needed it or not.[20] As a result, the Army of the Tennessee was more than abundantly supplied throughout the entire campaign with few surgeons complaining of shortage. Instead, they complained about paperwork.

Military procedures and regulations were intended to promote efficiency, assuming regular army physicians could get their volunteer counterparts to adhere to them. Medical officers were urged to keep extensive records while in the field. They were expected to track not only their supplies but also their patients, carefully listing complaints and treatments. Even combat did not excuse the medical staff from their administrative responsibilities. During the campaign, each division hospital was assigned a "historian" who documented each patient's name, rank, and regiment along with his injury, treatment, surgeon, and outcome.[21] Once evacuation procedures resumed, this process was repeated each time the soldier was admitted to a new hospital, ultimately providing surgeons in the general hospital with a complete record of their patients' medical care.[22] These detailed records demanded by the Medical Department generated a lot of paperwork. As surgeon-in-chief for the Third Division in McPherson's corps, Silas Trowbridge was required to report all surgeries from the time his division left Milliken's Bend until it captured Vicksburg. It was an immense undertaking. "I had but two clerks, and to give an idea of what we accomplished . . . I will say that from July 6th to October 21st, we consumed 10 reams of paper in my office."[23] Of course, many of the medical officers saddled with these responsibilities loathed them. That some even avoided them can be assumed from the various directives and special orders that circulated requesting surgeons to complete their reports.

It is understandable that surgeons might resent their administrative responsibilities. After all, they did not join the army to become desk clerks. "I have very little to do now in the practice of medicine or surgery," one surgeon complained, "but am pretty busy preparing reports, requisitions, and discharges."[24] This emphasis on administration and bureaucratic procedure must have been especially perplexing for volunteer surgeons, who saw a greater need in the practice of medicine than in the recordkeeping of it, for they, perhaps more than anybody else, were quick to realize that the medicine they practiced in the field hospital was not like anything they had encountered in civilian life.

The supplies and procedures supported by the Medical Department were intended to streamline service and provide medical officers with the means to successfully accomplish their duties as both medical providers and military personnel. However, these resources could not adequately prepare the medical corps for field service. The wounds were too horrific, the dead too numerous. And the challenge of practicing military medicine was nothing like its civilian counterpart. "How different are the means of treating injury in the field and in civil life!" declared former surgeon George Macleod. "Injuries which might be completely cured in stationary hospitals have often to be relieved by amputations, while others whose treatment might, under more favorable circumstances have afforded a fair prospect of success are placed beyond recovery." As a veteran of the Crimean War, Macleod was intimately acquainted with the chaos of battlefield medicine. "The ample space, established routine, careful nursing many comforts and appliances of a civil hospital contrast strongly with the temporary nature, hurried extemporized inventions, and incomplete arrangements of a military hospital in the field."[25] The key to becoming a good military surgeon, then, was learning to adapt to chaos, urgency, and perpetual shortage.

Thus, for the medical officers serving during the Vicksburg Campaign, isolation was both friend and foe. It created conditions that threatened soldiers' health, challenged evacuation procedures, and undermined surgeons' access to supplies and reinforcements. In doing so, however, the environment forced medical officers to turn inward, prompting them to rely on their own skills as well as on those of their colleagues and granting them the space to hone their trade without threat of outside interference. Sometimes this meant perfecting already established skills in order to increase efficiency and reduce suffering. In other instances, it meant innovation as surgeons solved unique problems with unconventional solutions. In the end, nearly all of the medical providers who served during the Vicksburg Campaign had adapted to the campaign's unique circumstances in some way. And it was by this process that they were transformed from raw recruit and civilian practitioners into experienced veterans of the US Army Medical Corps.

For hospital steward Charles Johnson, Port Gibson was the first opportunity to witness the carnage of war. Marching toward town in the midst of fighting, Johnson soon noticed a wounded soldier standing nobly by the side of the road. "His arm [was] in a sling and the bright blood ooz[ed] through the bandages over a wound on his breast otherwise bare." The "stalwart" man watched silently as the army passed. "His was the first blood I saw flow from a Confederate bullet." But if Johnson carried any fanciful notions of honor or glory forged in the trial of battle, they were soon dispelled. As the army moved closer to town, the land became broken and trampled. Debris from the day's fighting littered the field. "A little ahead broken wheels and dismounted cannon, and now and then a dead soldier, with here and there a disemboweled horse, showed that the advance of the Federals had met with resistance," he recalled. Johnson passed more field hospitals, as much a part of the war-torn landscape as the trampled corn and ruined fences. When the command paused, he visited one. "I stepped aside to see some Federal surgeons dressing the wounds of a young Confederate soldier. He was a stout-built young fellow but was pale and seemed exhausted from loss of blood. He was suffering from a large flesh wound in the calf of the leg." It was all too much. That night, haunted by all he had seen, Johnson was unable to sleep.[26]

Twenty-one days later, much had changed for Charles Johnson. Now a veteran of Champion Hill and the May 19 assault, Johnson cared for the wounded as part of his regular routine. Standing in front of a division hospital on the morning of May 22, he listened to the sound of cannon fire near Vicksburg and anxiously awaited patients. "About 2 pm through the trees was seen a long train of ambulances approaching, heavily loaded with mangled humanity," Johnson recalled. Upon their arrival, everyone went to work. The wounded were removed and laid upon blankets in the shaded yard. "One of the first that I assisted in taking from the ambulance was a tall, slender man, who had received a terrible wound in the top of his head... exposing the brains for three or four inches." The patient died shortly after his arrival, and Johnson moved on. Soon the yard was filled with long lines of wounded men, "and to attend to the wants of these kept all busy." To manage all these patients, surgeons divided the wounded into three categories. Those who were mortally injured were laid aside and made as comfortable as possible. One such man arrived having received a gunshot wound to the base of his brain. "When taken out of the ambulance, one side of his face was in convulsions," Johnson recalled. He and his colleagues removed the man from the ambulance and placed him under the shade trees, where the patient lived until the next day. "All night and till noon next day the convulsions continued; one eye was in constant motion, and the muscles of the same side of the face jerked and twitched in horrible contortions." Eventually, the poor soldier succumbed to his injuries.[27]

Soldiers whose injuries were not immediately pronounced mortal were cared for in order of the severity of their wounds. Mangled limbs and broken bones were privileged over patients presenting with simple flesh wounds. In many cases, this strategy of triage allowed the medical corps to manage the large number of casualties by quickly categorizing cases and prioritizing injuries that needed the most attention. Unfortunately, sometimes surgeons' judgment erred. Johnson recalled one man on May 22 who arrived at the hospital with only a small wound on his foot but admitted that "the number of dangling limbs and gaping wounds calling for immediate care seemed to justify the surgeons in putting him off for a time." The patient was eventually treated, and he was finally evacuated to Memphis, where his foot became gangrenous. The soldier died. Of course, surgeons had no way of knowing that the small foot injury would eventually prove fatal, and Johnson continued to assert, even decades after the war, that the delay in treatment did not result in the patient's death. Nevertheless, there had to be doubt, a restless wondering whether the patient would have lived had the wound been dressed sooner.[28]

The methodical examination, categorization, and treatment of patients practiced by Johnson's division was standard procedure throughout Grant's army. It involved much collaboration between ambulance drivers, hospital stewards, nurses, cooks, assistant surgeons, and surgeons. Medical care, after all, was not just surgery. Patients had to be fed and clothed. Their bandages had to be changed. Shortly after the battle at Champion Hill on May 16, Thad Smith observed the bustle of a nearby field hospital where the wounded were being "speedily collected.... There might be seen busy surgeons and attendants dressing wounds, amputating limbs, extracting balls, feeding and caring as circumstances best afforded to the unfortunate in battle."[29] The medical corps's ultimate goal was to operate with precision and efficiency, treating every wounded soldier as quickly as possible before consolidating the hospitals and moving out. This not only ensured the most favorable prognosis for the wounded but also helped medical providers manage their workload.

Unlike soldiers, surgeons' work was not finished when the last crack of gunfire rang across the battlefield. Instead, their duties continued for hours, even days after an engagement, and medical officers rarely rested until the work was done. Having driven the Confederates from Champion Hill, soldiers in the 46th Indiana made camp for the night near the battlefield. "It was covered with dead and wounded men. Rebel and Union soldiers lay almost as thickly as stood the living," recalled one soldier. "All night the ambulance corps with their torches of splinters came among the sleeping soldiers, hunting and carrying out those to whom surgical attention would benefit."[30] Knowing that the army would leave the battlefield at daybreak next morning, surgeon Silas Trowbridge personally rode over the battlefield three times, looking for anyone left behind.[31] Meanwhile, the soldiers slept.

Regrettably, extenuating circumstances often undermined the speed with which medical care could be administered. Wounded soldiers rendered immobile on the battlefield were often trapped until the fighting ceased. Because the battlefield remained occupied after the May 19 and May 22 assaults, it was exceptionally difficult to recover the wounded. Search parties had to wait for nightfall to protect them from enemy bullets.[32] Even then, sometimes it took days. Two days after the May 22 assault, patients were still arriving at the hospital for McPherson's Third Division. "[They] could not get to them before," explained Eugene Harrison. By then enough time had passed that some were "dreadfully fly blown when brought in."[33] Each new patient meant more work, another mouth to feed, another surgery to perform, another wound to dress.

Wartime sketch depicting a search party combing the battlefield for wounded soldiers. Note that night has fallen and the soldiers are working by firelight.
Harper's Weekly, May 30, 1863, 341. University of Michigan Library Digital Collections.

To make matters worse, surgeons' work became more difficult once the sun set. "Many operations were too delicate a character to be performed after night," Johnson remembered. Ideally, their surgeries were delayed until the next morning. If not, surgeons made use of small candles, which were relatively smokeless and did not drop wax.[34] This was at best makeshift. Trowbridge found operating by candlelight an extremely frustrating affair, declaring the candles "of the most inferior quality."[35] Consequently, when night fell, work effectively stopped, casting medical providers into a period of stasis. In some cases, the goal was simply to ease the suffering until sunrise. But this, too, was overwhelming. In the stillness of the night, the dark was isolating. It further separated medical providers from their comrades while thrusting them into even more intimate interaction with the day's casualties.

Therefore, in the wake of battle, the medical corps was routinely overworked and outnumbered. One historian has observed that more than 75 percent of the soldiers wounded during the Battle of Champion Hill—a number nearing 1,500 patients—were left in the care of just nineteen surgeons. Furthermore, at least four of those surgeons were not only caring for the Union wounded but tending to Confederates as well.[36] Given this, it is unsurprising that surgeons adopted techniques that could streamline patient treatment. One such strategy had to do with wound dressings. During the campaign, surgeons under William Forbes's supervision almost exclusively used water dressings in order to cover the stumps remaining after amputations. "These strips were applied just as the ordinary adhesive strips—and a wet bandage applied over the whole extremity of the stump and to some little above." Forbes was satisfied with the results produced by water dressing and on the whole preferred the method to using traditional adhesive plaster, which was more common in civilian practice. While adhesive strips were still used in the war, Forbes and his surgeons found them particularly onerous considering the dirty and dusty conditions on the battlefield and the challenge of keeping wounds clean every time the dressing was readjusted. Furthermore, water dressings were easier to apply, remove, and reapply. Considering that every wound was cleaned and redressed every day, this was a clear advantage.[37]

Because of the pressures of combat medicine, it was especially important that operating surgeons were knowledgeable about their craft so they could make quick and accurate decisions regarding their patients' treatment. This was especially challenging because the injuries faced by military surgeons were very different from those treated by civilian physicians. Prior to the war, few practitioners had the opportunity to refine their surgical skills through complicated procedures. Instead, most treated common complaints and set broken bones. And while William A. Hammond's Medical Department sought to facilitate the collection and transmission of information for the benefit of the profession, it was surgeons' responsibility to engage with the data.

Aware that their quick decisions at the operating table had life-altering implications for their patients, many operating surgeons spent time engaging the professional community over the efficacy of certain surgical treatments.[38] Surgeon Edmund Andrews used the information he collected on the wounded at Chickasaw Bayou to reflect on the utility of amputation. In doing so, he urged the readers of his *Complete Record of the Surgery of the Battles Fought near Vicksburg* to consider the location of the injury before deciding on a course of action. "The rule is now well established, that the military surgeon may go almost all lengths in his efforts to preserve superior extremities," he counseled.[39] Instead of amputating upper extremities, surgeons might consider resection. Charles Johnson recalled the procedure well: "If the joints were not involved, the wound was enlarged and the ragged ends of bones pared off smoothly, the arm put in a splint, and if the case resulted fortunately, fibrous tissue first and later a bony structure took the place of the original

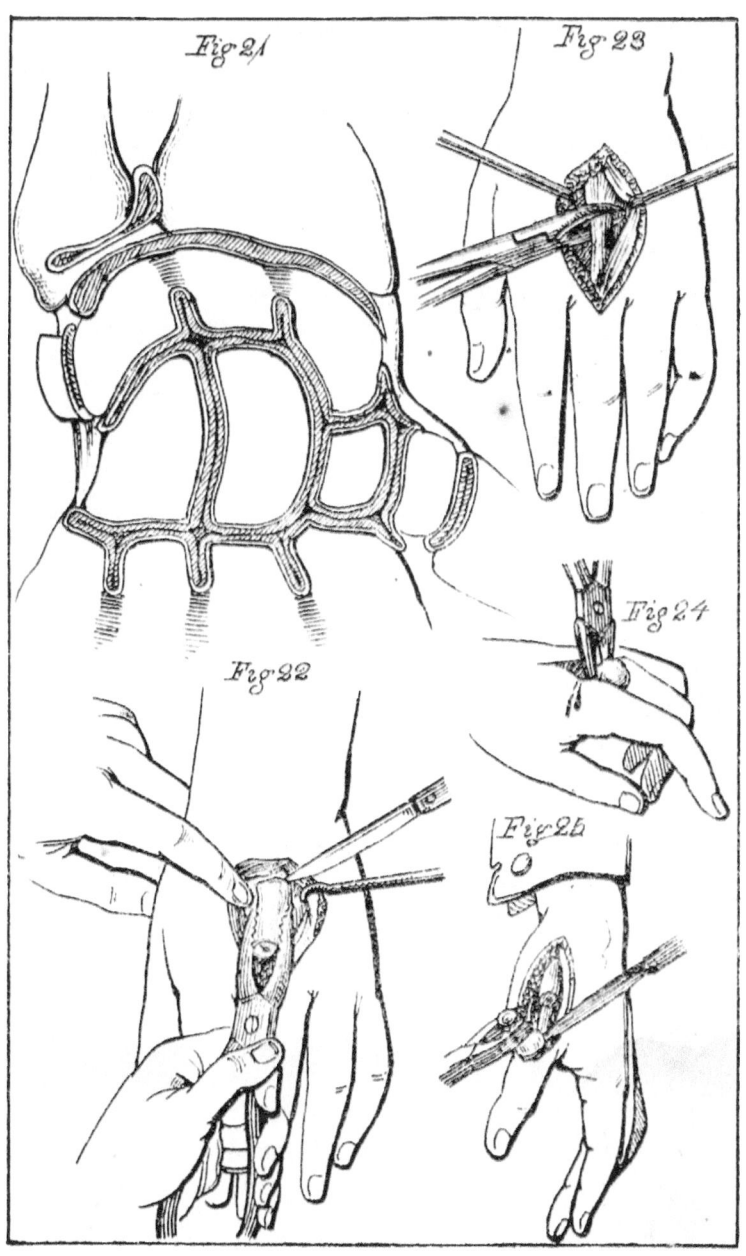

Resection plate demonstrating the proper procedure for the resection of bones in the hands. Confederate States of America, *A Manual of Military Surgery: Prepared for the Use of the Confederate States Army* (Richmond: Ayres and Wade, 1863), pl. 5. Thomas Jefferson University Digital Commons.

hard bone."[40] Resection was just as invasive as amputation, but surgeons made extensive effort to save the limb rather than remove it. This, of course, preserved the patients' quality of life to some extent, but Andrews was more concerned with the survival rate. Mortality rates for both operations consistently showed that resections were the preferable course of treatment for arm injuries.

Leg injuries, however, required more extensive deliberation. The proper course of treatment relied on a number of shifting variables and depended on the operating surgeons' expertise in interpreting those variables and responding. For example, Andrews observed that gunshot wounds to the tibia looked different depending on the direction that the bullet was moving. If the bullet entered the leg from the front, the "opening in the skin is small; but the fragments of the bone are driven back among the tissues of the calf, producing more danger of mortification than the first glance indicated." But when the bullet entered through the calf, the wounded appeared more "hideous." "It drives all the splinters outward through the skin in front, doing less real injury than the former case, but still tearing open the skin and everting the flesh over an area of two or three inches in diameter." Andrews believed that the real danger rested with the surgeon who, through inexperience, might fail to notice the severity of the first injury and select a more moderate treatment while pursuing amputations with the latter. To prevent this from happening, Andrews concluded that when it came to injuries of the leg, "amputation must be extensively practiced" in order to ensure the patients' greatest chance of survival: "By [amputating] 75 per cent of the patients may be saved; but if attempts are made to save the limb, almost every man will die."[41] This assertion placed Andrews at odds with many in his field who agreed with surgeon John Woods of the 99th Ohio that "amputation is almost never warrantable; but the prospect of success warrants the efforts to save the life with the limb."[42] Ultimately, there was an extensive rift in the field regarding the nature of amputation and when it should be practiced. Considerable literature emerged both during and after the war in an effort to find consensus, but none was found. At best, operating surgeons had the opportunity to consult with their assistants before deciding on a course of treatment.

Given the chaos of combat, surgeons' ability to examine patients and decide on appropriate treatment revealed their professional skill. Though some surgeons prided themselves on this, others lacked discretion, and their shortcomings often led to devastating consequences. Shortly after the battle at Port Gibson, Silas Trowbridge consulted at the bedside of a Confederate soldier. The man "had been wounded by a buck shot or pistol ball penetrating the thigh bone about two inches above the knee joint," wrote Trowbridge, who described the wound as "very simple" with no fractured bones. Still, the patient's Confederate surgeons insisted that the leg be amputated. Failing to convince the Confederate surgeons that the operation was unnecessary, Trowbridge appealed to the patient, telling him that "if he objected to the amputation, we would not permit it to be performed." When the patient did not object, the procedure went forward:

> They . . . applied the spiral tourniquet high on the thigh, to arrest the hemorrhage; and were operating by the flap methods. The operator had transfixed the thigh with his catline so closely to the tourniquet band that the blade came out above it on the inner thigh. He made his sweep forming the under and inner flap first, cutting, of course, the tourniquet strap in doing so, and severing the Femoral Artery at the same time. They attempted to impress the artery in the groin, but were so much excited that the loss of blood caused the death of the poor deluded soldier in a very few moments after the thigh was removed and before the dressing had been applied or he taken from the operating table.

A postmortem showed the femur intact, proving the operation unnecessary. Trowbridge was unsurprised. "So much for rebel surgery," he wrote.[43]

Certainly, sectional feelings influenced Trowbridge's perception of Confederate surgeons, but Union surgeons were just as critical of their own colleagues. A fiercely conservative operator, surgeon Alexander Hoff considered surgery little more than "mutilation" and was horrified when, after one particular battle, he found a surgeon "in the rear of the battlefield standing by the operating table, covered with blood, with a pile of legs and arms around him that could have been a good rifle pit, crying out 'bring on the next one.'" Endeavoring to stop the "butchery," Hoff suggested that "these limbs ought to be saved." When ignored, he forcibly removed the offending surgeon, "and a consulting board soon began to find plenty to save but few to mutilate."[44] It is difficult to explain why some surgeons were so free with the blade and others so discerning. Perhaps they were overwhelmed by the number of patients waiting for medical care or the speed with which they had to treat each soldier. Perhaps they were numb to their surroundings, operating mindlessly on the body before them. Maybe they were careless, or their skills of discernment were not up to the task. Regardless of the circumstances, by insisting on radical, often unnecessary operations, surgeons brought their expertise into question. For surgeons such as Hoff and Trowbridge, this not only violated professional standards but provided civilians with further reason to charge surgeons with butchery and barbarism.

Good surgeons did not take shortcuts when it came to treating their patients. Instead, they did what they could to offset the disadvantages that came with battlefield medicine. And for the medical officers participating in the Vicksburg Campaign, there were plenty of disadvantages. Although Mills's medical corps was well supplied with medicine and stimulants, there were other resources that surgeons could not feasibly carry in quantities large enough to sustain them throughout the campaign—tents, for instance, and beds. In addition to being dirty and overcrowded, field hospitals were often temporary sites with limited access to permanent structures. This was not a problem when the army was connected to a reliable evacuation route. However, this was not the case in Mississippi. Severely wounded or otherwise incapacitated soldiers had to remain in the field until evacuation lines were reestablished. As such, medical officers had to provide for their patients' long-term comfort, a difficult task without permanent shelter. To achieve this task, medical officers adopted soldiers' strategy of foraging supplies from the surrounding countryside. They turned to the dense cane that grew in nearby forests and ravines. Cane shelters appeared as early as Grand Gulf and were extensively used to protect injured and recuperating patients from the elements. Forbes wrote that "they consisted of a roof, twelve feet high, made of long cane . . . and supported by poles at the ends and along the ridges which were left open." The shelters were approximately 16 feet wide and 100 feet long and had a "covering of cane on the pole, holding up the roof." They protected patients from the morning dews as well as the blistering sun, and the cane leaves were particularly adept at shielding patients from the rain.[45]

Finding a way to increase patients' access to shelter was invaluable, but cane also provided another luxury: beds. Once shelters were erected, medical providers constructed simple beds by driving four stakes into the ground. These stakes were forked and connected with four poles through which cane and bark were woven to form a mattress. Forbes declared the makeshift beds admirable for hospital use, firm but flexible and "rendered very comfortable" when covered with a blanket. The beds were remarkably sturdy. Not only were they strong enough to hold the patient, but surgeons soon discovered that they could hang weights from the bed and improvise a traction device to treat compound fractures. Most importantly, however, all of the cane structures were so easy to construct that a group of 100 men could build them. And since cane grew abundantly through the countryside, there was no want for supplies. "These sheds and beds were used after the various battles and during the siege of Vicksburg and their utility was amply tested and well approved in this corps," Forbes wrote. There is no doubt that the cane structures provided wounded men with a level of comfort that was otherwise unattainable given the army's isolation.[46]

For the men in the Army of the Tennessee's medical corps, the Vicksburg Campaign was a professionally transformative experience. The rugged terrain and geographic isolation created a series of challenges that medical providers had to overcome in order to limit individual suffering and prolong the army's fighting strength. Like the soldiers, medical officers turned to local resources when inadequate supply lines followed them into Mississippi. They adapted some techniques and perfected others in order to ease pain, decrease infection, and preserve quality of life. In doing so, the medical corps bound together, functioning as a unit in order to care for an overwhelming number of patients as quickly as possible. Consequently, many medical officers found their work professionally gratifying. "It was most pleasant to contemplate the time saved when it was so precious at such a moment with acres of wounded men around pleading with their gaping wounds for help," wrote William Forbes.[47] However, the Vicksburg Campaign was not only professionally transformative but also personally transformative. After all, the men who labored as surgeons, assistant surgeons, hospital stewards, and ambulance drivers did not just experience the campaign as medical providers. They experienced the war as individuals vulnerable to the same physical and emotional hardships endured by soldiers.

The medical corps performed an important role during combat. As professionals, medical officers offered essential expertise on the care of wounded and dying men, and this expertise meant that they had responsibilities that set them apart from other officers and enlisted men. They were responsible for logistics like evacuation and triage. They performed operations, bandaged wounds, and eased pain. They monitored the dying. Perhaps more than anyone else, the medical corps bore witness to soldiers' suffering and sacrifice. Given this, it seems obvious that medical officers might be personally affected by their work. And yet, because they participated in the war as professionals rather than as private citizens, their emotional resilience remains overshadowed by their professional performance.

The tendency to emphasize medical officers' professional skills over personal experiences originated with the officers themselves. Encouraged by the Medical Department to contribute to a growing body of scientific knowledge, surgeons compiled extensive case studies and forwarded them to Washington. Unsurprisingly, these reports adopted a clinical tone and employed anatomical terminology to describe injuries and infections. As a result, they offer an account of the war that neglects the emotional and physical reality of human suffering. Take Iowa private Burton Ayres, for example. Labeled in the *Medical and Surgical History of the War of the Rebellion* as "case 94," Ayres was shot on May 19 during the first assault against the Vicksburg fortifications. The treating surgeon recorded that "a minié ball entered the left thigh through the center of Scarpa's triangle, passing to the inside of the vein and out at the lower part of the left nates." Initial observation found the wound in a "very dirty and sloughing condition." The patient had an elevated heart rate, suffered from diarrhea, was sweating profusely, and had a difficult time remaining conscious. Ayres's surgeon tried to counteract his symptoms by ordering a series of water dressings and placing Ayres on his abdomen to allow the wound to drain. At 7:00 p.m. on May 31, Ayres suffered a "haemorrhage from the anterior wound, which was checked by a compress." The following afternoon surgeons opened the wound "to the sheath of the femoral vessels and a darning needle [was] removed." At 8:00 on the night of June 1, Ayres hemorrhaged again. "Blood, in large quantities, burst forth in a jet, apparently from below; it was quite dark, but the exact shade was not observed. The femoral artery was immediately ligated, but with difficulty owing to the thickened and diseased condition of the parts." The patient died three hours later. Surgeons then conducted an autopsy where they observed "great sloughing in the course of the wound. There was a slough of the femoral vein of the size of a three-cent piece. The vein was pierced by the large needle alluded to above, two small holes existing opposite each other; the artery was healthy. It was observed that well marked symptoms of pyaemia existed several days before his death."[48] The record of Ayres's injury, treatment, and subsequent death is extensive. But the reality of his suffering remains evasive.

When crafting reports like Burton Ayres's, medical officers adopted a tone of clinical disinterest. This, of course, was more than appropriate given the document that they were creating and its intended audience. However, when nonmedical professionals engage these sources, they sometimes project the tone of emotional detachment onto the medical officers who wrote them. In doing so, they overlook the emotional challenges—the anxiety, stress, frustration, and grief—of treating and losing patients like Ayres. Failing to consider the emotional toil of caregiving can perpetuate the illusion that practicing medicine does not have emotional implications.[49] But it does. The spate of scientific studies examining physician burnout syndrome, mental toughness, and vicarious trauma attests to the fact that medical providers are emotionally affected by their work, whether they write about it or not.[50]

Like soldiers, members of the medical corps underwent an emotional transformation as they endured the fear, danger, confusion, and grief of combat.[51] Unlike soldiers, however, medical officers did not extensively process this transformation in writing. Considering the number of Americans who participated in the Civil War, medical officers were a small fraction of either army. The medical providers who left behind letters, diaries, and memoirs are fewer still. Writing about emotions is intensely reflective, and for those still caught amid the chaos of combat or for whom the war was not yet over, such reckoning was often unwelcome. Additionally, those who did write about their experiences were often under immense pressure to maintain a level of detachment from their patients, and failure to do so could reflect poorly on their professional reputation. Thus, there tends to be more emotional language in the memoirs written after the war than in the diaries and letters written during the conflict. This, of course, also presents challenges. Many memoirs were written for publication and thus crafted with a specific audience in mind. As such, medical officers rarely drew direct connections between their professional responsibilities and feelings of helplessness, fear, and frustration. Instead, they wrote vivid descriptions of combat, recounted harrowing tales of surgery performed under enemy fire, and carefully recorded the carnage produced by modern weaponry.[52]

Medical officers' emotional experiences, then, are often hidden, embedded into the types of stories they chose to tell and what they left unsaid. For every medical provider who left behind journals, memoirs, or letters home, there were unforgettable patients inscribed on the page. Of course, they did not always articulate that these patients were remarkable, but the fact that they wrote extensively about a select few cases in contrast to the tens of thousands whom they treated suggests that these patients were unique. The key to understanding their significance, then, is often inferred. Over time, as many members of the medical corps formed personal connections to the soldiers they cared for, they developed a keen sense of grief for the patients they lost. One of the patients Charles Johnson treated in the wake of the May 22 assaults left such an impression. The soldier was a "nice young fellow of eighteen" who had been "wounded in the bowels and was sitting against the root of a large tree, resting his head against its trunk." Part of what made this patient so memorable was the fact that Johnson knew the man and he, in turn, recognized Johnson. "His name was Banks and knowing me well, he recognized me and calling me by name, said: 'Ah, I am badly wounded.'" Banks knew Johnson as a member of the medical staff and, thus, as his potential healer. Unfortunately, there was nothing Johnson could do to save the man's life. This realization not only forced Johnson to grapple with his own helplessness but also led Banks to the realization that his wound was fatal. Slowly, Banks succumbed to shock. His lips turned an "ashy pale." His brow broke into a clammy sweat. And he sat against the tree with a "long knuckle" of intestines protruding from his abdomen. The young man's death was no doubt a personal blow to Johnson, but Johnson did not reflect on his own sorrow. Instead, he shifted attention to Banks's grieving father, a soldier in the same regiment who sat "sad and heartbroken" next to his son while the young man died. Johnson's instinct to deflect attention away from himself was common among medical providers.[53] When members of the medical corps wrote about their patients, their detachment protected them from processing their responsibilities—and failures—on a personal level.

In theory, medical providers assumed professional disinterest in order to insulate themselves from their immediate environment. This practice, of course, was not exclusive to military medicine. Even in civilian life, new physicians were trained to observe their patients' bodies, recommend treatment, and conduct procedures through a lens of dispassion. Doing so allowed them to privilege their patients' well-being over their comfort.[54] This need for separation, however, was even greater during combat, when wounds were more graphic and agony more extensive. By denying themselves the opportunity to reflect on their limitations and the overwhelming task before them, military practitioners could more easily move between patients.

Unfortunately, the professional disinterest practiced by medical officers did not endear them to their patients. Soldiers were already predisposed to view surgeons' trade negatively. To most, field hospitals were an extension of the battlefield, where the human body was mangled, mutilated, and distorted in a variety of grotesque ways.[55] Sometimes this was accomplished by enemy shot and shell, and other times it occurred at the end of a surgeon's blade. Surgeons' instruments, after all, were tools of destruction, not made to reassemble the body but to dismantle it. There were "long, bright, razor-edged knives for cutting through fleshy parts in amputation and sharp toothed, shining saws for sawing bone," wrote Charles Johnson. "Strong forceps for extracting bullets, bone pliers for snipping off jagged ends of bone and tourniquets for arresting hemorrhage."[56] Such instruments were wielded with fearful effectiveness as 2nd Lt. Daniel Ramsdell could attest. Shot through the hip during the May 22 assaults, Ramsdell was taken to a nearby field hospital, where he lay watching the surgeons work: "They would place a man on the table ... [and] commence looking him over. Whatever the trouble was, they attended to him in short order. If it was a leg or arm it was likely to come off. It was not a very pleasant sight to witness. Some of those on the table were still, some of them would pray, others would laugh and some would cry or curse."[57] The aftermath of these operations nearly made Charles Dana ill. Stumbling upon a field hospital several hours after the battle at Port Gibson, Dana was repulsed by the "heap of arms and legs which had been amputated and thrown into a pile." More than the sight of the dead and wounded, this grotesque mound gave Dana a "vivid sense of war such as I had not before experienced."[58]

That medical officers spent prolonged bouts of time in the field hospitals without seemingly being affected by their surroundings only contributed to the perception that they were heartless, callous, or cruel. And this assumption was strengthened by soldiers' personal experiences. After hours of watching the surgeons work on his comrades, Ramsdell endured their probing hands and scrutinizing gaze himself. "They got down on their knees one on each side, rolled me over onto my right side . . . then [one] ran his finger into my wound, could not feel anything then took a probe and run that into me four or five inches worked it around a while, pulled it out and then said to the other doctor, 'I don't find the ball, see what you can do?'" Ramsdell endured the procedure a second time with the same result: "[The surgeon] got to his feet and said, 'I don't think we can do anything for him. The ball has gone into his bowels. He will die before morning.'" And with that shattering prognosis, Ramsdell was taken to a tent to lie with other dying soldiers. He would remember the cold detachment with which his surgeons surveyed his wounds and declared his inevitable death for the rest of his life, which happened to last another sixty years.[59]

Within the context of war, medical officers' emotional detachment may have helped them perform their job efficiently, but it did not guarantee that they performed it compassionately. Furthermore, it hindered them from establishing the emotional bonds that soldiers routinely used to process their experiences. After all, men facing death on the battlefield were not interested in surgeons collecting data at a field hospital. They wanted comrades, and battle was where true camaraderie was formed.[60] Through combat, soldiers forged a bond founded on principles of courage and honor. These virtues were intimately tied to one's battlefield performance. Consequently, not only were the surgeons stationed at a field hospital excluded from the true combat experience, but the operations they performed also had the power to threaten the courage, honor, and masculinity soldiers sought to maintain.[61] This is not to say that soldiers never forged emotional bonds with their surgeons, only that they bonded better with surgeons who behaved more like good soldiers than good physicians.

Surgeon Christopher Blackall, for example, received the adoration of soldiers in his command during the siege of Vicksburg. When a sergeant in the 33rd Wisconsin was shot and left vulnerable to Confederate fire, Blackall organized a rescue mission. "With my green sash around my waist and over one shoulder to indicate that I am a surgeon, I crept to the nearest point for reaching [the sergeant]." After retrieving the wounded man, Blackall and his rescue party rushed back to the trenches, only to discover that the sergeant had already died. At that point, Blackall called for the dead man's gun, removed his surgeon's insignia, took aim at the opposing force, and emptied the sergeant's cartridge box. "My fellows cheered me, dubbing me their 'fighting surgeon.' In this way, I balanced the account without the least regret."[62] In so doing, Blackall won the respect of his soldiers, but he did so at the expense of his professional duty as a physician. According to orders issued by the United States Medical Department, surgeons were to remain at their assigned post, tend to patients, and keep thorough records for posterity. Any other behavior was outside surgeons' purview. By shooting at Confederates, Blackall was not healing but rather killing. His decision to remove his surgeon's insignia before doing so suggests that he was aware of the implications.

Compared to Blackall's experience, most medical providers had little opportunity to form emotional bonds with the soldiers in their command. Their combat experience, after all, was dramatically different from that of the common enlisted man. Surgeons rarely dashed headlong into enemy gunfire, and few were present to witness their acts of valor. Nevertheless, medical officers took pains to recognize their own courage. Three years after the war, medical director William Forbes recounted the death of one of his surgeons in an essay about the campaign: "He was at his post applying a bandage to the lower extremity of a wounded man of his regiment" when he was shot by a sharpshooter. The ball entered "the thorax just above the sternal extremity of the clavicle when he was in a stooping position[, penetrated] the thorax . . . and entering the abdomen passed through it and emerged just above the . . . illium."[63] Of course, this unnamed surgeon was not the only medical officer to lose his life during combat, but Forbes's description of the injury—even while maintaining a standard of professional detachment—highlights the event as a notable tragedy. After all, the surgeon's death was a direct result of his devotion to his patient, not only because of his proximity to the battlefield but also because of the position he was in at the time he was shot. He was bent over, administering aid. It was a defenseless position. Perhaps had the surgeon been standing, the ball would have taken a different trajectory. Perhaps he would have lived. Instead, he died caring for his patients.

For members of the medical corps, the death of a colleague produced a flurry of emotions. Grief was certainly one of them. Like anyone else, medical officers mourned the loss of friends and comrades with whom they worked closely, learned from, and taught. However, these deaths also reminded members of the medical corps that, although they were not soldiers fighting on the battlefield, their lives were still endangered. Considering this, many felt that their responsibility to the wounded and dying was a noble pursuit, particularly in light of the threat to their own lives. "No language better than the foregoing can convey the true idea of the position of the surgeon upon the battlefield," wrote one medical reporter. "He occupies 'the symbolized spot' around which are gathered the tokens of war's devastation, and to whom, as an angel of mercy, not of wrath, he is to minister. . . . No arm should be raised to strike him down. His life should be held as sacred as that of the minister to God." But there was a notable distinction between medical officers' interpretation of their wartime service and everyone else's. The reporter went on to lament that "instances have occurred to which surgeons of both contending parties have been taken, and, in some respects treated as prisoners of war, and subjected to all their privations and hardships," while still others had been "shot while in the performances of their duties." This was proof, he believed, that "we have not yet fully comprehended the surgeon's mission upon the battlefield."[64]

The fact that medical officers' sacrifices were not recognized by the general population was discouraging. Critics of the medical corps failed to take into consideration the unique demands and challenges of combat medicine, personnel shortages, supply needs, and evacuation procedures. Instead, they highlighted visceral images of pain, dismemberment, and neglect. "Individual cases in which there has been apparent neglect, and which from want of proper explanation are given as positive evidence of the heartlessness of our profession," complained one surgeon. As an example, he wrote of a friend who had recently died, "alone and at night." In fact, the surgeon had no idea what happened to his friend or the specific circumstances around his death. All he knew was that "somebody wrote to his wife that the nurses found him dead in his bed, and nothing can ever eradicate from her mind the belief that he was totally neglected and that the surgeons and hospital attendants were brutes." Such criticism grieved medical officers who held fast to their successes and believed their wartime contributions valuable. They were discouraged by the constant attention to their failures and Americans' refusal to consider their efforts within the larger context of the war. "The public knows that thousands of our soldiers are buried at Nashville; that ten thousand have found a final resting place on the banks of the Mississippi. . . . Without knowing or without stopping to consider, if the ration of deaths be less or greater in our armies than in others, this large mortality is associated in the minds of the public with want of capacity or want of attention on the part of surgeons."[65] Ultimately, the assumptions embedded in these complaints suggested that soldiers' suffering would be better remedied if only the Medical Department and its members were more competent managers, officers, and physicians.

Perhaps more than having their dedication recognized, medical officers needed to believe that their role in the war effort mattered, and at Vicksburg, it did. For the Army of the Tennessee, the Vicksburg Campaign was an unparalleled success, and the US Army Medical Corps played an invaluable role. It kept tired and overheated soldiers on their feet, cared for combat casualties, and made arrangements for the incapacitated and invalid. Ultimately, they kept Grant's army moving, and they did so while leveraging their experiences into a growing body of professional literature. When the medical corps received accolades for its wartime service, it was typically for these accomplishments. But medical officers' achievements extended beyond the logistical, bureaucratic, and professional successes of the battlefield. Theirs was a personal endurance, one that kept them on their feet and at their post.

Of course, not all surgeons could withstand the relentless demands of military medicine all the time. Just like with soldiers, the campaign demanded that medical officers push their minds and bodies to the brink of exhaustion in order to execute operations with speed and precision. The engagements fought between May 12 and May 22 created a compounding effect that brought medical providers into prolonged contact with the sights, sounds, and smells produced by hundreds if not thousands of unwashed, bleeding, and infected bodies. "The unutterable horrors of war most manifest in a hospital, *two weeks after* battle," moaned surgeon Seneca Thrall. "It is terrible [and] requires all of my will to enable me to properly dress some of the foul, suffurating, eryipelateus fractured limbs."[66] By June, the relentless march had turned into a siege. As operations progressed, medical officers' physical health and mental endurance began to collapse under the stress. Shortly after the May 22 assault, Henry Strong, in charge of the 14th Division hospital, wrote to his wife in despair. "The care and anxiety of this large hospital, the general oversight, a labor to provide tents, shelters, medicine, food, cooking, beds . . . is a work of no small amount," he wrote. "We have over 400 badly wounded men, most of whom have had amputations or other operations performed and constant attendance and labor is required."[67] At times, the responsibility of caring for so many soldiers was staggering, and despite his best efforts, patients still died. "Most of them are severely wounded and the means we have are very limited to use for their comfort or relief. We are all prostrate with loss of sleep and fatigue."[68] And yet, despite the challenges, Strong believed his work was important and continued to push himself to the breaking point. A little over a month later, he received a certificate of disability and tendered his resignation. In the end, it was not about how long medical officers could endure these trials but about the work they did while they could.

5

The Victorious Army

Spring transformed the Lower Mississippi River Valley. Flowers bloomed and fruit ripened. New crops inched their way through the silty topsoil, giving hope for a productive harvest. Everything turned a vibrant shade of green, and the forests chattered with life. But not all of the changes were welcome. As the season wore on, reliable rainstorms became more sporadic, eventually giving way to drought-like conditions. Mud dried into dust, and the sun grew fierce. "The very trees, fences, and stones were gray and heavy and yellow from the dust stirred up by the marching armies," recalled one Iowa soldier, lamenting that "the sun shone mercilessly upon us [and] water was scarce."[1] By the start of June, the heat was relentless.

The Vicksburg Campaign took place during the height of spring's transformation. It took four weeks to march from Milliken's Bend to Vicksburg. During that time the Army of the Tennessee covered nearly 200 miles. Soldiers navigated flooded bayous and dusty roads. They yearned for water under the broiling sun and foraged wherever they could. And though some luxuries—a dry place to sleep, ripe fruit, fresh honey—bolstered soldiers' bodies and lifted their spirits, the campaign was still demanding. On May 18, regiments of weary and footsore soldiers appeared along the edge of the Vicksburg defenses. They were exhausted by a week of near constant fighting, but they were eager. "The victorious army, which had so completely out fought its enemies in the open field, was in no mood to settle down amid heat and discomfort to trench and sap in a siege that would undoubtedly last until midsummer," wrote Ohioan Frank Mason.[2] Grant's men were ready to fight their way into the city. The final assault began at 2:00 p.m. the following afternoon. It was an abysmal failure.

There are many reasons the Union army failed to secure Vicksburg on May 19. For one, the attack was too rushed. Grant's orders gave his officers fewer than three hours to move their troops into position and survey the terrain before the charge began. Unfortunately, when they arrived at the front lines, soldiers discovered that the terrain around Vicksburg was broken and jagged, completely hostile to a direct assault against the Confederate fortifications. Centuries of erosion in loess soil had carved the landscape into thin, meandering ridges separated by deep ravines filled with cockleburs, cane, and vines.[3] Soldiers might descend the hill easily enough, but climbing out was another matter: "The soil, when cut vertically, will remain so for years," explained Iowa soldier George Crooke. "For this reason, the sides of the smaller and newer ravines were often so steep that their ascent was difficult to a footman unless he aided himself with his hands."[4] It was a difficult task under the best conditions but doubly so when under fire.

In addition to the daunting landscape, many Union soldiers reported being physically weaker than they might have been prior to the campaign. Most had not drawn full rations since they left Port Gibson the week of May 3, and hunger gnawed in their bellies even as the assault began. "We were getting pretty close to the end of endurance," confessed William Eddington.[5] To make matters worse, May 19 was an exceptionally hot day, and soldiers' hunger was compounded by debilitating thirst. During the melee, Crooke found himself pinned to the battlefield with an empty canteen. The following hours were agony; "the earth which we hugged so closely was like the floor of an oven," he recalled. "I was covered with dust and perspiration and hour after hour passed by with constant aggravation of suffering from thirst."[6] While none of the reports written in the wake of the May 19 assault indicate that Union soldiers fought with less vigor or stamina than on previous engagements, there is little doubt that their bodies had been negatively affected by the campaign.

The Army of the Tennessee never did manage to take Vicksburg by storm. Several days after the failed assault on May 19, Grant ordered another charge. The May 22 attack was even more costly, generating over 3,000 casualties. Although the two days' rest gave soldiers the opportunity to recover their physical stamina, it was detrimental in other ways. During the lull, Union morale began to wane. Soldiers once eager to fight through their hunger became disgruntled and riotous. On May 21, troops watched Grant and his staff make their rounds in preparation for the second assault. Soldiers' reaction to seeing their commander was initially subdued. "We were interested spectators," T. B. Marshall later wrote, "and our respect for General Grant prompted us to observe silence." But not everyone remained so reserved: "The gnawings of hunger overcame some of the ruder ones despite reproof from our officers." Slowly and in a low voice, one soldier began to chant, "Hard Tack, Hard Tack." Soon, the cry spread throughout the line: "Hard Tack! Hard Tack!" The scene left a lasting impression. Marshall recalled that the general finished his work before informing the men that the roads connecting the army to the Yazoo River were nearly complete and "as soon as [the wagons] can cover the distance, you will have all you want."[7] But along with allowing his men to sit with their defeat—and their hunger—Grant's delay only postponed the inevitable. There were certain environmental factors that would not change, no matter how long they waited. Any direct assault against Vicksburg would have to cross those ravines. Finally, when Grant did attack, the May 22 assault exposed significant flaws within the Army of the Tennessee's command structure. Because Grant allowed his generals the flexibility to organize and execute orders with their best judgment, the pressure applied to Confederate lines was inconsistent. Though fighting along some areas of the front was fierce, in others it was too lax. The effort collapsed. Five days later, on May 27, the siege of Vicksburg officially commenced.[8]

The Army of the Tennessee's transition to siege tactics marked an important change in its approach to the Vicksburg problem. Prior to May 22, Grant's intention was to take Vicksburg as quickly and efficiently as possible. Federal troops marched through the Mississippi countryside at lightning speed, consistently defeating Confederate forces on the battlefield and forcing their retreat into the protected confines of the Vicksburg fortifications. The assaults on May 19 and 22 were intended to use that same momentum to ensure that Union soldiers would indeed secure the city before the start of the sick season. Grant's siege orders abandoned the original strategy by shifting the focus from speed to endurance. "As long as we could hold our position," Grant later wrote, "the enemy was limited in supplies of food, men, and munitions of war to what they had on hand. These could not last always."[9] But the strategy also came with drawbacks.

Executing the siege would require more reliance on manual labor, picket duty, and the construction of semipermanent camps to house the army's growing population. In short, siege life would be far more reminiscent of soldiers' experiences working on the canals than of marching in the campaign. Similarly, soldiers' health would also become more vulnerable as the local environment—the jagged terrain, warm and humid climate, and deteriorating sanitation—facilitated the growth of parasites, bacteria, and other microorganisms apt to invade soldiers' bodies. If neglected, these factors could erode soldiers' health and generate another public outcry similar to the one from the previous March.

But the inland campaign had transformed the army's overall approach to soldiers' health and medical care. When combined with the logistical advantages that came with siege operations, these experiences bettered prepared the army to cope with a military strategy aimed at weaponizing the local environment. For one, medical officers' ability to shepherd soldiers' bodies through the Mississippi countryside, despite the isolation, was collectively viewed both by commanders and by civilians as evidence of their professional skill. No longer fighting to establish themselves as capable health care providers allowed the members of the medical corps to benefit from the additional resources offered by the United States Sanitary Commission and Western Sanitary Commission without undermining their professional authority over soldiers' bodies. Renewed contact with the supply base at Milliken's Bend enabled patient evacuation as well as access to important supplies. Still, medical officers retained their willingness to innovate new procedures to accommodate their present circumstances. Similarly, despite the hardships of campaign life, soldiers' physical and emotional well-being seemed to have improve while on the march. The warmer climate combined with soldiers' limited exposure to bacteria and increased access to fresh fruits and vegetables had bolstered soldiers' bodies. Likewise, the freedom to employ informal self-care strategies strengthened their resilience against the oppressive heat and mind-numbing tedium inherent to siege operations. Of course, none of this is to suggest that soldiers did not get sick. They did, by the thousands. But their suffering was no longer deemed gratuitous. Instead, it was justified. Victory was imminent. Vicksburg would fall.

In the nineteen days since crossing the Mississippi River, soldiers in the Army of the Tennessee had pushed their bodies to the extreme, marching somewhere between eleven and twelve miles a day. For a healthy soldier on full rations, consuming somewhere between 3,500 and 4,000 calories, this might have been a reasonable energy expenditure in which soldiers were not burning

Table 5.1. Disease in the Department of the Tennessee, February–May 1863

	February 1863	March 1863	April 1863	May 1863
Typhoid fever	666	716	405	219
Remittent fever	1,715	1,919	1,736	1,565
Intermittent fevers	4,566	5,076	4,695	3,911
Diarrhea (acute and chronic)	9,519	9,437	8,349	6,923
Dysentery (acute and chronic)	1,782	1,523	1,508	2,368
TOTAL	18,248	18,671	16,693	14,986

Source: United States Surgeon General's Office, Medical and Surgical History, 1:241.
Note: This is certainly not a comprehensive list of all the ailments and injuries treated in the Department of the Tennessee and it does not account for misdiagnosis, but it still demonstrates a general trend within the army during the campaign.

significantly more calories than they were taking in.[10] However, the soldiers marching toward Vicksburg were not consuming full rations. Instead, their diet was both insufficient and erratic. And soldiers were not just marching; they were fighting. Additionally, the rising temperatures and drought-like conditions made troops especially vulnerable to sunstroke and dehydration, and to make matters worse, the men were not getting enough sleep.

Given such a physically depleting campaign, it is unsurprising that when Union soldiers first appeared along the outskirts of Vicksburg on May 18, they looked worse for wear. Ohioan Frank Mason vividly recalled how soldiers arrived in camp with "their ragged clothing dirty and stained with rain and dust and their faces thin from long and arduous labor and insufficient food."[11] But even though soldiers arrived hungry, filthy, and exhausted, the statistics collected by the Medical Department suggest that the army's overall health had improved. A brief survey of the most common ailments demonstrates a consistent downward trend in diagnoses starting in April. Cases of diarrhea and typhoid often caused by poor sanitation and contaminated water dropped by nearly 30 percent between March and May. Similarly, cases of remittent and intermittent fever dropped by almost 22 percent. And while dysentery diagnoses increased, there were not enough new cases to disrupt the general pattern of decline. Cases did not grow at the same rate that others declined. When added together, episodes of typhoid fever, diarrhea, dysentery, remittent fever, and intermittent fever dropped from 18,671 in March to 14,986 in May. It was a change of nearly 20 percent.

There were several factors that contributed to this trend. During the campaign, soldiers constantly changed locations, offering little opportunity to contaminate their camps. Furthermore, the army's policy of leaving sick soldiers at Milliken's Bend increased the chances that the healthiest soldiers made the trek. Nevertheless, when these objective statistics are coupled with the soldiers' subjective experiences with hunger, thirst, and sunstroke, it becomes clear that health is a relative qualifier. There was no objectively healthy Civil War army. Instead, the army's fitness shifted depending on who was observing soldiers' bodies and how they defined health. For soldiers, hunger and thirst posed as much of a threat to their survival as dysentery or smallpox, but for commanders, soldiers might endure considerable hunger or thirst before the campaign failed. Medical officers often bridged the gap between these two extremes. As physicians they were concerned with the physiological threats to soldiers' bodies and believed it their responsibility to reduce suffering whenever possible. And yet, as military officers, those in the medical corps were learning that war meant suffering and that sometimes soldiers' failing health was incidental to defeating the enemy.

Members of the civilian population—most notably agents working for the USSC and the WSC—were yet another group of people critically observing soldiers' bodies for signs of sickness or health. Prior to the campaign, civilians' anxiety for soldiers' well-being was the origin of a growing conflict with military officials. While the army was still stationed at Young's Point and De Soto Point, soldiers' deteriorating health attracted the attention of the USSC and Northern newspapers and even elicited an inspection from the US Army Medical Department. No formal censure came from the complaints, but many Americans, whether they were civilians, soldiers, or members of the USSC, remained wary of both Grant's commitment to soldiers' safety and the medical corps's competency to care for soldiers' bodies. As news spread of the Vicksburg Campaign and of Grant's ultimate decision to limit contact with his supply line, the concerns only grew. "Supplies in anything approaching sufficient quantities cannot be conveyed to the front by any existing method," complained Dr. Henry Warriner, an inspector for the USSC. Warriner fretted that intense fighting coupled with the onset of summer would mean a rapid decline in soldiers' health. Even worse, he feared that the USSC's inability to access soldiers directly in the field would contribute to unnecessary suffering.[12]

Limited contact with the front meant that civilians could hardly intervene on behalf of soldiers if they believed health conditions were lacking. But it was not for want of trying. Anxious to be of some help, sanitary agents waited for word of the army's condition and cobbled together reports with whatever information they had. On May 18, one day after the Confederates were defeated at the Big Black River Bridge, Dr. Warriner reported on the battle to the best of his abilities: "The direction seemed to be southeast from Vicksburg, distances not exactly calculable. I have just enquired at headquarters the meaning and upshot of it. No report has yet reached them in regard to it." Throughout the course of the campaign, Warriner had received word—sometimes amounting to little more than hearsay—about the various battles and casualties. This information was of limited use. Try as he might, Warriner could not access the army while it was in the Mississippi interior.[13] Instead, he was forced to wait.

The first reliable news regarding the army's well-being came with its arrival at Vicksburg and the establishment of supply depots that linked General Sherman's position north of the city to the base at Milliken's Bend. Despite their fear that isolation would contribute to the collapse of soldiers' health and lead to gratuitous suffering, the sanitary agents who first encountered the Army of the Tennessee were shocked to find soldiers in such good health and spirits. "It is indeed not a little remarkable that the health and vigor of the troops should have been kept up to so high a pitch through such adverse circumstance," Warriner proclaimed. "The rations furnished by the Government during the last five weeks have been confined to hard bread, salt pork, and coffee, and not full rations at that." In addition to the troop health, Warriner praised the medical corps's skill. Having visited the field hospitals shortly after the May 22 assault, he reported them to be "vastly better than I anticipated. And now that all manner of supplies—or at least such supplies as the army gets at any points—are fairly accessible, there should be no special hardships, so long as they remain in their present condition."[14] Warriner's assessment was supported by other members of the USSC who admitted that there had been too much haste in judging the medical corps's dedication and skill: "It only remains for us to say that, in view of all difficulties—necessary and otherwise—the medical staff has accomplished all that could be reasonably expected of it."[15]

The praises did not end there. Along with celebrating the medical corps's achievements, sanitary agents with both the USSC and the WSC commented on commanding officers' remarkable dedication to soldiers' health, provision, and sanitation. "I saw General Sherman going through the camp on foot, giving particular directions in regard to sanitary regulation," wrote a pleased James Yeatman, who declared that "no one could look after his men more carefully than he does." Yeatman, founder and president of the Western Sanitary Commission, was particularly impressed with how gentle Sherman was with the sick. "He is as delicate and tender as a woman," he wrote, offering similar praise to Grant for being "determined to have provision made for the sick equal to any contingency that may arise."[16] Yeatman's assessment was a dramatic transformation from the accusations of heartlessness and neglect leveled at the generals the previous winter and suggests a newfound respect for the high-ranking command. This respect was grounded with a sense of cooperation and recognition that the commanders of the Army of the Tennessee were, in fact, invested in their soldiers' health and safety.[17]

Of course, both Sherman and Grant had to be aware that this image—the tender general, devoted and concerned with the well-being of his command—would draw support. After all, it offered proof that officers recognized their soldiers' sacrifice and validated their suffering. However, it is also significant that while Warriner and Yeatman recognized soldiers' suffering, they did not rail against commanding officers as they had done the previous winter. Instead, their reaction legitimized commanders' authority to conduct the campaign as they saw fit. After all, Vicksburg was closer to falling than it had ever been before. The army only needed more time. Thus, the victory was worthy of the sacrifice.

Between this recognition and the acknowledgment that the medical corps was capable of managing and restoring the bodies of sick and wounded men, the sanitary commissions transformed their relationship with the Army of the Tennessee. No longer struggling to establish his medical corps as the primary health care provider for his army, Grant offered a compromise. In March 1863, he had issued a request for the Quartermaster Department to set aside a small steamboat for exclusive use by the USSC. According to Grant, the boat was "for the conveyance of goods calculated to prevent disease and supplemental to the Government supply of stores for the relief of the sick and wounded."[18] The decision was praised by those within the commission as "unusual" and "exceptional" and taken as a sign that Grant had come to appreciate not only the "remarkable zeal, capacity, and judgement of the Agents" but also the commission's ability to "meet the needs of the suffering."[19] More likely, Grant realized that there was no use trying to prevent the USSC's involvement. But he could control its contribution. To be fair, Grant knew that his soldiers benefited from resources that only sanitary agencies could supply in sufficient quantity. But even though the USSC had the freedom to move supplies between the home front and front lines, Grant's orders allowed him to retain authority over what and who made that journey. He ordered that "no persons will be allowed to travel on said boat except officers of the army and navy (and they only on permits from their proper commanding officer), discharged soldiers, and employees of said Sanitary Commission."[20] He further instructed sanitary agencies to inventory every shipment and provide a weekly statement to his medical director. When the Army of the Tennessee reestablished contact with its supply base in Milliken's Bend, interaction with the sanitary commissions resumed under these orders. For the rest of the siege, the USSC and the WSC supplied the army with much-needed resources. However, these actions were always supplementary and facilitated by the army. The sanitary commissions did not directly interfere with soldiers' care and treatment as they had at Shiloh.

With the campaign now over, life did not get easier for the Army of the Tennessee. Conducting a siege was hard work. Soldiers did not just sit and wait for their enemy to capitulate. Instead, sieges employed a strategy that depended on a complex infrastructure of roads, trenches, batteries, and camps, all of which soldiers had to build.[21] Construction began with a series of artillery batteries and rifle pits that surrounded the Confederate lines. Breastworks were dug into the earth and reinforced with gabion—large bottomless baskets woven from cane, grapevine, or willow. With the Union position reinforced, approach trenches and mines were employed to undermine the Confederate breastworks. Over the course of the siege, Union soldiers dug more than 60,000 feet of trenches and constructed eighty-nine batteries.[22] Just as important, however, were the roads. Stretching from Warrenton in the south to Haines Bluff in the north and offering direct access to river transportation, these routes provided Federal forces with access to ammunition, rations, and medicine. Perhaps most importantly, however, the new roads supplied reinforcements. Having finally established contact with his base, Grant's army swelled to approximately 77,000 men.[23]

Unsurprisingly, siege life more closely resembled soldiers' previous experience working along the Young's Point and De Soto Point canals than it did the campaign. Not only were they engaged in more fatigue and picket duty and less combat, but the transition back to semipermanent camps introduced a host of new environmental threats to undermine soldiers' physical and mental well-being. Of course, the exact nature of these threats was not necessarily the same. The canal project was marked by wet, cold weather, while the siege was characterized by the region's infamous hot and humid climate. Nevertheless, soldiers' bodies responded the same when faced with fever, infection, and deteriorating sanitation.

The Army of the Tennessee's position around Vicksburg's outer perimeter meant that soldiers were not confined to the trench lines. Instead, troops took advantage of the opportunity to scatter into nearby ravines, where they established camps along the steep gradient.[24] The geography provided natural protection against Confederate shelling, but it also harbored unseen threats. "Our camp is between two hills," complained surgeon Robert Jameson, "low and swampy."²⁵ Rainwater drained into the gullies of nearby ravines, mixing with a thick deposit of silt. Within this boggy tract grew bamboo, which merged into thick tangles woven with honeysuckle, greenbrier, and poison ivy.²⁶ Such terrain undoubtedly recalled the untamed swamps and bayous that had characterized soldiers' experiences around Young's Point, Milliken's Bend, and Chickasaw Bayou. And just as they had before, soldiers misidentified the true threat. They feared that the putrid miasmas emanating from the decaying organic material would poison their bodies and make them sick. And with air circulation blocked by the hillsides, surgeons were particularly concerned that many of the camps were subject to poor ventilation.²⁷ But it was not the air that threatened their lives—it was the mosquitoes.

Although mosquitoes were present throughout much of the United States, they were especially pervasive below the thirty-fifth parallel, where mild winters and marshy lands prolonged the breeding season.²⁸ The ravines around Vicksburg offered the perfect environment for the insects, which lay their eggs in warm, stagnant pools of water. These eggs, in turn, hatched as the weather became warmer and more humid. By summer, their gestation was complete, and the mosquitoes took flight. Of course, their presence was not unnoticed. Soldiers wrote about mosquitoes constantly, identifying them as yet another example of the land's undesirability. "Mosquitoes are certainly bloodthirsty and ravenous monsters," wrote surgeon Seneca Thrall. "At night they swarm by the hundred in my tent . . . each of them humming sweetly all the time."²⁹ Thrall was not the only one annoyed by the pests. Camped along the banks of the Yazoo River, hospital steward Thomas Barton complained that the mosquitoes were not only "very troublesome" but huge, "some of these insects being as large as the common house fly." On several occasions, Barton found the buzzing so vexing that he abandoned his tent and climbed to higher ground in order to sleep.³⁰ However annoying though they may have been, mosquitoes themselves were not necessarily the problem. Instead, the true danger lay with the malaria parasite that was transmitted by the female *Anopheles* mosquito, which swarmed through the ravines.

In total, there are five different malarial parasites: *Plasmodium falciparum*, *Plasmodium malariae*, *Plasmodium vivax*, *Plasmodium ovale*, and *Plasmodium knowlesi*. Of these, infections caused by *P. falciparum* are generally the most life-threatening, though *P. vivax* and *P. ovale* also cause severe infections. Regardless of the exact protozoan, all malarial infections share the same life cycle. The parasite is introduced into its host's bloodstream by a mosquito bite. Once in the body, the protozoan migrates to the host's liver where it takes anywhere from five to twenty-one days to reach maturity.³¹ At that point, the parasite moves into the bloodstream, where it invades the red blood cells, replicating itself until the cells burst, leaving the protozoa free to invade other cells.[32] This rupturing process is cyclical, occurring roughly every forty-eight to seventy-two hours, and is responsible for the intense fever and chills that characterize malarial infections.

Even with the cyclical nature of symptoms, it is surprisingly difficult to track malaria among Civil War soldiers. This is largely because the Medical Department did not include malaria as its own category of diagnosis. Instead, medical officers categorized soldiers' ailments based on the presence of fever and the frequency with which that fever recurred. A quotidian intermittent fever, for example, occurred every twenty-four hours, whereas a tertian fever spiked every forty-eight. Diagnoses of remittent fevers are even more vague because they suggest that the patients' symptoms did not wane like the intermittent fevers. Of course, the recurring fever is often a good indicator that Civil War soldiers had malaria, but it was not their only symptom. Patients endured violent chills, nausea, headaches, muscle pain, and, in some cases, diarrhea. Not only were these symptoms painful, but their fluctuations seemed unending. Affected soldiers languished miserably, desperate for relief, and they grew discouraged by their protracted suffering. By the end of the siege, Barton's health had rapidly deteriorated: "My robust constitution and powerful frame were shaken with disease," he wrote. Two months later, he was still ill. Entirely confined to his tent, his body was racked with fever, chills, and severe diarrhea. He was convinced that his only hope was to apply for a furlough and go home.[33] Barton's experience is reminiscent of thousands of Civil War soldiers who endured similar symptoms during the war. By comparing these stories with the medical records and case reports collected by the Medical Department, scholars are confident that most cases of remittent and intermittent fever were caused by malarial infections.[34]

In many instances, malarial infections themselves did not prove fatal, but they did weaken the body, making patients more susceptible to secondary infections produced by other microorganisms that were flourishing in the vicinity. For example, patients suffering from malaria, already weak and fatigued, also became dehydrated. Desperate to relieve their thirst, they would drink whatever they could, regardless of the consequences. Sixteen-year-old Chauncey Cooke was stricken with intermittent fever during the latter half of the siege. One day he found himself in close proximity to a spring marked with an ominous sign: "Don't drink this water, poison." "It is as big as the spring at the head of our coulee and as pure looking," he wrote to his mother in Wisconsin. But despite the warning, sick soldiers, "burning up with fever and thirst," flocked to the water's edge. "[They] stagger down here and fill up with water and go back to their tents and die."[35] By consuming contaminated water, patients already suffering from malarial infections ingested harmful bacteria that exacerbated their failing health.[36] In doing so, they contributed to the slowly deteriorating sanitation.

As their bodies became weaker due to diarrhea and dehydration, sick soldiers were either unable or unwilling to properly use the latrines.[37] This happened to Pvt. True Morrill, who suffered from fever for nearly a month before he developed diarrhea. He spent the last days of the siege shuffling between the hospital and the camp, working when he had the energy, but by July 18 his bowels were so loose he could hardly move. "I feel pretty easy when lying still, but a diarrhea is running when I stir about much."[38] Without round-the-clock care and help to keep himself clean, it must have been difficult for Morrill to maintain a sanitary environment. Consequently, his failing health endangered everyone else in his vicinity. True Morrill died on August 21, 1863, forty-eight days after Vicksburg fell.

As May melted into June, cases of acute and chronic diarrhea as well as dysentery were on the rise. This was the natural result of 77,000 men living clustered together without benefit of proper sewage disposal, drainage, and permanent shelter. After all, maintaining a sanitary camp took effort. In addition to caring for their own personal hygiene, communal latrines required constant attention. "[The latrines] should be at least four feet in depth and the bottom should be covered with charcoal," advised Union surgeon general William A. Hammond. "When the matter reached within two feet of the surface, cover with charcoal, and fill up with earth a little above the level of the adjacent surface." At that point, soldiers should dig new latrines.[39] This was the ideal, but it was not always the practice. An inspection of the Union camps and field hospitals in June revealed that soldiers often avoided the latrines. "The men have been in the habit of going out into the bushes, and not unfrequently only thirty- or forty-feet from some of their tents, and relieving themselves," complained Medical Inspector John Summers. He added that "human excrement has been promiscuously deposited in every direction, until the atmosphere, as the dampness of evening and night approaches, is so heavily loaded with the effluvia that it is sickening."[40] There were many reasons that soldiers avoided using the latrines. In some cases, they were inconveniently located too far from camp or in the sun. Privacy was limited and the smell horrific. And, of course, ailing soldiers did not always have the energy to travel far. Whatever the reason, Summers was worried about the overall effect on the command's health, and he was especially concerned about the water supply.[41]

Gastrointestinal ailments were among the most common complaints throughout the war. In fact, they were so common that affected soldiers did not always consider themselves sick. Two months after the fall of Vicksburg, James Forbis of Illinois seemed stunned by his increasing feebleness. "I ain't sick," he insisted while at the same time acknowledging that "nearly everything sours on my stomach." Despite his protestations, Forbis was sick. In fact, he had been suffering with diarrhea for nearly seven weeks and would continue to suffer for another four before he died.[42] All told, Forbis is one of an estimated 40,000 Union soldiers who died as a result of diarrhea and dysentery during the war.[43] Of those fatalities, 770 deaths were recorded in the Department of the Tennessee during May and July of 1863. These soldiers' deaths were attributed to their dominant symptom—similar to the way remittent and intermittent fevers were recorded—but the cause of that symptom was often unrecorded.

Certainly, many soldiers developed diarrhea and dysentery after drinking contaminated water. Those suffering from infections of *Salmonella*, *Shigella*, or *Escherichia coli* eliminated the bacteria from their bowels, easily infiltrating nearby water sources. Similarly, bacteria were also transported throughout the camp by the swarms of flies that, encouraged by the warm climate, laid their eggs on excrement, rotting food, and other decaying substances. When the eggs hatched and the flies took flight, the insects deposited the pathogens that clung to their bodies onto soldiers' clothing, skin, and food.[44] Of course, bacterial infections were not responsible for all cases of diarrhea and dysentery. Certain viral infections as well as dietary deficiencies contributed to increased cases of diarrhea or dysentery or both, as did the presence of *Entamoeba histolytica*, an intestinal parasite commonly found in warmer climates where sanitation is poor.[45] Consequently, soldiers' prolonged sojourn in humid, filthy, overcrowded, fly-infested camps contributed to a rapid decline in the command's health.

Between May and June, the cases of diarrhea diagnosed and treated in the Department of the Tennessee grew 71 percent, from 6,923 cases to 11,865. The most startling increase, however, was among cases of intermittent fever, which grew from 3,911 cases in May to 9,715 cases in June: an increase of over 148 percent. In fact, when comparing the same cases treated in the army in June with the previous March, the siege produced over 9,116 more patients in the same five categories. Furthermore, the numbers for July seem to highlight which ailments were circumstantial, owing to deteriorating sanitation and other temporary conditions, and which ones were endemic, resulting from environmental circumstances that extended beyond human control.

Table 5.2. Disease in the Department of the Tennessee, May–July 1863

	May 1863	June 1863	July 1863
Typhoid fever	219	217	324
Remittent fever	1,565	3,266	4,370
Intermittent fevers	3,911	9,715	17,132
Diarrhea (acute and chronic)	6,923	11,865	9,718
Dysentery (acute and chronic)	2,368	2,724	2,920
TOTAL	14,986	27,787	34,464

Source: United States Surgeon General's Office, Medical and Surgical History, 1:241, 390.
Note: This is not a comprehensive list of all the ailments and injuries treated in the Department of the Tennessee and it does not account for misdiagnosis. However, it does highlight the general deterioration of health during the siege.

The 34,464 patients nearly doubled the cases treated in February. And yet, there was no public outcry. There was no investigation. The army, after all, was victorious.

By the end of June, disease and sickness had ravaged the Army of the Tennessee. Union surgeon James Whitehill estimated that a little more than 3,000 soldiers in Brig. Gen. Nathan Kimball's division were under medical care. According to Whitehill, this represented 1 in every 2.48 men in the command: "There have been twenty deaths, three officers, and seventeen enlisted men; being a mortality of one in 152.6 of the cases treated, and one in 379.95 of the command."[46] This growing sick list combined with the casualty count meant that a substantial portion of the Army of the Tennessee required medical attention at some point during the siege. In addition to the 3,986 Union soldiers killed or wounded during the May 19 and May 22 assaults, another 523 soldiers were killed or wounded between May 23 and July 4. Furthermore, the medical corps was still responsible for the continued care of nearly 3,390 soldiers wounded during the campaign, at least until arrangements were made to evacuate them out of Mississippi.[47] Given such demand on the medical corps's resources, it is unsurprising that the army's hospital structure evolved dramatically between May 18 and July 4.

Because the May 19 assault was so hurried, the medical corps defaulted to the same temporary field hospitals that they had constructed during the previous weeks' battles. The field hospital for Maj. Gen. John A. McClernand's Ninth Division, for example, was established at a local farmstead located about four miles from the front lines. The log house sat high on a hill, in the center "of a large yard that sloped down in nearly every direction." The hospital's location was significant for several reasons. For one, it was far enough removed from the fighting to protect habitants from active shelling. But it was also a functioning farm, which meant that it had access to reliable water. Furthermore, the permanent structures on the property promised privacy for operations, and the yard was filled with large shade trees that could shield the wounded from the sun. The dead were buried behind the garden.[48]

Once the siege commenced, however, Union field hospitals became more complex, transforming into a semipermanent system. Eleven division hospitals were established around Vicksburg's perimeter. Located near farmsteads, they spread across the ridgetops, offering patients fresh air and ventilation.[49] Here, Union casualties from the May 19 and 22 assaults, as well as those from the previous battles, were consolidated for further treatment. Still, as the siege wore on and the sick list grew, these hospitals slowly filled with more and more patients, forcing medical officers to rethink the system. Prior to June the division hospital was the largest hospital in the field, but by the end of the month the medical corps had established three corps hospitals to accommodate overflow.[50] Louise Maertz, a nurse who arrived to care for the soldiers near Vicksburg, wrote that each corps hospital consisted of "three parallel rows of tents opening one into the others and accommodate[ed] three hundred patients. In the center of the broadest avenue between the rows our mess dining table is shaded by the roof tent and flanked with benches for the other surgeons and steward." The surgeons' tents were pitched along one side of the mess table, while Maertz's and the corps medical director's tents were located opposite.[51]

The corps hospitals were in keeping with Grant's determination to keep as many able-bodied soldiers as possible under the authority of the Army of the Tennessee. Rather than send sick and wounded soldiers upriver to convalesce in a general hospital, Grant expected the medical corps to manage soldiers' treatment in the field when practicable Still, with growing confidence in the siege's success and access to reinforcements, evacuation policies became more lenient.[52] Soldiers with severe injuries who were unlikely to recover in the field were transported to the river, where a network of hospital boats was employed to evacuate soldiers out of the region. As it had the previous winter, the floating ship the USS *Nashville* operated as a receiving hospital, providing a permanent structure to shelter patients until they could be placed aboard the *D. A. January* and evacuated to Milliken's Bend. If cases were deemed particularly severe, they were placed aboard the *City of Memphis* or the *R. C. Wood*, which relocated soldiers to general hospitals in Memphis and St. Louis.[53]

Between May 4 and July 5, the *City of Memphis* made six such trips from either Milliken's Bend or the near vicinity, transporting approximately 400 patients to Northern hospitals.[54]

Evacuation was just one step in what was otherwise a growing triage process. Soldiers' access to medical care largely depended on their injury or illness. "All slightly wounded cases were directed to be kept in camp under charge of their own regimental surgeon," wrote Medical Director Madison Mills, adding that it was "the desire of the commanding general that the sick and wounded of this army should not be removed from his department." Division hospitals, then, cared for patients who were incapable of remaining with their regiment in the field, while the corps hospitals were reserved for soldiers who sustained injuries so severe that they could not endure evacuation. To qualify for evacuation, soldiers had to receive written instructions from the corps medical director, after which they were escorted to the surgeon in charge of hospital transportation, where further arrangements were made.[55]

Unfortunately, for many soldiers, evacuation from Vicksburg was not the end of their ordeal but the beginning. Soldiers slated for removal had to first endure a harrowing ambulance ride from the ravines, through the bluffs, and down to the riverbanks, where they were loaded onto a boat for transfer to Milliken's Bend. For those who had recently sustained life-threatening injuries and, in many instances, emergency surgery, the journey was nothing short of agony. "I was in fearful pain," wrote Daniel Ramsdell; "every time I was moved it was like running a knife into my hip." To get to the river, Ramsdell endured an eleven-mile ambulance ride that started at 9:00 a.m. and ended with his arrival at 3:00 p.m. "The pain and misery that I endured during that ride will remain in my memory as long as life shall last," he swore. But the ordeal was not over. Ramsdell was taken aboard a steamer for transportation upriver and placed in a stateroom. Confined to the sweltering, dark room, Ramsdell lay "crying and moaning with pain" for hours before the wound in his hip opened and began to bleed: "I was laying in the matter. I was saturated with the filthy stuff." Somehow, he mustered the energy to call for help and a nurse came to his assistance, but that was not the last indignity. After arriving in Memphis, attendants had to carry Ramsdell off the ship. Covered in dirt, sweat, and blood, he was paraded from the cabin and across the deck where men and women—civilians—leisurely stood. "I don't know whether they were paying attention or not. I know I did not want to see them." If anything, by the time Ramsdell arrived in Memphis, he was in a worse condition than when he had left Vicksburg.[56]

While the specifics of Ramsdell's story remain his alone, in general his experience was not unusual. In fact, stories like his—marked by agony, blood loss, and physical deterioration—were yet another reason that Mills encouraged his surgeons to practice discernment when considering patients for evacuation. "Some deaths have occurred by removing the wounded at too early a period," he admitted.[57] William Forbes, medical director for the XIII Army Corps, made a similar observation, noting that the men who were wounded during the campaign and left where they were until after May 18 generally fared better than those subject to immediate evacuation. The problem, in part, lay with the rural countryside, limited roads, and jagged terrain that separated the hospitals from the river. With no rail lines to facilitate their evacuation, soldiers endured unnecessary trauma on an overland trip. But the terrain was only part of the problem. Forbes believed that his patients' suffering was also exacerbated by "the evils which always exert and cannot be separated from the removal of large bodies of men, particularly when their removal as is most usually the case, is performed in haste."[58] For Forbes, this was the great lesson of the Vicksburg Campaign—that medical officers had the resources and skills to care for sick and wounded soldiers in the field. Rather than evacuate soldiers from the field hospitals, the Medical Department should bring the hospital and supplies to the patients whenever possible.[59]

Thus, the hospital system depended on the transportation lines not only to evacuate patients out of Vicksburg but to bring supplies in. As always, the success of these efforts was largely contested. Mills claimed that "abundant supplies were at hand," particularly once "communication [was] opened with the Yazoo River and Young's Point[;] transports loaded with medical and subsistence stores were only six miles distance from the center of our lines."[60] And while hospital steward Charles Johnson complained that the corps hospitals acquired fuller orders of supplies, even he admitted that all the hospitals enjoyed access to "delicacies" such as fruits and wine as well as ample clothing.[61] Even S. W. Butler, a reporter for the *Medical and Surgical Reporter*, praised Mills's administration, observing that "all supplies have been in great abundance; at all times on hand for emergencies in the rapid and peculiarly arduous campaigns of the war, and far beyond the wants of the army."[62]

Of course, not all of these stores came from the army. Many of the supplies were furnished by the sanitary commissions, which established a depot at Milliken's Bend for easy distribution.[63] Surgeons were particularly grateful because these supplies were often badly needed in quantities greater than what the army could consistently provide. "I have never before fully realized the immense good done by 'aid societies,'" declared surgeon Seneca Thrall.

"Anyone being in our field hospitals after battle" could see "the wounded brought in bloody and dirty, their clothing frequently necessarily cut from them ... [and] then see them, a few hours after sanitary supplies, sent by the ladies through 'aid societies.'" With "the clean shirts, drawers, sheets, etc. then only can you realize the good done."[64] The sanitary commissions also had access to materials that might otherwise be considered luxuries. Each USSC ship that transported supplies to Vicksburg included 10 tons of ice, and another 100 tons were sent on a separate barge. Unfortunately, once the ice arrived, medical officers disagreed over the proper procedure for its distribution.[65]

However, more than clothes, food, ice, and bandages, medical officers needed access to quinine. An alkaloid remedy derived from cinchona bark, quinine prevents the parasite causing malaria from multiplying in the bloodstream. In fact, quinine was so effective at managing malaria symptoms that nineteenth-century physicians tended to administer it for a variety of other ailments, including non-malarial-related fevers, erysipelas, stomach ailments, and exhaustion.[66] Civil War surgeons were no different. Not only did they rely on the drug to treat a wide array of symptoms, but they also administered it as a prophylactic to prevent the onset of malaria.[67] For the surgeons in Grant's army who had to maintain soldiers' health through the sick season, access to sufficient quantities of quinine was essential. Thomas Madison Reece, surgeon of the 118th Illinois, prescribed copious amounts of the drug to the soldiers under his command. Reece noted in his records for June that it "was not unusual to dispense one or two ounces of quinine every day to a regiment of 300." In fact, the medicine was so important to his patients' health that Reece constantly felt the squeeze of shortage. Consistent among all his supply requests for June and July was the need for more quinine, and he expressed frustration at Medical Director Mills for tightly rationing surgeons' access.[68] Upon arriving in Vicksburg after the siege, surgeon John Moore, who replaced Mills as medical director of the Army of the Tennessee on July 12, quickly discovered the reason for Mills's rationing—a breakdown in the supply line between Vicksburg and Memphis. The mistake was quickly remedied. Shortly after his arrival, Moore submitted a request for the medical storekeeper in Memphis to forward 6,000 ounces of quinine, which he estimated would keep the army supplied for about a month.[69]

All told, the medical care provided to soldiers engaged in the siege of Vicksburg was not without its challenges. Certainly, some of the trials were beyond human control. The rural nature of the Mississippi interior, for instance, remained a problem for surgeons attempting to consolidate field hospitals and evacuate patients to the river. And the mosquito-laden ravines ensured that cases of malaria would continue to increase while soldiers remained in their camps. Other challenges, however, were avoidable. With better access to the river, there was no reason that surgeons should struggle to access sufficient quantities of quinine or ice. Nevertheless, it is important to recognize that the Army of the Tennessee's medical corps was actively adapting to soldiers' needs as they evolved. Rather than imposing a standard model for medical care onto the siege and forcing medical officers to conform, the hospital system employed the use of corps hospitals and hospital ships in order to allocate patient care more evenly among medical providers and locations. Renewed access to Milliken's Bend facilitated the distribution of medicine, clothing, and other stores to the front lines. Furthermore, it cultivated a symbiotic relationship with civilian relief organizations that supplemented military resources. Consequently, even though siege life closely resembled soldiers' experiences from the Young's Point and De Soto Point canals, their medical care was notably different.

In their most basic form, siege operations reduced the need for Federal troops to fight their way into Vicksburg. While arrangements were still made for a direct assault against Confederate lines in late June and early July, the siege worked to weaponize the local environment against the Confederate garrison—and the civilian population—trapped inside the city.[70] But Confederates were not the only ones to suffer amid the increasingly oppressive conditions. Nearly every soldier stationed around Vicksburg was susceptible to thirst, hunger, sunstroke, and exhaustion: conditions that threatened to undermine not only their physical health but also their mental stamina. These factors were pervasive, intimately tied to the daily realities of siege life. However, Union soldiers had an advantage. They sought to mitigate their ordeal by employing informal self-care strategies to help sustain their bodies, just as they had during the campaign. After all, soldiers' freedom to forage for food and comfort was a distinguishing feature of the campaign and was largely responsible for maintaining the army's fighting strength. Now that the army had reestablished its supply base, self-care was less about meeting soldiers' physical needs than it was about alleviating the tedium of siege life.

Union soldiers laboring in the trenches quickly fell into a routine. George Hale's regiment, the 33rd Wisconsin, typically began picket duty in the afternoon, when they could dig in the rifle pits without detection. They worked through the night and often the next day before being relieved.[71] "There was not much change in the routine of duty during the siege," recalled Isaac Elliot, one of Hale's comrades. "Two companies were furnished daily for duty on the works where each man disposed of forty rounds."[72] For those on duty, days alternated between monotony and excitement, digging and shooting, all under the blistering sun. Soldiers marveled at how exhausted they were. "Unless you have experience[d] it, you can not *even imagine* the enervating effect that the hot and sultry weather of this Southern climate has upon one's system," declared George Remley of the 22nd Iowa. "The entire system—mental, physical and nervous—is weakened and prostrated to such a degree that I never felt, nor even had any idea of before."[73] In fact, soldiers were often so tired that they sometimes struggled to meet other, basic needs. Taylor Pierce, also from Iowa, wrote that "the heat is so weakening that it seems impossible for . . . at least one of us to muster up energy enough to cook a little victual." He was grateful for the cool evenings that brought some relief, or else "we would be unable to do anything at all."[74]

For most soldiers, the distinguishing feature of the siege was the heat. Having first become an issue during the campaign, temperatures only increased through the month of June. "It really is awful hot," wrote Wisconsin native James Newton. "In the middle of the day the sun actually scorches a person."[75] The sweltering sun proved particularly worrisome for Northern soldiers, many of whom were used to more temperate climates. They feared their bodies were not acclimated to the excessive heat and thus would be more vulnerable to sickness. Their fears were exacerbated by the Confederates who taunted them from across siege lines. When a Confederate asked a soldier in George Crooke's Iowa regiment "how we like their 'Sunny South,'" the young soldier responded, "Oh, bully! . . . We wear our overcoats all day."[76] That Union soldiers might endure the Southern heat at least as well as Confederates became a point of pride. "The men, coming from a northern climate, endured a heat which even an acclimated person avoids," wrote one soldier from the 48th Ohio, declaring that "a heartier or more robust set of men probably never passed in review."[77] In reality, it did not matter whether the men were from the North or the South; the heat affected them the same. By stripping the body of much-needed fluids, the heat undermined the body's capacity to regulate its internal temperature. As a result, soldiers' ability to counter the heat's deleterious effects and protect themselves from sunstroke and dehydration was essential, and to this end Federal troops had an important advantage.

Unlike their Confederate counterparts who lay exposed in the trenches for most of the siege, Union soldiers were not permanently confined to the siege lines. Reinforcements arriving from the river allowed Grant the opportunity to rotate fresh troops to the front every few days.[78] When it came time to rest, soldiers retreated from the trenches and into the safe confines of their camp. Alexander McDonald of the 33rd Wisconsin relished these moments of freedom: "Got relieved and . . . stayed in camp and did not do anything." Indeed, there were frequently entire days where McDonald and his comrades were not required for picket duty.[79] When not on duty, Union soldiers spent their time searching for shade, as it was "absolutely necessary to comfort," according to Lt. Anthony Burton.[80] Yet even in the shade it was uncomfortably warm. Surgeon Thrall estimated that temperatures ranged between ninety and ninety-five degrees.[81]

While the Union camps provided a vital physical reprieve from the heat, they also offered an important mental break from the monotony of shooting and digging. Soldiers invested a lot of time into making their camps comfortable and homey, creating spaces that facilitated a psychological separation from the front lines.[82] Satisfied with the location of their camp, T. B. Marshall and his comrades in the 83rd Ohio immediately set about making their space as enjoyable as possible. Because they were not on level ground, extensive modifications were needed in order to make the site habitable. Soldiers used shovels to level sleeping grounds and carve benches.[83] Given the limited number of tents, they crafted temporary shelters—known as shebangs—into the hillside and reinforced their construction with excess timber. To Phineas Underwood, a relief worker arriving with the United States Sanitary Commission in June, the camps looked like small cities, stretching as far as the eye could see. "In the ravines and on the side hills we would see regiment after regiment encamped, occasionally riding by a group of tents in a pleasant grove with a U.S. flag erected which were headquarters of some of the Generals, or with a red flag which indicated the hospitals." Underwood was scheduled to camp with the 72nd Illinois, but his journey had taken longer than expected, and he arrived late in the night. "They were all asleep in their shebangs—the Colonel's large one in the center." Settling in for the night, Underwood found his surroundings deceptively tranquil. He was less than one mile from the Confederate breastworks, yet "there was a fine breeze drawing through the ravine and the moon in all its splendor rode above us and my first thought was of a huge happy picnic party."[84]

Within the shelter of their camps, soldiers indulged in recreational luxuries. They filled their free time with card games and letter writing. Some took naps while others read.[85] One of the most popular ways to escape the heat was swimming, though this activity posed a peculiar danger: Soldiers shared their swimming holes with all the local fauna. According to several reports,

This wartime photograph shows numerous "shebangs" built down the hill east of Wexford Lodge. *Quarters of Logan's Division in the Trenches in Front of Vicksburg*, 1863. Library of Congress, Prints and Photographs Division.

alligators tended to be especially prevalent in the bayous and streams near Haines Bluff and the Yazoo River. On several occasions, bathing soldiers were injured when they came too close to the large reptiles: "There was one bit the arm off from a soldier swimming," announced Oscar McLouth of the 20th Michigan. The incident was corroborated by Capt. Charles B. Haydon of the same division, who quipped, "If the soldiers would keep out of the river, they would not be eaten."[86] In most cases, though, soldiers and animals could amicably coexist. Wisconsin corporal John Wesley Largent's regiment, for example, swam in a nearby pond filled with snakes, frogs, lizards, leeches, turtles, and birds. "It feels kinder slimy to get in and squirm around among them," he told his sister. Largent's swimming hole sounds like a welcome treat until he admitted to drinking from the same pond. Predictably, by the end of the siege, Largent and many of his comrades were suffering from chronic diarrhea. He died in September.[87] Sometimes, it was the unseen microbes that accompanied the animals into the water that posed the greatest danger.

Water not only cooled the body externally, providing welcome relief from the oppressive heat, but was also needed to replenish lost fluids and stave off dehydration. Ponds like the one near Largent's camp were especially tempting because they offered the illusion of convenience. Enterprising soldiers crafted ways to maximize their access to water while expending as little energy as possible. "When we want a drink it is but little trouble, I'll tell you why," wrote Largent. "One of the boys went down to the slough and grabbed up a handful—drug it up to the tent—tied one end around the center pole, so when we want a drink we loosen the end and drink as much as we want."[88] T. B. Marshall's regiment improvised a similar strategy for their camp by modifying a nearby stream with a barrel "so that not only our regiment but the whole brigade had a good supply of water, clear, and freed from contamination."[89] Clean or contaminated, that Largent's and Marshall's regiments even had access to water was a growing luxury. By the middle of June when the days reached their hottest and the rain was infrequent, the water supply was dwindling.

It was ironic, really, that after a winter characterized by an excess of water, soldiers would suffer from its shortage. While the entire Lower Mississippi River Valley was susceptible to water's carving force, there was a drastic difference between the river's east and west banks. Perkins' Plantation and Milliken's Bend were surrounded by swamps and bayous, but the land around Vicksburg was jagged and dry. Having left the clay-rich soil of the Mississippi forests, the soldiers surrounding Vicksburg were now camped atop deposits of relatively impermeable loess. These hills had little groundwater, and now that both armies were stationary, they were drawing from the same supply.[90] Water resources were rapidly depleted, sometimes lasting only days before drying up completely.[91] Creeks and ponds ran full during the winter and spring when rains were frequent, but as summer wore on many slowed to a trickle or faded into a sporadic network of puddles. Most farmsteads did not rely on these streams. Instead, inhabitants drew from cisterns, while stock ponds served the livestock. Consequently, plantations and farmsteads were the safest choice when searching for potable water, since there was usually a nearby source to sustain the local population. But even these sources threatened to disappear by the end of the dry season. Drought-like conditions meant that soldiers had little control over what kind of water they consumed.

The most obvious source of water was the Mississippi River, and both armies took advantage of it. But the logistics of supplying water from the river were staggering. One scholar has estimated that the Union army needed over 338 wagons solely devoted to collecting and transporting water to meet soldiers' minimum needs.[92] This process could be dangerous. The regularity of soldiers' trips to the river made them subject to enemy fire. On May 23,

General Sherman complained to Rear Adm. David Dixon Porter that his "men get water out of the Mississippi at the cattle pens. The enemy has a 32 par[rot] which sometimes reaches that point."[93] But the water was clean—at least, that is what the locals claimed. Charles Johnson was dubious. "There was so much sediment that a bucket dipped in the current would be filled with water which, after a time would have moved more than an inch of settling in the bottom," he wrote. Johnson eventually learned to wait until after sedimentation to drink his fill and ultimately declared the water "pleasant to drink."[94]

Nevertheless, many regiments preferred to supplement their resources with water foraged from recently dug wells or newly discovered springs.[95] Like the river, these sites were difficult to access and often required soldiers to risk their lives for a simple drink. The closest spring to Thomas Barton's regiment was situated directly between the contending armies, forcing thirsty soldiers to expose themselves to enemy fire. "It was like running a blockade to get a drink of water," wrote Barton. "I frequently made the dangerous journey and about the time I reached the spring would hear the sharp report of the enemy's guns. Sometimes I would remain half an hour to throw them off their guard, and then double quick back with a small supply of water."[96] Illinois private Job Yaggy was one of thirty men from his regiment sent over the next hill to dig a well. Yaggy and his comrades labored for two hours before he was sent to fetch them something for lunch. He was shot returning to camp.[97] Most devastating of all, however, were soldiers who expended their time and energy to locate a source only to find it dry or, worse, unpalatable. When William Eddington's Illinois regiment pitched camp at a creek where they expected to find water, the men found instead "a few little holes covered with green scum about an inch thick." According to Eddington, "You could smell it long before you got to it."[98] Tired and thirsty, they had to decide if the water was worth drinking.

Ultimately, there was no consensus as to whether drinking water from wells and springs was safer than consuming water from the river. Charles Dana and Thomas Barton both believed that excellent water could be found in the ravines, but Robert Jameson declared the water "awful."[99] Capt. William T. Rigby of Iowa was troubled about the water produced by his regiment's well. "It is seep water," he wrote, "and all of it is more or less affected by the clay soil of the country."[100] Like Rigby, most soldiers were concerned about the organic material that filtered through their water. Decaying material was considered poisonous regardless of whether it was ingested or inhaled.[101] But water could also be misleading. Most soldiers would have characterized the deep blue waters of the Yazoo River healthier than the muddy Mississippi, but locals knew better. They warned Joseph Thatcher Woods's regiment, the

Wartime sketch showing the rear of the Union siege lines. Note the city of Vicksburg in the far distance. This view offers some context to the separation between soldiers' camp and the front lines as well as to the space afforded them for forage. *Harper's Weekly*, June 27, 1863, 404. University of Michigan Library Digital Collections.

96th Ohio, away from the river, but the regiment did not pay heed. "We soon learned the value of the advice we had scouted," Woods wrote. "In the hundreds of men [that] became suddenly and very seriously ill was demonstrated that insidious poison may lurk in sparkling sweets."[102] Indeed, the Yazoo was so characterized by sickness that soldiers took to calling it the "River of Death."[103] But if locating and identifying reliable sources of clean water was not intuitive, soldiers had better results when foraging for food.

During the campaign, Union soldiers had better access to fresh fruits and vegetables, which were more desirable and better tasting than the desiccated foodstuff traditionally found in soldiers' rations. But while the quality of food accessible to soldiers during the campaign was preferable, the quantity was limited. Soldiers were restricted to what they could forage, and as the campaign progressed, soldiers at the back of the advancing column found themselves traveling greater distances to find fresh forage. Once troops arrived in Vicksburg, these items slowly returned to their diet with more consistency. New supply lines meant that the Union army returned to full rations with supplemental subsistence provided by the sanitary commissions. However, this did not necessarily end soldiers' foraging opportunities. Instead, foraging continued, but the primary motive between foraging soldiers and the officers who sanctioned their behavior changed. For one, foraging parties took on a defensive role during the siege. Worried that an army of relief commanded by Confederate general Joseph Johnston would launch an attack from Jackson, Grant sent soldiers to strip the land of any resources that would sustain such an assault. In doing so, he transformed the barren land into an accomplice working to undermine and defeat the Confederates.[104]

Additionally, foraging continued as an informal activity, one that supported soldiers' mental health as much as their physical needs. As surgeon John Ordronaux pointed out, "the conquering races of the earth have always been the best fed races," not because they participated in "luxurious indulgences" but because they consumed food that "impressed upon the system a vigorous tone, and thus developed physical courage." Since the mind and body were integrated, the same diet that encouraged physical strength also promoted mental fortitude. As a result, Ordronaux believed that one of the greatest dangers of a soldiers' diet was "monotonous uniformity." He asserted that "however good any single article may in itself be, its continued and exclusive use for any length of time is sure to inspire disgust, and consequently to impair its nutritive character."[105] In other words, a repetitive diet could undermine morale.

Spurred by a combination of restlessness and distaste for desiccated vegetables, soldiers wandered to nearby farmsteads and took their fill. "An hour's march brought us into a man's vegetable garden, where we pitched our tents, much to the injury of the green stuff," wrote William Reid of the 15th Illinois. "The men found Irish potatoes as large as hen's eggs here." Reid and his comrades loved their "vegetable camp" and spent days feasting on potatoes, peas, and beans, "all at the expense of the natives who live on the place."[106] Freshly ripened fruits and vegetables were especially tempting. "I frequently met soldiers coming into camp with buckets full of mulberries, blackberries, and red and yellow wild plums," recalled Charles Dana.[107] Nearly everyone went berrying at some time or another, and when they returned they made delicious pies.[108]

Still, gorging on fresh fruit did have its drawbacks. "Soldiers are like children," Sherman complained; they "eat, eat, eat, all the time." And despite his efforts, he could not make them stop. The overabundance of fruit and corn was too tempting. They gave "our soldiers an additional tendency to sickness—advice, order, and remonstrances are all idle."[109] Surgeon Thomas Blackwell was perplexed by the number of soldiers whose diarrhea seemed perfectly avoidable. "I do not believe that a man who becomes a soldier has the same control of his physical appetites that he has, at home, in civil life, or they would not, while suffering apparently the utmost of their endurance from diarrhea, gormandise such quantities of melons, peaches, apples, etc."[110] Nevertheless, if the overabundance of fresh fruits and vegetables rectified nutritional deficiencies at the expense of introducing too much fiber or sugar into a soldier's diet, many medical officers were willing to deal with the consequences. Surgeon Frank Hamilton informed the Medical Department that benefits of fresh produce outweighed the detriments: "If they occasionally increased or produced diarrhea they have also cured or prevented many more."[111] To that end, Isaac Elliot and the men of the 33rd Illinois used the fresh berries that grew wild around their camp to treat their own intestinal complaints. Elliot remembered quite clearly that "the water was bad and hard to get, and brought on a camp trouble for which most fortunately the abundant blackberries on the nearby hills were almost a specific."[112]

While Union soldiers' diets improved with the siege, Confederate diets declined. "Vicksburg had not been prepared," admitted Confederate surgeon John Leavy. "Our breadstuffs were soon exhausted. . . . We had bacon that was not fit to eat; we had no vegetable supply." Perhaps worse, there was no means to supplement the meager rations. There was little forage left within the city—aside from rats and mules—and soldiers were generally not permitted to leave the front lines. "Our men were exhausted for want of rest and nourishment and the hospitals and field infirmaries were filled by those unable for military duty." By the end of the siege, even Leavy was "barely able to walk."[113] Confederate soldiers suffered from scurvy, a condition caused by a lack of vitamin C. As with many deficiencies, scurvy contributed to a breakdown in soldiers' muscle mass, an increase in apathy and listlessness resulting from cellular degeneration, and the collapse of their immune system. In short, while Union soldiers foraged for fresh fruits and vegetables, sought access to clean water, swam in ponds, and lounged in the shade, Confederates were starving.

By the time Federal troops arrived at Vicksburg, field medical care in the Union army had become more orderly and proficiently executed. The medical corps retained authority over its own supplies and transport, received supplementary donations from the sanitary commissions, and was generally supported by the army's commanding officers. Discipline had evolved to include greater flexibility for soldiers to participate in formal and informal methods of self-care, and troops enjoyed the freedom to forage for fresh food and clean water. For the first time in a month, the siege afforded them the luxury of relaxation. While deteriorating sanitation and the growing sick season threatened the command's health, there were enough reinforcements to sustain the siege. Hardship was relative when Vicksburg was the prize.

None of this could be said of the Confederates. As the siege progressed, sick and emaciated men poured from the trenches, quickly filling the hospitals, and soon surgeons began searching for new places to house the infirm. Civilians saw their homes completely overtaken for use as a field hospital. Vicksburg resident Rowland Chambers's home was already filled with the sick when Confederate soldiers informed him that they needed more space. "Before I knew it, they had the shed nearly cleaned out to use as a hospital. The sick were taken from the house to the shed and the house filled with wounded, many of them badly."[114] Permanent structures soon became a limited commodity and medical officers turned to tents, but Mississippi soldier James West Smith questioned whether these tents could be considered hospitals at all. "The word hospital ever presented a different idea from what is realized here. I thought it properly meant a building furnished with bunks and many other conveniences for the accommodations of the sick and wounded. . . . But alas, not so here." Ill himself, Smith left his command in search of medical care, but when he arrived at a nearby hospital, he found disorder. "I look around and find the tents are filled to over-flow, besides are several pale and weakly looking fellows living promiscuously on the ground, under a very thin willow shade. I take my blankets and after selecting my 'position,' throw them down, and being exceedingly fatigued, sweetly repose."[115] Eventually, space became so limited that there was nowhere for the sick to go. When H. M. Compton forwarded the "very sick and badly wounded" of Maj. Gen. Carter L. Stevenson's division to a nearby general hospital, many of them were returned. "The surgeons say that they cannot obtain admission for all whose conditions required hospital care," Compton complained, finding this unacceptable. "The sick of the brigade are as well cared for as they can be by the Medical Officers of the brigade," but this was not enough. The medical officers near the front lines did not have the equipment to treat the "very sick and badly wounded whose condition required permanent hospital care."[116] With nowhere to go, men stayed in the trenches.

By the start of July, disease was ubiquitous throughout the Confederate army. Nearly one-third of the garrison was hospitalized, and the remaining two-thirds were in questionable health. Realizing that his army was near the end of its endurance, Lt. Gen. John C. Pemberton sent a dispatch to his generals, inquiring whether their soldiers were strong enough to fight their way out of the city. The answer was a resounding "no." "The command suffers greatly from intermittent fever and is generally debilitated from the long exposure and inaction of the trenches," reported Brig. Gen. Seth Barton. He went on to say that one-half of the soldiers reporting for duty were "undergoing treatment" and should not even be in the field. Barton's assessment was echoed by Brig. Gen. Alfred Cumming, who reported that 50 percent of his troops were unfit for duty. Alexander Reynolds reported that two-thirds of his troops were so weak that they would not make it ten miles.[117] Unable to fight and with no relief in sight, Pemberton surrendered. On July 4, 1863, the first Federal troops entered the city.

Epilogue

The fight for Vicksburg ended on July 4, but the medical crisis did not. Having "laid waste" to the country, General Grant made arrangements to provide for the material needs of local residents "to prevent [their] actual starvation and suffering."[1] This corresponded with the arrival of new tents, cooking utensils, and fresh clothes for his men.[2] Corps and division hospitals were consolidated as they transitioned into permanent facilities. And though the summer drought gave way to heavy rains, the heat persisted. With the city in ruins, sanitation collapsed. The streets were filled with standing pools of stagnant water, rotting excrement, and decaying carcasses.[3] According to one Ohioan, "The air was laden with miasmatic vapors, and sickness spread through the camp, attacking nearly a third of some companies, and deaths were frequent."[4] The fighting had stopped, but the medical battles continued. By the end of August, thousands of refugees—Black and white—had flooded into the town searching for food, shelter, and medical care.[5]

The practical challenges of occupying a crumbling and destitute city notwithstanding, the capture of Vicksburg was a strategic triumph. Following the Confederate defeat at Port Hudson, Louisiana, on July 9, Federal forces gained control of the Mississippi River. This not only allowed river traffic to flow freely from Memphis to New Orleans but also severed Texas, Arkansas, and Louisiana from the rest of the Confederacy. Nevertheless, the war continued for another twenty-one months. Following the capture of Chattanooga in November, the Union army was poised to invade Georgia from the northwest. By early 1864, Grant had transferred east, where he launched a six-week campaign through the Virginia wilderness. The Overland Campaign began in Spotsylvania County and ended at Cold Harbor. From there, the Army of the Potomac maneuvered into a 292-day siege of the Confederate breastworks around Petersburg. In the South, General Sherman and the Army of the Tennessee carved a path from Atlanta to Savannah and north toward the Carolinas.

The medical corps's performance in the campaign and siege for Vicksburg encouraged greater cooperation between the Union army and civilian relief organizations, but the relationship would continue to wax and wane. In the months to come, civilian involvement would persist, challenging the boundaries of military authority when approval of the war effort lagged. By 1864, Americans were once again growing weary of the war and the sacrifices it demanded, particularly as the casualties mounted in Virginia. US Sanitary Commission agents became more critical of the Medical Department's performance, again accusing medical officers of recklessness. Much of the suffering, they alleged, was avoidable, the deaths unnecessary. Some military officials pushed back. Already wary of civilian interference, Sherman restricted the USSC's transportation to the front. "Our Sanitary Dept. is now so systematized that there is no use of any one male or female going south of Nashville," he wrote to his brother, just prior to the Atlanta Campaign. "You have no idea of the crowds of men & women who come here on seeming errands of charity, but they might as well stay at home for they simply aggravate the trouble." Later he would add that "the Sanitary Commission should limit its operations to the hospitals at the rear and should never appear at the front."[6] Others were more diplomatic. In early 1865, Henry Bellows, president of the USSC, observed that Grant and the commission enjoyed a beneficial relationship. Consequently, Bellows "troubled him very little."[7]

In early 1864, tensions between USSC agents and military officials were exacerbated by Surgeon General William Hammond's court-martial. Hammond's Medical Department had been characterized by reform, research, and increasing efficiency, but he often clashed with Secretary of War Edwin Stanton. As the senior medical officer of the United States Army, Hammond believed that he held ultimate authority over the Medical Department and its officers, but Stanton viewed the surgeon general's cooperation with the USSC with suspicion.[8] Conflict came to a head in May 1863. After receiving reports that soldiers at Vicksburg displayed symptoms of mercury and calomel overdose, Hammond issued Circular No. 6, which prohibited the use of calomel and tarter emetic. Unfortunately, both substances were widely prescribed and considered integral to the pharmacopeia, particularly by the more senior members of the medical community. As a result, there was public backlash as military surgeons and civilian physicians took offense at the surgeon general's orders. The Ohio State Medical Society, for example, issued a statement demanding that the circular be revoked, noting that "the Society believed that the surgeons and assistant surgeons from this State are well qualified, and that Circular No. 6 not only implies that they were not qualified to administer safely two remedies, but raises a doubt in the public mind as to their general skill or ability." Two of the society's members went a step further and requested "the speedy trial and expulsion of Dr. W. A. Hammond, for the growing injustice done the profession of medicine by his foolish and quackish order." For once, public outrage worked in Stanton's favor. He quickly leveraged the controversy into an investigation that led to Hammond's removal from office in August 1864.[9]

Though Hammond was no longer with the Medical Department, the impact of his policies and reforms continued to shape Civil War medical care. As military operations became increasingly complex, so too did the demands of battlefield medicine. Later campaigns shared many of the challenges faced by the medical corps at Vicksburg. Making its way from Nashville to Chattanooga, medical officers in the Army of the Cumberland had to decide between dragging sick and convalescent soldiers along, scattering them among various temporary hospitals located between the front and Nashville, or consolidating them into a central location easily supplied by the army's base.[10] Similarly, the increasing casualties of Grant's Overland Campaign mimicked and even exceeded the ten days in May 1863 when medical officers in the Army of the Tennessee collected, triaged, and treated over 8,064 casualties. Between the Battle of the Wilderness on May 5 and Cold Harbor on June 12, the Overland Campaign included at least ten separate engagements and produced nearly 55,000 casualties in the Union army alone. However, the strongest connections might be drawn between the Vicksburg Campaign and Sherman's March to the Sea. Having seen the speed and devastation with which foraging armies moved across the land, Sherman abandoned his supply line in Atlanta and ordered his men to "forage liberally on the country." As at Vicksburg, soldiers indulged in the freedom to manage their own physical and emotional needs, and reports indicated that the army's health improved on the march.[11] More studies dedicated to highlighting the medical corps's centrality to field operations would only serve to strengthen these connections and more.

The campaign and siege of Vicksburg is not merely a story of military conquest. It is a story about the conflict between health care providers and reluctant patients, confrontations over individuals' right to care for their own bodies, and the physical and emotional suffering generated by war. The veterans who lived and fought along the Lower Mississippi River Valley recognized that the Army of the Tennessee's success at Vicksburg was not only about defeating Confederates but about overcoming the environmental and medical challenges of the region. Thirty-eight years after Pemberton's surrender, Christian Riebsame was eager to contribute his memories to the growing body of veterans' accounts collected by the Vicksburg Military Park Commission. A former captain of the 116th Illinois, Riebsame was intimately familiar with all the threats to soldiers' survival. He had faced each enemy himself. Having charged the bluffs at Chickasaw Bayou, he and his comrades labored along the canal, foraged through the country, and charged the battlefield at Champion Hill. Shortly after the assault on May 22, Riebsame developed intermittent fever and was removed to a hospital in the rear, where he remained for the rest of the siege. Although undoubtedly trying at the time, by 1901 Riebsame remembered Vicksburg as one the army's greatest accomplishments. He yearned to return to the city before his "final muster out" so that he might remember the summer he spent in Mississippi "fighting johnnies, fevers, and mosquitoes."[12]

Notes

ABBREVIATIONS

ALPL	Abraham Lincoln Presidential Library, Springfield, IL
LOC	Library of Congress, Manuscripts Division, Washington, DC
NARA	National Archives and Records Administration, Washington, DC
OR	United States War Department, *The War of the Rebellion: A Compilation of the Official Records of the Union and Confederate Armies*, 128 vols. (Washington, DC: Government Printing Office, 1880–1901)
RFHL	Reynolds-Finley Historical Library, University of Alabama at Birmingham
RG 94	Record Group 94: Records of the Adjutant General's Office, National Archives and Records Administration, Washington, DC
RG 112	Record Group 112: Records of the Office of the Surgeon General, National Archives and Records Administration, Washington, DC
SHI	State Historical Society of Iowa, Des Moines
USAHEC	US Army Heritage and Education Center, US Army War College, Carlisle, PA

USGPL Ulysses S. Grant Presidential Library,
       Mississippi State University, Starkville
VNMP   Vicksburg National Military Park, Vicksburg, MS
WHS   Wisconsin Historical Society, Madison

INTRODUCTION

1. Clampitt, *Occupied Vicksburg*, 24–25; Mahan, *Memoirs of James Curtis Mahan*, 133.

2. Christopher R. Blackall, "In the Tornado: Days of '62–64: From the Diary and Letters of an Army Surgeon to His Family," 96, Christopher R. Blackall Memoirs, WHS.

3. Charles Dana to Edwin Stanton, July 5, 1863, Edwin McMasters Stanton Papers, Correspondence, 1831–1870, June 16–August 6, 1863, LOC.

4. Cooke, *Badger Boy in Blue*, 76, 79.

5. Devine, *Learning from the Wounded*, 3–4. For more on the relationship between formal medical care and informal domestic care, see Valenčius, *Health of the Country*. Over the years, many historians have examined the evolution of the medical profession as well as its changing reputation. See Kaufman, *American Medical Education*; Starr, *Social Transformation of American Medicine*; Duffy, *From Humors to Medical Science*; Humphreys, *Marrow of Tragedy*; Meier, *Nature's Civil War*; and Sappol, *Traffic of Dead Bodies*, 47–48.

6. The United States Army Medical Department is the healthcare organization for the United States Army. It is headed by the Surgeon General of the US Army, who is responsible for the bureaucratic oversight of personnel, supplies, and patient care. The United States Medical Corps, by contrast, comprised the healthcare providers directly involved with patient care. In many instances, the term "medical corps" is used to refer specifically to surgeons. As a result, this book utilizes the term "field medical service" as a broader classification referring to anyone involved in patient care. This includes but is not limited to surgeons, assistant surgeons, hospital stewards, nurses, etc.

7. The US Medical Department's limitations during the first years of the war is well documented in Cunningham, *Field Medical Services*; Adams, *Doctors in Blue*; Bollet, *Civil War Medicine*; and Rutkow, *Bleeding Blue and Gray*.

8. For an overview, see Linderman, *Embattled Courage*; Hess, *Liberty, Virtue, and Progress*; Sheehan-Dean, *View from the Ground*; Reardon, *With a Sword in One Hand*; Meier, *Nature's Civil War*; and Carmichael, *War for the Common Soldier*. Meier and Carmichael also extend this conversation into the realm of soldiers' health and medical care. Meier, *Nature's Civil War*, 33, 66–70; and Carmichael, *War for the Common Soldier*, 145–46.

9. For a general overview of the United States Sanitary Commission, see Maxwell, *Lincoln's Fifth Wheel*. Meier, "U.S. Sanitary Commission Physicians," offers an overview of the USSC as a reforming arm for the Medical Department. Meier, *Nature's Civil War*, 70–72.

10. G. Jones, "Medical History of the Fredericksburg Campaign"; Bollet, *Civil War Medicine*; Rutkow, *Bleeding Blue and Gray*. The notable exception is Adams, *Doctors in Blue*.

11. Saikku, *This Delta*, 27; and "LMVJV Geography," Lower Mississippi Valley Joint Venture, accessed January 20, 2025, www.lmvjv.org/lmvjv-geography.

12. Grabau, *Ninety-Eight Days*, 14; C. Morris, *Big Muddy*, 2–4. Morris is quick to point out how humans have sought to tame the Mississippi, thereby posing restrictions on the river's natural changes. These efforts culminated by the twentieth century with the work of the US Army Corps of Engineers, which maintains stewardship of the river in present day.

13. Grabau, *Ninety-Eight Days*, 16–19.

14. Grabau, *Ninety-Eight Days*, 14, 20–22; Noe, *Howling Storm*, 241.

15. Nearly every scholar who has written about Vicksburg has highlighted how the region's demanding geography thwarted Grant's efforts to take the city. See Bearss, *Campaign for Vicksburg*; Grabau, *Ninety-Eight Days*; Ballard, *Vicksburg*; Solonick, *Engineering Victory*; Hess, *Storming Vicksburg*; D. Miller, *Vicksburg*; and T. B. Smith, *Bayou Battles for Vicksburg*. Smith's work is one of five volumes, all of which emphasize the region's difficult geography. However, *Bayou Battles for Vicksburg* is perhaps the most extensive environmental analysis of the Union army's movements against Vicksburg to date.

16. "Mississippi Climate," Mississippi State University Department of Geosciences, accessed January 20, 2025, www.geosciences.msstate.edu/state-climatologist/mississippi-climate. ; Saikku, *This Delta*, 28; Grabau, *Ninety-Eight Days*, 16–19.

17. Several works have explored the relationship between the environment and disease. Works like Valenčius's *Health of the Country* and Brady's *War upon the Land* deal with popular perception of the diseased landscapes and their relationship to human health. Bell's *Mosquito Soldiers* and Meier's *Nature's Civil War* explore how environmental factors such as mosquitoes, heat, shade, and water compromised soldiers' bodies. Finally, Browning and Silver's *Environmental History of the Civil War* explores how environmental conditions create the breeding ground for microorganisms such as bacteria and viruses to grow and spread.

18. Though many studies have examined the environment's role in shaping military operations near Vicksburg, many incorporate their analysis into a study focused on broader themes. See, for example, Bell, *Mosquito Soldiers*; Brady, *War upon the Land*; Browning and Silver, *Environmental History of the Civil War*; and Noe, *Howling Storm*.

19. By the 1860s, bacteria had been observed, but physicians did not understand the causal relationship between bacteria and their patients' ailments. Furthermore, while Lister's germ theory was published in 1867, it would not be widely accessible to American physicians until a decade later. For more on the development of laboratory-based medicine, see Cunningham and Williams, *Laboratory Revolution in Medicine*; and Bynum, *Science and the Practice of Medicine*. For an overview of the early scholarship on Civil War medicine, see Brookes, *Civil War Medicine*; Shryock, "A Medical Perspective on the Civil War," in *Medicine in America*; and Steiner, *Disease in the Civil War*.

20. To date, Humphreys's *Marrow of Tragedy* remains the most comprehensive treatment of Civil War medicine, while Devine's *Learning from the Wounded* is among the first works to consider the medical corps' scientific contributions. For more on how Civil War era physicians influenced gender and racial ideologies of the era as well as contemporary understandings of disability, mental illness, and addiction, see B. Miller, *Empty Sleeves*; Downs, *Sick from Freedom*; Handley-Cousins, *Bodies in Blue*; Carroll, *Invisible Wounds*; and J. S. Jones, *Opium Slavery*.

21. Meier, *Nature's Civil War*; B. Miller, *Empty Sleeves*; Carmichael, *War for the Common Soldier*; Handley-Cousins, *Bodies in Blue*.

CHAPTER 1

1. Scott, *History of the 67th Regiment*, 13.
2. Quoted in Halsell, "Sixteenth Indiana Regiment," 69.
3. Mason, *Forty-Second Ohio Infantry*, 152–53.
4. Scott, *History of the 67th Regiment*, 16.
5. For more on soldiers' perceptions of the wilderness, see Brady, *War upon the Land*; and Petty, *Battle of the Wilderness*.
6. Schuler Coe to Parents, January 6, 1863, Schuler Coe Letters, box 24, folder 2, Civil War Document Collection, USAHEC.
7. Charles McMillan, "Circular," December 20, 1862, published in Andrews, *Complete Record of the Surgery*, 5–7.
8. Freemon, "Lincoln Finds a Surgeon General," 6.
9. Rutkow, *Bleeding Blue and Gray*, 6–9.
10. Russell, *Battle of Bull Run*, 5–6.
11. Cunningham, *Field and Medical Services*; A. B. Shipman, "The Battle of Bull Run," *American Medical Times* 3 (August 1861): 111–12; "The Horrors of War," *Boston Herald*, August 6, 1861; "Improved Military Science and the Duties of the Army Surgeon," *American Medical Times* 3 (November 1861): 539–40.
12. Beach, "Army Surgeons."
13. Draft of Powers Asked from the Government by Sanitary Delegation to the President and the Secretary of War, May 23, 1861, p. 3, Sanitary Commission collection no. 2, RFHL.
14. Maxwell, *Lincoln's Fifth Wheel*, 5; Draft of Powers Asked from the Government by Sanitary Delegation to the President and the Secretary of War, May 23, 1861, Sanitary Commission no. 2, RFHL. For more on the USSC's relationship to the US Medical Department and its reforms, see Blustein, "To Increase the Efficiency of the Medical Department"; and Meier, "U.S. Sanitary Commission Physicians."
15. Forman, *Western Sanitary Commission*, 7.
16. Maxwell, *Lincoln's Fifth Wheel*, 97–100.
17. J. S. Newberry, "A Visit to Fort Donelson, Tenn., for the Relief of the Wounded of Feb'y 15, 1862," 5–6, Sanitary Commission no. 42, RFHL.
18. Newberry, "Visit to Fort Donelson."
19. Newberry, "Visit to Fort Donelson."
20. Stillé, *History of the United States Sanitary Commission*, 147–50; Forman, *Western Sanitary Commission*, 26.
21. *United States Sanitary Commission*, 165.
22. Stillé, *History of the United States Sanitary Commission*, 57–58.
23. S.-M. Grant, "'Mortal in this Season,'" 698.
24. Boos and White, "Civil War Diary."
25. Sherman, *Sherman's Civil War*, 291–92.
26. Stillé, *History of the United States Sanitary Commission*, 57–58.
27. Marshall, *History of the Eighty-Third Ohio*, 54.
28. Devine, *Learning from the Wounded*, 14.
29. Shiepko, "William Alexander Hammond's Transformation," 83–89. For more on Stanton's relationship with Hammond, see Marvel, *Lincoln's Autocrat*, 156, 313–25.

30. John H. Brinton, "Transportation of Sick and Wounded and Medical and Hospital Supplies," entry 621, Medical Records: Reports of Disease and Individual Cases, 1841–1893, file A and bound manuscripts, 1861–65, box 12, A442, RG 94.

31. *OR*, ser. 3, 2:22. (All following citations from the OR are from series 1.) This reform was strongly encouraged by Robert Murray after seeing medical officers' struggle to obtain supplies firsthand at Pittsburg Landing. Murray, "Report from the Union Medical Director."

32. United States Surgeon General's Office, *Medical and Surgical History*, 5:972; Alexander H. Hoff, "Relative to Hospital Transports on the Mississippi River," entry 621, Medical Records: Reports of Disease and Individual Cases, 1841–1893, file A and bound manuscripts, 1861–65, box 12, A444, RG 94.

33. For a general overview, see Adams, *Doctors in Blue*; Bollet, *Civil War Medicine*; and Rutkow, *Bleeding Blue and Gray*. For more specific analysis regarding the US Sanitary Commission, see Maxwell, *Lincoln's Fifth Wheel*; and Meier, "U.S. Sanitary Commission Physicians."

34. Duffy, *From Humors to Medical Science*, 133–34, 140; Starr, *Social Transformation of American Medicine*, 40–45; Devine, *Learning from the Wounded*, 3; Kaufman, *American Medical Education*, 68.

35. A more thorough overview of the sectarians may be found in Haller's *Sectarian Reformers*.

36. "Army and Navy. Regulations for Admission and Promotion in the Medical Department of the Army," *American Medical Times* 5 (October 1862): 206.

37. Shyrock, "Empiricism versus Rationalism"; Meier, "U.S. Sanitary Commission Physicians," 24.

38. Devine, *Learning from the Wounded*, 21–22, 29–33; Circular No. 2, May 21, 1862, 23, entry 63, Central Office Issuances and Forms: Circulars and Letters of the Surgeon General's Office, box 1, RG 112.

39. For an overview of the Medical Department's professional reputation in the decades after the Civil War, see Wintermute, *Public Health and the U.S. Military*.

40. For more on Surgeon General William Alexander Hammond and the reform of the Medical Department, see Blustein, "To Increase the Efficiency of the Medical Department"; Freemon, "Lincoln Finds a Surgeon General"; Flannery "Another House Divided"; and S.-M. Grant, "'Mortal in this Season.'" Each of these studies contextualizes Hammond's work as being in line with the USSC's reform efforts. Similarly, Kramer, "Effect of the Civil War," and Meier, "U.S. Sanitary Commission Physicians," also focus on the alignment between the USSC's reform efforts and Hammond's vision for the Medical Department.

41. Thomas Williams to his wife, June 28, 1862, in G. Williams, "Letters of General Thomas Williams," 322. The details of Farragut's naval bombardment and Williams's canal have been recounted several times. See Steiner, *Disease in the Civil War*, 186–200; Messner, "Vicksburg Campaign of 1862"; and McPherson, *Battle Cry of Freedom*, 420–22.

42. United States Navy Department, *Official Records of the Union and Confederate Navies*, 23:240, 237, 240, 239, 272.

43. United States Navy Department, *Official Records of the Union and Confederate Navies*, 23:272.

44. Sherman, *Memoirs*, 285; Sherman, *Sherman's Civil War*, 258–59.

45. George T. Allen to R. C. Wood, December 18, 1862, entry 12, Office of the Surgeon General, Letters Received, 1818–1870, box 108, RG 112.

46. Sherman, *Memoirs*, 304; Bearss, *Campaign for Vicksburg*, vol. 1, *Vicksburg Is the Key*, 114–15; Hess, *Civil War in the West*, 113.

47. Hess, *Civil War in the West*, 118–21.

48. D. Porter, *Incidents and Anecdotes*, 95–96.

49. Allen to Wood, December 18, 1862, entry 12, Office of the Surgeon General, Letters Received, 1818–1870, box 108, RG 112.

50. Alexander H. Hoff, "Relative to Hospital Transports on the Mississippi River," entry 621, Medical Records: Reports of Disease and Individual Cases, 1841–1893, file A and bound manuscripts, 1861–65, box 12, A444, RG 94.

51. Allen to Wood, December 17, 1863, entry 12, Office of the Surgeon General, Letters Received, 1818–1870, box 108, RG 112.

52. Mason, *Forty-Second Ohio Infantry*, 150.

53. Black, *Soldier's Recollections*, 25.

54. Bearss, *Campaign for Vicksburg*, vol. 1, *Vicksburg Is the Key*, 155, 158–59.

55. Schuler Coe to Parents, January 6, 1863, Schuler Coe Letters, box 24, folder 2, Civil War Document Collection, USAHEC.

56. Buegel, "Civil War Diary," 328.

57. Illinois Infantry 55th Regt., *The Story of the Fifty-Fifth Regiment*, 188.

58. Bearss, *Campaign for Vicksburg*, vol. 1, *Vicksburg Is the Key*, 160.

59. Henry C. Davisson to Wife, January 3, 1863, box 1, folder 1, Henry C. Davisson Collection, Mississippi Department of Archives and History, Jackson.

60. McMillan, "Circular," published in Andrews, *Complete Record of the Surgery*, 5–7.

61. *OR* 17 (1): 654.

62. Buegel, "Civil War Diary," 329.

63. Black, *Soldier's Recollections*, 27.

64. Douglas Ritchie Bushnell to Unknown, December 31, 1862, box 19, folder 10, Civil War Documents Collection, Douglas Ritchie Bushnell Letters, USAHEC.

65. Buegel, "Civil War Diary," 329.

66. Andrews, *Complete Record of the Surgery*, 9.

67. Charles McMillan, "List of Casualties, Vicksburg, December 27, 28, 29, 1862," entry 621, Medical Records: Reports of Disease and Individual Cases, 1841–1893, file A and bound manuscripts, 1861–65, box 21, A273, RG 94.

68. "City of Memphis: December 28, 1862–October 2, 1863," register 9, *City of Memphis*, entry 544, Field Records of Hospitals, 1821–1912, RG 94.

69. Andrews, *Complete Record of the Surgery*, 3–4.

70. Andrews, *Complete Record of the Surgery*, 47–48.

71. Douglas Ritchie Bushnell to Unknown, December 31, 1862, USHEC.

72. *OR* 17 (1): 667.

73. John A. McClernand to Edwin M. Stanton, January 3, 1863, box 18, January 1–5, 1863, John A. McClernand Papers, ALPL.

74. "The Vicksburgh Failure," *New York Times*, January 19, 1863.

75. "The Mississippi Expedition," *New York Times*, January 20, 1863.

76. "From Vicksburg," *Chicago Tribune*, January 13, 1863.

77. "Later," *Chicago Tribune*, January 14, 1863.

78. Henry Davisson to Wife, January 3, 1863, Henry C. Davisson Collection, Mississippi Department of Archives and History.

CHAPTER 2

1. Henry Clemons to Wife, February 20, 1863, Henry Clemons Civil War Letters, WHS.
2. Quiner, *Military History of Wisconsin*, 711. Quiner states that by the time the 23rd left Milliken's Bend, they had lost 150 men by death and another 113 by discharge.
3. John G. Jones to Parents, February 7, 1863, John G. Jones Civil War Letters, WHS.
4. Quiner, *Military History of Wisconsin*, 711.
5. Henry Clemons to Wife, February [?] 1863 and February 2[?], 1863, WHS.
6. Henry Clemons to Wife, February 20, 1863, WHS.
7. United States Surgeon General's Office, *Medical and Surgical History*, 4:97.
8. *OR* 24 (3): 109.
9. Henry Clemons to Wife, February 20, 1863, WHS.
10. "Registers of Deaths of Volunteers, Compiled 1861–1865, Wisconsin, A–G, 77," accessed January 20, 2025, Ancestry.com.
11. The most thorough examination of Grant's efforts to take Vicksburg between January 1 and April 30, including the canal project and bayou expeditions, is chronicled in T. B. Smith, *Bayou Battles for Vicksburg*.
12. U. Grant, *Personal Memoirs*, 1:369–70.
13. *OR* 24 (1): 8.
14. William T. Sherman to Ellen Sherman, January 28, 1863, in Sherman, *Sherman's Civil War*, 377.
15. Valenčius's *Health of the Country* is the most thorough study examining how nineteenth-century Americans saw themselves connected to the land. Meier, *Nature's Civil War*, examines how that relationship shaped soldiers' wartime experiences.
16. U. Grant, *Personal Memoirs*, 1:383–84. In his memoirs, Grant singles out both Maj. Gen. Henry W. Halleck and President Lincoln for their unconditional support.
17. Grabau, *Ninety-Eight Days*, 18.
18. Seneca Thrall to Wife, January 28, 1863, Seneca B. Thrall Civil War Letters, SHI.
19. Valenčius, *Health of the Country*, 109–32. Domestic medical books such as Folger's *Family Physician* regularly emphasized the importance of pure and hygienic air.
20. In the terminology of the day, rotting organic matter of vegetable origin was sometimes referred to as kiono-miasmata. If it was animal in origin, it was referred to as idio-miasmata. Hammond, "Miasmatic Fevers," in *Military Medical and Surgical Essays*, 207–8; D. Smith, "Rise and Fall of Typhomalarial Fever," 216; Woodward, *Outlines of the Chief Camp Diseases*, 28–57.
21. United States Surgeon General's Office, *Medical and Surgical History*, 6:331; Woodward, *Outlines of the Chief Camp Diseases*, 32, 37, 42.
22. Ordronaux, *Hints on Health*, 52–55; United States Sanitary Commission, "Camp Inspection Return," 6–7, Sanitary Commission Series, no. 19, RFHL; United States Sanitary Commission, "Revised General Instructions," 11–12, Sanitary Commission Series, no. 51, RFHL.
23. At the time, McArthur's division was a part of the XVII Army Corps. It was the only division from that corps located at Young's Point.

24. Frank Blair's 1st Brigade and John Thayer's 3rd Brigade were the two located at the canal. The reserve brigade was under the command of Charles Hovey.

25. Bering and Montgomery, *History of the Forty-Eighth Ohio*, 71–72; Bearss, *Campaign for Vicksburg*, vol. 1, *Vicksburg Is the Key*, 438–39.

26. Seneca Thrall to Wife, January 28, 1863, SHI.

27. "Special Orders No. 141," January 23, 1863, John A. McClernand, filed in Published Files, Ulysses S. Grant to J. A. Hammond (WA Hammond), July 10, 1863, USGPL; May 25, May 27, and May 29, 1863, box 64, folder 1, Orrin Albert Kellam Diary, Civil War Documents Collection, USAHEC.

28. Wells, *Siege of Vicksburg*, 31–33.

29. OR 24 (3): 17; William T. Sherman to Ellen Sherman, February 6, 1863, in Sherman, *Sherman's Civil War*, 394.

30. Illinois Infantry 55th Regt., *Story of the Fifty-Fifth Regiment*, 220.

31. Ulysses S. Grant to Willis A. Gorman, February 1, 1863, in Simon, *Papers of Ulysses S. Grant*, 7:276; Ulysses S. Grant to Willis A. Gorman, February 4, 1863, filed in Published Files, Ulysses S. Grant to W. A. Gorman, February 1, 1863, USGPL.

32. Woodward, *Outlines of the Chief Camp Diseases*, 42, 48–49.

33. J. Woods, *Services of the Ninety-Sixth Ohio Volunteers*, 26.

34. Ritner, *Love and Valor*, 114.

35. OR 24 (3): 10.

36. Bearss, *Campaign for Vicksburg*, vol. 1, *Vicksburg Is the Key*, 441.

37. Wells, *Siege of Vicksburg*, 33.

38. Bearss, *Campaign for Vicksburg*, vol. 1, *Vicksburg Is the Key*, 444–45; OR 24 (1): 20.

39. Bering and Montgomery, *History of the 48th Ohio*, 71–72; Bearss, *Campaign for Vicksburg*, vol. 1, *Vicksburg Is the Key*, 438–39.

40. Henry Strong to unknown, March 31, 1863, Henry P. Strong Letters, WHS.

41. Seneca Thrall to Mollie, Annie, Frank, Nellie, and Etc., February 25, 1863, Seneca B. Thrall Civil War Letters, SHI.

42. Scott, *History of the 67th Regiment*, 25.

43. Mayo Clinic Staff, "Hypothermia," Mayo Clinic, last modified April 16, 2024, www.mayoclinic.org/diseases-conditions/hypothermia/symptoms-causes/syc-20352682.

44. Winschel, *Civil War Diary of a Common Soldier*, 35.

45. Seneca Thrall to Wife, February 3, 1863, SHI.

46. Meier, *Nature's Civil War*, 2–15, 99–125.

47. Barton, *Autobiography*, 95–96.

48. Winschel, *Civil War Diary of a Common Soldier*, 39.

49. Bollet, "Medical Problems of the Civil War," 128; "Body Lice," Centers for Disease Control and Prevention, last modified June 24, 2024, www.cdc.gov/lice/about/body-lice.html?CDC_AAref_Val=https://www.cdc.gov/parasites/lice/body/index.html; "Parasites: Scabies," Centers for Disease Control and Prevention, last modified February 9, 2024, www.cdc.gov/scabies/about/?CDC_AAref_Val=https://www.cdc.gov/parasites/scabies/disease.html.

50. United States Surgeon General's Office, *Medical and Surgical History*, 6:31.

51. Ritner, *Love and Valor*, 133–34.

52. By the middle of the nineteenth century, the idea of immersion baths was becoming popular after centuries of disuse, and the hygienic benefits of clean clothes was also recognized. See K. Brown, *Foul Bodies*. Additionally, Meier discusses the popularity of bathing among Civil War soldiers and contextualizes it as one of their more favorable self-care strategies. Meier, *Nature's Civil War*, 100–104.

53. Pitts, "Civil War Diary," 33, 36–38.

54. Sperry, *History of the 33rd Iowa*, 19.

55. OR 24 (3): 18.

56. John A. McClernand to Major [?], January 25, 1863, filed in Published Files, Ulysses S. Grant to J. A. McClernand, January 31, 1863, USGPL.

57. OR 24 (3): 19.

58. For more information on the tension between regular line officers and the Medical Department, see Wintermute, *Public Health and the U.S. Military*, 5–6.

59. McClernand had a tendency to be abrupt and rigid in his decision-making. One subordinate officer complained that he was "dictatorial," "disagreeable," and "unreasonable." However, McClernand's effort to negotiate a solution is in keeping with his character as a political general. To side fully with the colonel would have caused a public outcry that reflected badly upon him. To side with the medical director could be read as a betrayal by subordinate line officers. For better insight into McClernand's personality and his relationship with Grant and other officers, see Kiper, *Major General John Alexander McClernand*; and Meyers, *Union General John A. McClernand*.

60. John A. McClernand to Major [?], January 25, 1863, USGPL.

61. OR 24 (3): 18.

62. Assistant Surgeon B. S. Chase to Medical Director B. B. Brashear, February 27, 1863, box 21, February 25–27, 1863, John A. McClernand Papers, ALPL.

63. The comparison between army camps and cities is also used in scholarship on prison camps. See Marvel, *Andersonville*.

64. OR 24 (3): 74–75. Returns for the month of February indicated that there were 45,938 present for duty in the XIII and XIV Army Corps.

65. Assistant Surgeon B. S. Chase to Medical Director B. B. Brashear, February 27, 1863, ALPL.

66. D. Smith, "Rise and Fall of Typhomalarial Fever," 182–83.

67. Bell, *Mosquito Soldiers*, 11. For more information on symptomatic fevers and how they were classified, see Wilson, "Fevers and Science in Early Nineteenth Century Medicine," 386–407.

68. United States Surgeon General's Office, *Medical and Surgical History*, 1:xvi–xvii, 4–718.

69. Steiner, *Disease in the Civil War*, 60. Occurrences of acute respiratory distress syndrome among military personnel was first studied during World War II. At that time, researchers found distinct patterns with regard to seasonality as well as transmission. Since then, acute respiratory distress syndrome has been routinely examined within the US military. Sanchez et al., "Respiratory Infections in the U.S. Military"; Mayo Clinic Staff, "ARDS," Mayo Clinic, last modified July 30, 2024, www.mayoclinic.org/diseases-conditions/ards/symptoms-causes/syc-20355576.

70. Barton, *Autobiography*, 142–43.

71. Bollet, *Civil War Medicine*, 272–73; Mayo Clinic Staff, "Typhoid Fever," Mayo Clinic, last modified January 28, 2023, www.mayoclinic.org/diseases-conditions/typhoid-fever/symptoms-causes/syc-20378661.

72. Bollet has written extensively about evidence of amebiasis outbreaks among Civil War soldiers; see *Civil War Medicine*, 367–68.

73. Ordronaux, *Hints on Health*, 58.

74. Don [?] to W. B. Scates, February 25, 1863, box 21, February 25–27, 1863, John A. McClernand Papers, ALPL. Is should be noted that Edward C. Franklin practiced homeopathic medicine, a fact that could have made him unpopular among other members of the Medical Department. For more information on Franklin, see Rutkow and Rutkow, "Homeopaths, Surgery, and the Civil War." He is also mentioned briefly in Flannery, "Another House Divided."

75. It is estimated that this is the case for 2–3 percent of survivors. Bollet, *Civil War Medicine*, 274.

76. Scott, *History of the 67th Regiment*, 25.

77. J. A. McClernand to Ulysses S. Grant, February 2, 1863, filed in Published Files, Ulysses S. Grant to G. W. Deitzler, February 2, 1863, USGPL.

78. Willison, *Reminiscences of a Boy's Service*, 45.

79. Abernethy, "Incidents of an Iowa Soldier's Life," 409.

80. Folgers, *Family Physician*, 53.

81. Stillé, *History of the United States Sanitary Commission*, 332.

82. The army's extensive control over soldiers' bodies is considered one of the hallmarks of modern warfare. See Bourke, *Dismembering the Male*; and Cooter et al., *Medicine and Modern Warfare*.

83. Ambrose, *Wisconsin Boy in Dixie*, 72–73.

84. For further study regarding soldiers' struggle to prove illness as a disability, see Handley-Cousins, *Bodies in Blue*.

85. Ambrose, *Wisconsin Boy in Dixie*, 72–73.

86. For more on tensions between soldiers and officers, see Carmichael, *War for the Common Soldier*, 145–46. See also Meier, *Nature's Civil War*, 33, 66–70; and L. Thompson, *Friendly Enemies*, 21–24.

87. Mason, *The Forty-Second Ohio Infantry*, 168.

88. T. Marshall, *History of the Eighty-Third Ohio*, 54.

89. Black, *Soldier's Recollections*, 37.

90. Henry Ankeny to wife, February 4, 1863, in Ankeny, *Kiss Josey for Me!*, 129.

91. Untitled document, box 3, Thomas Madison Reece Papers, ALPL.

92. "Special Orders No. 262," February 21, 1863, box 21, folder 7, John A. McClernand Papers, ALPL.

93. R. C. Wood to Ulysses S. Grant, March 14, 1863, filed in Published Files, Ulysses S. Grant to R. C. Wood, March 5, 1863, USGPL.

94. Ulysses S. Grant to G. T. Allen, March 8, 1863, filed in Published Files, Ulysses S. Grant to G. T. Allen, March 8, 1863, USGPL.

95. J. K. to Editors Patriot, June 19, 1863, Quiner Scrapbooks: Correspondence of the Wisconsin Volunteers, 1861–1865, 10:268, WHS.

96. Charles O. Musser to Father, January 26, 1863, in Popchock, *Soldier Boy*, 20.

97. Oak, *On the Skirmish Line*, 93.

98. Grecian, *History of the Eighty-Third Regiment*, 22.

99. J. Woods, *Services of the Ninety-Sixth Ohio Volunteers*, 26.

100. Douglas Ritchie Bushnell to wife, March 8, 1863, box 19, folder 10, Civil War Documents Collection, Douglas Ritchie Bushnell Papers, USAHEC.

101. Mason, *Forty-Second Ohio Infantry*, 182–83.

102. Oak, *On the Skirmish Line*, 93; Mason, *Forty-Second Ohio Infantry*, 150; Willison, *Reminiscences of a Boy's Service*, 48.

103. Recent scholarship has revealed how the Civil War disrupted the notion of the "good death" popularly held by most nineteenth-century Americans. There is an extensive historiography on the cultural and social rituals of death. Faust, *This Republic of Suffering*, is perhaps best known among Civil War historians. However, Nudelman, *John Brown's Body*, and Schantz, *Awaiting the Heavenly Country*, offer valuable discussions regarding the cultural meaning of death and how it might be wielded to encourage soldiers' sacrifice in battle. Ariès's *Hour of Our Death* takes a long durée approach, examining how people's relationship to death and the dying process changed between the Middle Ages and the nineteenth century. More specialized studies such as Ferrell's *Inventing the American Way of Death* and Jalland's *Death in the Victorian Family* examine the religious, social, and cultural shifts that transformed the rituals surrounding death in Anglo-American society during the nineteenth century. Undoubtedly, the Civil War played a significant role in this process.

104. Willison, *Reminiscences of a Boy's Service*, 45.

105. Willison, *Reminiscences of a Boy's Service*, 9.

106. Winschel, *Civil War Diary of a Common Soldier*, 35, 36.

107. Black, *Soldier's Recollections*, 37.

108. Illinois Infantry 55th Regt., *Story of the Fifty-Fifth Regiment*, 220.

109. Grecian, *History of the Eighty-Third Regiment*, 22–23.

110. Willison, *Reminiscences of a Boy's Service*, 44.

111. B. B. Brashear to W. B. Scates, February 15, 1863, box 20, February 15–16, 1863, John A. McClernand Papers, ALPL.

112. Bering and Montgomery, *History of the 48th Ohio*, 72.

113. McClernand to unknown, February 23, 1863, box 21, February 25–27, John A. McClernand Papers, ALPL.

114. John A. Rawlins to Maj. Gen. Stephen A. Hurlbut, February 15, 1863, in Simon, *Papers of Ulysses S. Grant*, 7:394.

115. Simon, *Papers of Ulysses S. Grant*, 7:393.

116. "Monstrous Medical Abuses!," *Milwaukee Daily Sentinel*, February 21, 1863.

117. Illinois Infantry 55th Regiment, *Story of the Fifty-Fifth Regiment*, 217–18.

118. *OR* 24 (1): 18.

119. William T. Sherman to Thomas Ewing, February 17, 1863, in Sherman, *Sherman's Civil War*, 400.

120. Thomas Townsend to Mattie Van Ness, January 18, 1863, in Puck, *Sacrifice at Vicksburg*, 43–45.

121. John G. Jones to Parents, February 7, 1863, WHS.

122. James Wright to James Harlan, March 5, 1863, entry 12, Office of the Surgeon General, Letters Received, 1818–1870, box 108, RG 112.

123. Murat Halstead to Salmon P. Chase, February 19, 1863, reprinted in Logan, *Proposed Ohio Senatorial Investigation*, 28.

124. Halstead to Chase, February 19, 1863. Halstead refers to Grant's army as "The Army of the Mississippi." This is potentially a mistake owing to the recent consolidation and renaming of Grant's army. In early January, McClernand had been placed in charge of the Army of the Mississippi. However, upon conferring with Sherman and Adm. David Porter after the Battle of Arkansas Post, both commanders expressed doubt regarding McClernand's capabilities. With Halleck's support, Grant issued General Orders No. 13 on January 30, assuming the command of the Vicksburg expedition, thus creating the Army of the Tennessee. Bearss, *Campaign for Vicksburg*, vol. 1, *Vicksburg Is the Key*, 432–34; T. B. Smith, *Bayou Battles for Vicksburg*, 95; OR 24 (1): 11. Other reports make a similar mistake. See note 134 below.

125. Fingerson, "William Tecumseh Sherman Letter."

126. United States Congress, *Journal of the House of Representatives*, 408.

127. George H. Pendleton to R. C. Wood, February 24, 1863, Series 1: General Correspondence and Related Documents, 1833–1916, Abraham Lincoln Papers, LOC.

128. "Special Orders 109," March 7, 1863, filed in Published Files, Ulysses S. Grant to R. C. Wood, March 6, 1863, USGPL.

129. R. C. Wood to Montgomery Blair, March 5, 1863, Series 1: General Correspondence and Related Documents, 1833–1916, Abraham Lincoln Papers, LOC.

130. R. C. Wood to U. S. Grant, March 14, 1863, in Simon, *Papers of Ulysses S. Grant*, 7:394.

131. U. S. Grant to E. B. Washburne, March 10, 1863, folder 3, Ulysses S. Grant Papers, ALPL.

132. U. S. Grant to R. C. Wood, March 5, 1863, entry 12, Office of the Surgeon General, Letters Received, 1818–1870, box 108, RG 112.

133. R. C. Wood to W. A. Hammond, March 18, 1763, entry 12, Office of the Surgeon General, Letters Received, 1818–1870, box 108, RG 112.

134. "Army of the Mississippi," *Medical and Surgical Reporter* 4, no. 23, 24 (1863): 416. See note 117 above.

135. William Shurtleff to Mattie Van Ness, March 2[?], 1863, in Puck, *Sacrifice at Vicksburg*, 55–56.

136. Bearss, *Campaign for Vicksburg*, vol. 1, *Vicksburg Is the Key*, 447–49; OR 24 (1): 23.

137. Ingersoll, *Iowa and the Rebellion*, 159.

CHAPTER 3

1. S. Jones, *Reminiscences of the Twenty-Second Iowa*, 26.

2. U. Grant, *Personal Memoirs*, 1:388–89.

3. William T. Sherman to John Sherman, April 26, 1863, in Sherman, *Sherman's Civil War*, 461.

4. Crooke, *Twenty-First Regiment of Iowa Volunteer Infantry*, 50.

5. While often overlooked, this aspect of the campaign is not entirely neglected. See T. B. Smith, *Bayou Battles for Vicksburg*, 266–335, 364–88.

6. To date, the most thorough study on soldiers' self-care techniques remains Meier, *Nature's Civil War*. Meier's work focuses on Union and Confederate soldiers who fought in

the Shenandoah Valley. While specific environmental factors might be different, soldiers' coping strategies were largely similar.

7. Because this study is interested in the interplay between the local environment and soldiers' health, it offers an abbreviated narrative of the tactical decisions, troop movements, and military engagements that took place between May 1 and May 22, 1863. For a more thorough study, see T. B. Smith, *Inland Campaign for Vicksburg* and *Union Assaults at Vicksburg*.

8. OR 24 (3): 212–13, 232.

9. U. Grant, *Personal Memoirs*, 1:392.

10. OR 24 (1): 128.

11. There were other reasons to replace Hewitt as well. He had been the army's medical director through the winter health crisis at Young's Point and Milliken's Bend and was in charge during the Medical Department's March investigations. Hewitt would remain with the Army of the Tennessee for the duration of the campaign, establishing field hospitals and serving as inspector. OR 7:241; OR 10 (1): 110; United States Surgeon General's Office, *Medical and Surgical History*, 1:1, 330–31; King, "Shoulder Straps for Aesculapius," 217.

12. U. S. Grant to William A. Hammond, July 10, 1863, filed in Published Files, Ulysses S. Grant to J. A. Hammond (WA Hammond), July 10, 1863, USGPL.

13. Adams, *Doctors in Blue*, 93.

14. OR 24 (3): 231, 212–13; Madison Mills to Surgeon General's Office, June 20, 1863, entry 624, Medical Records, 1861–1889, file F, box 3, 169, RG 94; OR 24 (3): 264.

15. Special Orders No. 6, March 11, 1862, filed in Published Files, Ulysses S. Grant to L. Thomas, June 12, 1863, USGPL; and King, "Shoulder Straps for Aesculapius," 217–18.

16. Mills to Surgeon General's Office, June 20, 1863, entry 624, file F, box 3, 169, RG 94; OR 24 (3): 264, 231, 212–13.

17. U. Grant, *Personal Memoirs*, 1:469–70.

18. April 26–April 27, 1863, Charles Foster Diary, box 41, folder 10, Civil War Document Collection, USAHEC.

19. Newberry, *U.S. Sanitary Commission*, 89–91.

20. OR 24 (3): 233.

21. Ichabod Frisbie to wife, May 4, 1863, Ichabod Frisbie Papers, box 43, folder 3, Civil War Document Collection, USAHEC.

22. April 12–April 29, 1863, Hezekiah Baughman Diary, SHI. Ultimately, how soldiers defined their health was not as important as how surgeons defined their health. Medical officers' authority to label men's bodies as convalescent, invalid, or healthy generated a lot of tension within the ranks. See Handley-Cousins, *Bodies in Blue*.

23. OR 24 (3): 231.

24. John Holston to John A. McClernand, April 24, 1863, box 24, April 23–24, 1863, John A. McClernand Papers, ALPL.

25. Walter Scates to John McClernand, April 30, 1863, box 24, April 29–30, 1863, John A. McClernand Papers, ALPL.

26. King, "Shoulder Straps for Aesculapius," 218–19; OR 24 (3): 198; Simon, *Papers of Ulysses S. Grant*, 8:81–82; OR 24 (3): 238.

27. Scates to McClernand, April 30, 1863, John A. McClernand Papers, ALPL.

28. Special Orders No. 449, April 29, 1863, box 24, April 29–30, 1863, John A. McClernand Papers, ALPL.

29. Bearss, *Campaign for Vicksburg*, vol. 2, *Grant Strikes a Fatal Blow*, 318.

30. *OR* 24 (3): 248; U. Grant, *Personal Memoirs*, 1: 402.

31. Bearss, *Campaign for Vicksburg*, vol. 2, *Grant Strikes a Fatal Blow*, 318–19; Greene, *The Mississippi*, 125.

32. Regimental Association, *History of the Forty Sixth Regiment*, 57.

33. S. Jones, *Reminiscences of the Twenty-Second Iowa*, 29.

34. Crooke, *Twenty-First Regiment of Iowa Volunteer Infantry*, 57. See also Diary, C. A. Hobbs, 99th Illinois files, VNMP, quoted in Bearss, *Campaign for Vicksburg*, vol. 2, *Grant Strikes a Fatal Blow*, 345.

35. Crooke, *Twenty-First Regiment of Iowa Volunteer Infantry*, 59; Elliot, *History of the Thirty-Third Regiment Illinois*, 38.

36. Bearss, *Campaign for Vicksburg*, vol. 2, *Grant Strikes a Fatal Blow*, 356.

37. U. Grant, *Personal Memoirs*, 1:485.

38. Crooke, *Twenty-First Regiment of Iowa Volunteer Infantry*, 59.

39. May 1, 1863, Israel Ritter Diary, box 98, folder 15, Civil War Document Collection, USAHEC.

40. Longacre, "'Dear and Mutch Loved One,'" 51.

41. William R. Eddington Memoirs, "My Civil War Memoirs and Other Experiences," 10, ALPL; Black, *Soldier's Recollections*, 44.

42. John A. McClernand to John A. Rawlins, June 17, 1863, Report on Operations of the 13th Army Corps since March 30, Series 1: General Correspondence and Related Documents, 1833–1916, Abraham Lincoln Papers, LOC.

43. Charles Dana to Edwin Stanton, May 4, 1863, 1863, Edwin McMasters Stanton Papers, Correspondence, 1831–1870, February 12–May 4, 1863, LOC.

44. *OR* 24 (3): 270, 285.

45. *OR* 24 (3): 285.

46. John A. McClernand to John A. Rawlins, June 17, 1863, Abraham Lincoln Papers, LOC.

47. There is a growing body of scholarship dedicated to investigating the interaction between military campaigns and their environment. See Brady, *War upon the Land*; Meier, *Nature's Civil War*; Drake, *Blue, the Gray, and the Green*; Browning and Silver, *Environmental History of the Civil War*; and Noe, *Howling Storm*.

48. The idea of regional medical distinctiveness held that an individual's health was adapted to familiar surroundings and therefore unable to adequately deal with the conditions of another region without a substantial seasoning process. Thus, it became one of the main components of the states' rights medicine debate prior to the war. For more on acclimation, regional distinctiveness, and states' rights medicine, see Breeden, "States-Rights Medicine"; Numbers and Savitt, *Science and Medicine*; Valenčius, *Health of the Country*; and Willoughby, "His Native, Hot Country: Racial Science and Environment in Antebellum American Medical Thought," 328–51.

49. Bering and Montgomery, *History of the 48th Ohio*, 105.

50. Bell, *Mosquito Soldiers*, 9–20. For more on the relationship between yellow fever, malaria, and the South, see Humphreys's studies *Yellow Fever and the South* and *Malaria*.

51. Dowdey, *Wartime Papers of R. E. Lee*, 43; Bell, *Mosquito Soldiers*, 68–69; Brady, *War upon the Land*, 29–31.

52. Brady, *War upon the Land*, 35–48; T. B. Smith, *Bayou Battles for Vicksburg*, xiii–xvii.

53. Geologist Phillip R. Kemmerly has carefully estimated the length of time it would take for supply wagons to reach Grant's army at various stages during the campaign. Traveling at a rate of twenty-four miles per hour, Kemmerly estimated that supply wagons would need five days for a round trip to supply the army at Jackson, the farthest distance from Grand Gulf. Kemmerly, "Logistics of U. S. Grant's 1863 Mississippi Campaign," 590.

54. C. Johnson, *Muskets and Medicine*, 88.

55. Foraging is prominently featured in many veterans' memoirs. See Billing, *Hardtack and Coffee*. Scholars have also emphasized foraging as an important part of army life. See Wiley, *Life of Johnny Reb* and *Life of Billy Yank*; Robertson, *Soldiers Blue and Gray*; and Meier, *Nature's Civil War*.

56. In addition to targeting civilian morale, foraging orders were also employed as retaliation tactics against enemy policies deemed inappropriate or uncivilized; see Foote, *Rites of Retaliation*. For more on Union military strategy and its impact on Confederate civilians, see Grimsley, *Hard Hand of War*.

57. Several scholars have highlighted the pragmatism behind Grant's foraging orders and observed the relationship between the Vicksburg Campaign's more formal "hard war" policy that Grant and Sherman would come to embrace. Grimsley, *Hard Hand of War*, 4, 142–62; Shea and Winschel, *Vicksburg Is the Key*, 119, 208; Dougherty, *Vicksburg Campaign*, 99–101.

58. Meier notes that foraging is one of the fundamental components of soldiers' self-care routines, enabling them to achieve a more balanced diet than if they were to depend on government rations. Meier, *Nature's Civil War*, 112–13.

59. Bentley, *History of the 77th Illinois*, 138.

60. O'Hara, "Susceptibility of Ground Water."

61. Dana, *Recollections of the Civil War*, 50.

62. Wells, *Siege of Vicksburg*, 60.

63. William T. Sherman to Ellen Ewing Sherman, May 6, 1863, in Sherman, *Sherman's Civil War*, 468.

64. Wells, *Siege of Vicksburg*, 60.

65. Longacre, "'Dear and Mutch Loved One,'" 52.

66. C. Johnson, *Muskets and Medicine*, 88.

67. William T. Sherman to John Sherman, April 3, 1863, in Sherman, *Sherman's Civil War*, 439.

68. T. Marshall, *History of the Eighty-Third Ohio*, 77.

69. C. Johnson, *Muskets and Medicine*, 88–89.

70. Bering and Montgomery, *History of the 48th Ohio*, 81.

71. T. Marshall, *History of the Eighty-Third Ohio*, 10–11.

72. Eddington Memoirs, "My Civil War Memoirs and Other Experiences," 10–12, ALPL.

73. Blake, *Succinct History of the 28th Iowa*, 14.

74. Longacre, "'Dear and Mutch Loved One,'" 52.

75. Bentley, *History of the 77th Illinois*, 138.

76. The value of domestic space to soldiers' physical and psychological well-being is well examined in Nelson, *Ruin Nation*, 62, 66, 71–72.

77. Illinois Infantry, 13th Regiment, *Military History and Reminiscences*, 308–9.

78. Kellogg, *War Experiences*, 23.

79. Henry Strong to unnamed, May 7, 1863, Henry P. Strong Letters, WHS.

80. Cyrus Wilson to father, May 30, 1863, Cyrus Wilson Civil War Papers, SHI; Elliot, *History of the Thirty-Third Regiment*, 39.

81. Eddington Memoirs, "My Civil War Memoirs and Other Experiences," 10, ALPL.

82. Ordronaux, *Hints on Health*, 60, 53–54; Hammond, *Military Medical and Surgical Essays*, 165, 166.

83. Sleep remains an understudied topic within Civil War scholarship. White's *Midnight in America* remains the foundational work in the field. Some studies, however, do highlight sleep and sleep deprivation, particularly as it relates to combat stressors. See Reardon, *With a Sword in One Hand*, 104–14.

84. Fred Grant, Vicksburg Observations, Series II: Speeches, Frederick D. Grant and Ida Honore Grant papers, USGPL.

85. The importance of cheerfulness as a coping mechanism is extensively examined in Carmichael, *War for the Common Soldier*, 81–82.

86. The relationship between heat and the American South has a long and complicated history and is well explored in Hauser, "By Degree." Hauser contends that the Southern heat played a significant role in creating a regional distinction between the American South and the rest of the country while also creating physical separation among the nation's populace.

87. Winschel, *Civil War Diary of a Common Soldier*, 43, 47.

88. Crooke, *Twenty-First Regiment of Iowa Volunteer Infantry*, 84; Elliot, *History of the Thirty-Third Regiment Illinois*, 46; May 16, 1863, William Lewis Robert Papers, Alabama Department of Archives and History, Montgomery.

89. James C. Whitehill Memoirs, 2, box 33, folder 10, Civil War Document Collection, USAHEC.

90. Megan Kate Nelson, "The Difficulties and Seduction of the Desert," in Drake, *Blue, the Gray, and the Green*, 44.

91. Further elaboration on humoral theory and the quest for balance can be found in Valenčius, *Health of the Country*, 53, 58–60,143.

92. Valenčius, *Health of the Country*, 53, 58–60, 143.

93. April 23, 1863, Isaac Vanderwarker Diary, box 117, folder 12, Civil War Document Collection, USAHEC; June 29, 1863, Robert Edwin Jameson Diary and Letters, LOC. It should be noted that there are few reports in the *Medical and Surgical History* regarding sunstroke for the Army of the Tennessee during the months of May, June, and July. These numbers compared with soldiers' and surgeons' discussion of sunstroke suggest either that the reports are incomplete or that cases were reported as a different complaint. United States Surgeon General's Office, *Medical and Surgical History*, 1:243.

94. Philip Roesch Memoirs, 7, box 99, folder 21, Civil War Document Collection, USAHEC.

95. Ordronaux, *Hints on Health*, 45.

96. Ordronaux, *Hints on Health*, 45–46.

97. *OR* 24 (3): 286.

98. William T. Sherman to John Sherman, April 23, 1863, in Sherman, *Sherman's Civil War*, 459.

99. Bellows, *How Not to Be Sick*, 335.

100. Eddington Memoirs, "My Civil War Memoirs and Other Experiences," 15, ALPL. Three pints is approximately 48 ounces of water. The recommended water intake for a

250-pound man with no physical exercise is 125 ounces; Ordronaux, *Hints on Health*, 46; Hammond, *Military Medical and Surgical Essays*, 169.

101. Browning and Silver, *Environmental History of the Civil War*, 12–13.
102. Hammond, *Military Medical and Surgical Essays*, 4–5.
103. Hammond, *Military Medical and Surgical Essays*, 4–5.
104. Tripler, *Handbook for the Military Surgeon*, 16.
105. *OR* 24 (3): 308.
106. For more on straggling as an important self-care strategy, see Meier, *Nature's Civil War*, 125–50; and Carroll, *Invisible Wounds*, 86–92.
107. Meier, *Nature's Civil War*, 126–46.
108. King, "Shoulder Straps for Aesculapius," 220.
109. Cooke, *Badger Boy in Blue*, 61, 63.
110. The soldiers' response to the tension created by the regimentation of military life is more thoroughly studied in Meier, *Nature's Civil War*, 126–46.
111. General Orders No. 68, May 5, 1863, box 24, May 5, 1863, John A. McClernand Papers, ALPL; *OR* 24 (3): 308.
112. Cooke, *Badger Boy in Blue*, 63.
113. Blake, *Succinct History of the 28th Iowa*, 14.
114. T. Marshall, *History of the Eighty-Third Ohio*, 83.

CHAPTER 4

1. Henry Strong to unnamed, April 6, 1863, Henry P. Strong Letters, WHS.
2. Henry Strong to unnamed, May 10, 1863, Henry P. Strong Letters, WHS.
3. Bearss, *Campaign for Vicksburg*, vol. 2, *Grant Strikes a Fatal Blow*; Winschel, *Triumph and Defeat*; Ballard, *Vicksburg*; Kemmerly, "Logistics of U. S. Grant's 1863 Mississippi Campaign"; and T. B. Smith, *Inland Campaign for Vicksburg*, examine how Grant's limited supply line affected troop movement, soldier stamina, and the army's overall fighting strength.
4. *OR* 24 (1): 600, 619.
5. United States Surgeon General's Office, *Medical and Surgical History*, 1:appendix, 331; King, "Shoulder Straps for Aesculapius," 220; William S. Forbes, "An Essay on the Treatment of the Wounded Men, after the Battles of Port Gibson, Champion Hill, Black River Bridge, and during the Siege of Vicksburg Belonging to the 13th Army Corps of the Army of the Tennessee—1863. For the Degree of Doctor of Medicine in the University of Pennsylvania by W. S. Forbes County of Philadelphia, State of Pennsylvania. Residence in the City no. 241 So. 17th Street," 4, Rare Book Collection, Kislak Center for Special Collections, University of Pennsylvania, Philadelphia.
6. While many of Grant's decisions seemed to undermine soldier health and challenge the medical corps's performance in the field, several historians have observed that among his peers Grant had a reputation of being more supportive of his medical directors. See Adams, *Doctors in Blue*, 62.
7. Forbes, "Essay on the Treatment of the Wounded Men," 7, Rare Book Collection, Kislak Center for Special Collections.

8. James' Plantation, located just north of the Federal base at Perkins' Plantation, was established in late April as the army made its way toward the river. The hospital at Hard Times was created just prior to Grant's crossing.

9. Simon, *Papers of Ulysses S. Grant*, 8:153.

10. May 2, 1863, Eugene Harrison Diary, box 52, folder 12, Civil War Document Collection, USAHEC; United States Surgeon General's Office, *Medical and Surgical History*, 1:331–33.

11. H. S. Hewitt, Special Orders, May 2, 1863, Orders and Letters before the Battle of Vicksburg, entry 621, Medical Records: Reports of Disease and Individual Cases, 1841–1893, file A and bound manuscripts, box 5, A161, RG 94.

12. Simon, *Papers of Ulysses S. Grant*, 8:172–73.

13. Mills finally joined Grant's army at Rocky Springs on May 5. Mills to Surgeon General's Office, June 20, 1863, entry 624, file F, box 3, 169, RG 94. John Holston to H. S. Hewitt, May 6, 1863, Orders and Letters before the Battle of Vicksburg, entry 621, Medical Records: Reports of Disease and Individual Cases, 1841–1893, file A and bound manuscripts, box 5, A161, RG 94; Complete Index to Records on File from Mississippi, 5–6, entry 544, Index to Field Records of Hospitals, 1821–1912, box 4, RG 94.

14. Several works offer more detailed overviews of these battles. The most thorough are Bearss, *Vicksburg Campaign*, and T. B. Smith, *Inland Campaign for Vicksburg*, but Ballard, *Vicksburg*; Woodworth and Grear, *Vicksburg Campaign*; and D. Miller, *Vicksburg*, are also valuable contributions. See also *OR* 24 (3): 348.

15. "Responsibility of an Army Surgeon," *Sanitary Reporter* 1, no. 4 (1863): 28.

16. These hospitals were located at Raymond, Jackson, and the Big Black River. Madison Mills, Report Accompanying Tabulated Statements of Wounded in the Army of the Department of the Tennessee for the Month of May 1863, entry 624, Medical Records, 1861–1889, file F, box 3, F169, RG 94; United States Surgeon General's Office, *Medical and Surgical History*,1: appendix, 331–32; King, "Shoulder Straps for Aesculapius," 221–22; Gillett, *Army Medical Department*, 217.

17. Michael Mahr, "The Story of Camp Letterman," National Museum of Civil War Medicine, last modified July 1, 2022, https://www.civilwarmed.org/camp-letterman.

18. Rubenstein, "Study of the Medical Support," 42.

19. Madison Mills, Report Accompanying Tabulated Statements of Wounded in the Army of the Department of the Tennessee for the Month of May 1863, RG 94; *OR* 3:128, 357; King, "Shoulder Straps for Aesculapius," 216.

20. United States Surgeon General's Office, *Medical and Surgical History*, I: I appendix, 331; King, "Shoulder Straps for Aesculapius," 220.

21. H. S. Hewitt, Special Orders, May 2, 1863, Orders and Letters before the Battle of Vicksburg, entry 621, Medical Records: Reports of Disease and Individual Cases, 1841–1893, file A and bound manuscripts, box 5, A161, RG 94; Circular No. 4, March 25, 1863, 3, entry 63, Central Office Issuances and Forms: Circulars and Letters of the Surgeon General's Office, box 1, RG 112.

22. Hospital registers still exist for a number of the Vicksburg field hospitals in addition to hospital steamers like the *City of Memphis*. Entry 544, Index to Field Records of Hospitals, 1821–1912, box 4, RG 94.

23. Trowbridge, *Autobiography*, 151.

24. Watson, *Letters of a Civil War Surgeon*, 17. While Watson did not serve at Vicksburg, his experience was shared among military surgeons regardless of their post.

25. After the war, Macleod wrote a treatise on military surgery designed to help other surgeons while in the field. This work became one of the foundational texts for the medical corps in the early years of the Civil War. Macleod, *Notes on the Surgery*, 7.

26. C. Johnson, *Muskets and Medicine*, 81, 84–85.

27. C. Johnson, *Muskets and Medicine*, 102–4, 99.

28. C. Johnson, *Muskets and Medicine*, 102–4.

29. T. L. Smith, "Twenty-Fourth Iowa Volunteers, Part 2," 118–19.

30. Regimental Association, *History of the Forty Sixth Regiment*, 62.

31. Trowbridge, *Autobiography*, 139–40.

32. C. Johnson, *Muskets and Medicine*, 99.

33. May 24, 1863, Eugene Harrison Diary, box 52, folder 12, Civil War Document Collection, USAHEC.

34. C. Johnson, *Muskets and Medicine*, 99–100.

35. Trowbridge, *Autobiography*, 139–40.

36. King, "Shoulder Straps for Aesculapius," 221.

37. Forbes, "Essay on the Treatment of the Wounded Men," 11–12, 13–14, Rare Book Collection, Kislak Center for Special Collections; C. Johnson, *Muskets and Medicine*, 104–5.

38. Surgeon General William A. Hammond viewed the Civil War as an unprecedented opportunity to further medical science. The Medical Department's efforts to strengthen surgeons' professionalism through the national collection, transmission, and dissemination of medical research is thoroughly examined in Devine, *Learning from the Wounded*.

39. Andrews, *Complete Record of the Surgery*, 40.

40. C. Johnson, *Muskets and Medicine*, 98–99.

41. Andrews, *Complete Record of the Surgery*, 45.

42. For a full conversation regarding the necessity of performing amputations on inferior limbs, see United States Surgeon General's Office, *Medical and Surgical History*, 6:335–41, 339.

43. Trowbridge, *Autobiography*, 119–21.

44. Alexander Hoff to Alden March, October 9, 1863, Hoff Papers, National Library of Medicine, Washington, DC, quoted in Brodman and Carrick, "American Military Medicine," 67.

45. Forbes, "Essay on the Treatment of the Wounded Men," 8–10, Rare Book Collection, Kislak Center for Special Collections; C. Johnson, *Muskets and Medicine*, 107.

46. Forbes, "Essay on the Treatment of the Wounded Men," 8–10, Rare Book Collection, Kislak Center for Special Collections.

47. Forbes, "Essay on the Treatment of the Wounded Men," 13–14, Rare Book Collection, Kislak Center for Special Collections.

48. United States Surgeon General's Office, *Medical and Surgical History*, 5:43; register 9, *City of Memphis*, 101, entry 544, Field Records of Hospitals, 1821–1912, RG 94.

49. In December 2009, *Isis: Journal of the History of Science in Society* dedicated an issue toward this question of integrating emotions history within the history of science and medicine. Notable articles include P. White, "Focus"; Alberti, "Bodies, Hearts, and Minds"; and Dror, "Reflection." See also Alberti, *Medicine, Emotion, and Disease, 1700–1950*; Acton and Potter, *Working in a World of Hurt*; and Payne, *With Words and Knives*.

50. A few examples of these studies include Hartley et al., "Dead on the Table"; Percy et al., "Mental Toughness in Surgeons"; and Rodrigues et al., "Burnout Syndrome among Medical Residents."

51. Historians have long been fascinated with how Civil War soldiers were shaped by their wartime experiences. The earliest studies on the subject are Wiley's classics *Life of Johnny Reb* and *Life of Billy Yank*. This grew into a burgeoning field of scholarship beginning in the 1980s with the publication of works such as McPherson's *For Cause and Comrades*; Linderman's *Embattled Courage*; Costa and Khan's *Heroes and Cowards*; and Sheehan-Dean's *View from the Ground*. For the most part, these works are interested in the inner world of Civil War soldiers, examining concepts such as virtue, honor, courage, and bravery. Yet, while this scholarship coincided with a growing interest in the history of emotions, few of these scholars explicitly connected these concepts to soldiers' emotional regimes, focusing instead on issues such as morale and camaraderie. This has recently begun to change as historians are becoming more interested in examining the emotional worlds in which Civil War era Americans lived. See M. Woods, *Emotional and Sectional Conflict*; Sommerville, *Aberration of Mind*; Carmichael, *War for the Common Soldier*; Broomall, *Private Confederacies*; and Elder, *Love and Duty*. For more on emotions history, see Stearns and Stearns, "Emotionology"; Rosenwein, "Worrying about Emotions"; and Matt and Stearns, *Doing Emotions History*.

52. Eustace, *Passion Is the Gale*, 12; Acton and Potter, *Working in a World of Hurt*, 12–13.

53. C. Johnson, *Muskets and Medicine*, 103. This tendency was not unique among those who served in the Civil War. Historians have recognized it among those who served in other wars as well. See Acton, *Working in a World of Hurt*.

54. For more on physicians' professional dispassion, see Payne, *With Words and Knives*.

55. Linderman, *Embattled Courage*, 28–29.

56. C. Johnson, *Muskets and Medicine*, 97.

57. Daniel Ramsdell Papers, 70, WHS.

58. Dana, *Recollections of the Civil War*, 45. The image of amputated limbs piled high at field hospitals remains an enduring legacy of Civil War medicine. For more on amputees and amputated limbs' social significance, see B. Miller, *Empty Sleeves*; and A. Johnson, *Scars We Carve*.

59. Daniel Ramsdell Papers, 70–72, WHS.

60. The relationship between camaraderie and courage under fire has an extensive scholarship. See Linderman, *Embattled Courage*; McPherson, *For Cause and Comrades*; Costa and Khan, *Heroes and Cowards*; Hamner, *Enduring Battle*; and Gordon, *Broken Regiment*. In each of these works, battlefield performance defined soldiers' understanding of themselves and their comrades.

61. B. Miller, *Empty Sleeves*, 50–90; Carmichael, *War for the Common Soldier*, 140–49. See also Hess, *Liberty, Virtue, and Progress*; and Costa and Khan, *Heroes and Cowards*.

62. Christopher R. Blackall Memoirs, "In the Tornado: Days of '62–64," 86, WHS.

63. Forbes, "Essay on the Treatment of the Wounded Men," 19–20, Rare Book Collection, Kislak Center for Special Collections.

64. "The Surgeon on the Battlefield," *Medical and Surgical Reporter* 7, no. 23 (1862): 548.

65. "Army Surgeons: Their Character and Duties," *Sanitary Reporter* 1, no. 6 (1863): 41–42.

66. Seneca Thrall to Wife, May 18, 1863, Seneca B. Thrall Civil War Letters, SHI.

67. Henry Strong to wife, May 27, 1863, Henry P. Strong Letters, WHS.

68. Henry Strong to wife, May 25, 1863, Henry P. Strong Letters, WHS.

CHAPTER 5

1. Byers, "How Men Feel in Battle," 439.
2. Mason, *Forty-Second Ohio Infantry*, 217.
3. Grabau, *Ninety-Eight Days*, 20–25. Loess is a rather unusual soil, and its properties played an important role during the siege; Bentley, *History of the 77th Illinois*, 151.
4. Crooke, *Twenty-First Regiment of Iowa Volunteer Infantry*, 79.
5. William R. Eddington Memoirs, "My Civil War Memoirs and Other Experiences," 11–12, ALPL.
6. Crooke, *Twenty-First Regiment of Iowa Volunteer Infantry*, 84–85.
7. T. Marshall, *History of the Eighty-Third Ohio*, 84–85; Barton, *Autobiography*, 127–28; U. Grant, *Personal Memoirs*, 1:236.
8. Hess, *Storming Vicksburg*, xv, 87, 110.
9. U. Grant, *Personal Memoirs*, 1:446.
10. Browning and Silver, *Environmental History of the Civil War*, 13, 58; Hess, *Storming Vicksburg*, 14.
11. Mason, *Forty-Second Ohio Infantry*, 217.
12. Dr. Warriner's Report, Milliken's Bend, May 4, 1863, *Sanitary Reporter* 1, no. 2 (1863): 13–14.
13. Report, Young's Point, LA, May 18, 1863, *Sanitary Reporter* 1, no. 3 (1863): 20.
14. Report, Haines Bluff, May 27, 1863, *Sanitary Reporter* 1, no. 3 (1863): 20–21.
15. "Responsibility of the Army Surgeon," *Sanitary Reporter* 1, no. 3 (1863): 28.
16. Quoted in Forman, *Western Sanitary Commission*, 72.
17. "The Western Medical Department," *Medical and Surgical Reporter* 10, no. 11 (1863): 167.
18. Special Orders No. 8, *Sanitary Reporter* 1, no. 2 (1863): 15.
19. Stillé, *History of the United States Sanitary Commission*, 333–34, 339–40.
20. Special Orders No. 8, *Sanitary Reporter* 1, no. 2 (1863): 15.
21. Solonick, *Engineering Victory*; and T. B. Smith, *Siege of Vicksburg*, offer the most detailed examination of the strategy employed by the Army of the Tennessee between May 22 and July 4.
22. Bearss, *Campaign for Vicksburg*, vol. 3, *Unvexed to the Sea*, 953.
23. U. Grant, *Personal Memoirs*, 1:448–49; *OR* 24 (3): 350.
24. May 24, 1863, William M. Reid Diary, ALPL.
25. T. Marshall, *History of the Eighty-Third Ohio*, 88–89; Bell, *Mosquito Soldiers*, 11; June 18, 1863, Robert Edwin Jameson Diary Letters, LOC.
26. Grabau, *Ninety-Eight Days*, 22.
27. June 4, 1863, Charles Foster Diary, box 41, folder 10, Civil War Documents Collection, USAHEC; Ordronaux, *Hints on Health*, 54–55.
28. Bell, *Mosquito Soldiers*, 11.
29. Seneca Thrall to Mollie, August 6, 1863, Seneca B. Thrall Letters, SHI.
30. Barton, *Autobiography*, 158, 157, 158.

31. This process takes longer in the case of *P. vivax* and *P. ovale*, in which maturation may be delayed for up to two years.

32. "Malaria," MedlinePlus, last modified May 19, 2023, https://medlineplus.gov/ency/article/000621.htm; James M. Crutcher and Stephen L. Hoffman, "Malaria," in Baron, *Medical Microbiology*; Humphreys, *Malaria*, 8–11; Schlagenhauf, "Malaria."

33. Barton, *Autobiography*, 160.

34. For more information on symptomatic fevers and how they were classified, see Wilson, "Fevers and Science in Early Nineteenth Century Medicine"; and D. Smith, "Rise and Fall of Typhomalarial Fever."

35. Cooke, *Badger Boy in Blue*, 79.

36. Bollet, *Civil War Medicine*, 368.

37. July 18, 1863, True Morrill Diary, SHI.

38. June 24, July 18, and July 20, True Morrill Diary, SHI.

39. Hammond, *Military Medical and Surgical Essays*, 22–23.

40. United States Surgeon General's Office, *Medical and Surgical History*, 4:95.

41. United States Surgeon General's Office, *Medical and Surgical History*, 4:95.

42. James Forbis to William T. Forbis, September 6, 1863, James Forbis Letters, box 40, folder 18, Civil War Document Collection, USAHEC.

43. Bell, *Mosquito Soldiers*, 2.

44. Bollet, *Civil War Medicine*, 303; Khamesipour et al., "Systematic Review of Human Pathogens."

45. Bollet, "Major Infectious Epidemic Diseases"; "Parasites-Amebiasis-*Entamoeba histolytica* Infection," Centers for Disease Control and Prevention, last modified May 2, 2024, www.cdc.gov/amebiasis/about/?CDC_AAref_Val=https://www.cdc.gov/parasites/amebiasis/general-info.html. Bollet suggests that some of the liver abscesses that appear in the autopsy reports published in the *Medical and Surgical History of the War of the Rebellion* indicate the presence of *E. histolytica* among some Civil War soldiers. Bollet, *Civil War Medicine*, 297; Bollet, "Medical Problems of the Civil War," 129.

46. United States Surgeon General's Office, *Medical and Surgical History*, 1:334.

47. *OR* 24 (2): 167.

48. C. Johnson, *Muskets and Medicine*, 99–100, 107.

49. United States Surgeon General's Office, *Medical and Surgical History*, 1:331–33.

50. "Reports, Department of the Tennessee," June 23, 1863, *Sanitary Reporter* 1, no. 5 (1863): 37; William S. Forbes, "An Essay on the Treatment of the Wounded Men, after the Battles of Port Gibson, Champion Hill, Black River Bridge, and during the Siege of Vicksburg Belonging to the 13th Army Corps of the Army of the Tennessee—1863. For the Degree of Doctor of Medicine in the University of Pennsylvania by W. S. Forbes County of Philadelphia, State of Pennsylvania. Residence in the City no. 241 So. 17th Street," 26, Rare Book Collection, Kislak Center for Special Collections, University of Pennsylvania, Philadelphia.

51. Maertz, "Midland War Sketches IV," 82.

52. King, "Shoulder Straps for Aesculapius," 221–22.

53. Circular, June 13, 1863, entry 624, Medical Records, 1861–1889, file F, box 3, F169, RG 94.

54. Register 9, *City of Memphis*, 101, entry 544, Field Records of Hospitals, 1821–1912, RG 94.

55. Circular, June 13, 1863, entry 624, file F, box 3, F169, RG 94.

56. Daniel Ramsdell Papers, 75–77, WHS.

57. Madison Mills, "Report of the Medical Director of the Army of the Tennessee from May 1 to July 4, 1863," in United States Surgeon General's Office, *Medical and Surgical History*, 1:1139, appendix, 331–33.

58. Forbes, "Essay on the Treatment of the Wounded Men," 34–35, Rare Book Collection, Kislak Center for Special Collections.

59. Forbes, "Essay on the Treatment of the Wounded Men," 34–35, Rare Book Collection, Kislak Center for Special Collections.

60. Madison Mills, "Report of the Medical Director of the Army of the Tennessee," 1:1139, appendix 331–33.

61. C. Johnson, *Muskets and Medicine*, 106.

62. S. W. Butler, "Army and Navy News," *Medical and Surgical Reporter* 10, no. 11 (1863): 167.

63. *Report of the Western Sanitary Commission*, 25.

64. Seneca Thrall to Wife, May 28, 1863, Seneca B. Thrall Papers, SHI.

65. "Report on the Operations of the U.S. Sanitary Commission in the Valley of the Mississippi, Made September 1, 1863," in United States Sanitary Commission, *Documents of the U.S. Sanitary Commission*, 2:3; *Chicago Tribune*, June 26, 1863. In late June, there was growing disagreement over the proper procedures for surgeons to follow in order to obtain ice for use in the field hospitals. Frustrated by what were seemingly arbitrary rules, several surgeons forwarded their correspondence to the *Chicago Daily Tribune* for publication.

66. Flannery, *Civil War Pharmacy*, 118–19; C. Johnson, *Muskets and Medicine*, 97.

67. United States Surgeon General's Office, *Medical and Surgical History*, 6:185. When used as a prophylactic, quinine does not prevent malarial infections. It just reduces the threat of a malarial attack. Flannery, *Civil War Pharmacy*, 118–19.

68. June 1863, box 4, BV, Thomas Madison Reece Papers, ALPL.

69. John Moore to William Hammond, September 1, 1863, and August 4, 1863, box 66, entry 12, Office of the Surgeon General, Letters Received, 1818–1870, RG 112.

70. Certainly, siege operations were not about sitting and waiting for Vicksburg to fall. Federal troops were constantly employed to dig trenches, mines, and "zigzag" approaches that might facilitate a final assault on the Confederate lines. One mine was detonated under the 3rd Louisiana Redan on July 25 with subsequent plans to widen the resulting crater in preparation for another assault sometime after July 4. For more on the technicalities of siege operations, see Solonick, *Engineering Victory*.

71. May 26–27 and June 1–2, 1863, George Hale Diary, WHS.

72. Elliot, *History of the Thirty-Third Regiment Illinois*, 65.

73. Holcomb, *Southern Sons*, 76.

74. Kiper, *Dear Catharine*, 117–18.

75. Ambrose, *Wisconsin Boy in Dixie*, 83.

76. Crooke, *Twenty-First Regiment of Iowa Volunteer Infantry*, 109.

77. Bering and Montgomery, *History of the 48th Ohio*, 105.

78. Dana, *Recollections of the Civil War*, 78.

79. June 1, 1863, Alexander McDonald Civil War Diaries, 1862–1865, WHS.

80. May 29, 1863, Anthony Burton Diary, ALPL.

81. Seneca Thrall to Mollie, June 28, 1863, Seneca B. Thrall Civil War Letters, SHI.

82. See Nelson, *Ruin Nation*, 103–59.

83. T. Marshall, *History of the Eighty-Third Ohio*, 88–89.

84. P. L. Underwood to William Underwood, June 12, 1863, Benjamin Underwood Letters, Old Courthouse Museum, Vicksburg, MS.

85. S. Jones, *Reminiscences of the Twenty-Second Iowa*, 41.

86. Oscar McLouth to Phobe, undated, Oscar McLouth Letters, box 78, folder 18, Civil War Document Collection, USAHEC; Sears, *For Country, Cause, and Leader*, 332; June 18, 1863, Robert Edwin Jameson Diary Letters, LOC.

87. John Wesley Largent to sister and family, June 25, 1863, John Wesley Largent Civil War Letters, WHS; Estabrook, *Wisconsin Losses in the Civil War*, 164. Estabrook lists Largent as having died "from disease." While it is possible that Largent contracted another illness that ultimately caused his demise, chronic diarrhea or even dysentery was likely an added complication.

88. John Wesley Largent to sister and family, June 25, 1863, WHS.

89. T. Marshall, *History of the Eighty-Third Ohio*, 88–89.

90. Grabau, *Ninety-Eight Days*, 21, 25.

91. United States Surgeon General's Office, *Medical and Surgical History*, 4:95; Grabau, *Ninety-Eight Days*, 443. Grabau estimates that the Union army needed 120 full cisterns a day to keep the army properly supplied.

92. Grabau, *Ninety-Eight Days*, 443–44. Grabau estimates that the Union army required about 81,240 gallons of water each day starting in May, when Grant's army numbered around 42,000 men. By the end of the siege, the Army of the Tennessee had swelled to 77,000 soldiers.

93. William T. Sherman to David Dixon Porter, May 23, 1863, James McClintock Signal Corps Messages, LOC. Sherman is referring to a parrot gun.

94. C. Johnson, *Muskets and Medicine*, 69.

95. Charles Dana to Edwin Stanton, June 16, 1863, Edwin McMasters Stanton Papers, Correspondence, 1831–1870, 1863, June 16–August 6, 1863, LOC; Ordronaux, *Hints on Health*, 53.

96. Barton, *Autobiography*, 155.

97. June 28, 1863, Job H. Yaggy Diary, ALPL.

98. Eddington Memoirs, "My Civil War Memoirs and Other Experiences," 15, ALPL.

99. Dana, *Recollections of the Civil War*, 52; Barton, *Autobiography*, 130; June 18, 1863, Robert Jameson Diary and Letters, LOC.

100. William T. Rigby to brother, July 1, 1863, box 1, folder 18, William T. Rigby Series, VNMP.

101. Hammond, *Military Medical and Surgical Essays*, 207–8.

102. J. Woods, *Services of the Ninety-Sixth Ohio Volunteers*, 20.

103. This nickname is pervasive and appears in several sources; see Black, *Soldier's Recollections*, 30; Cooke, *Badger Boy in Blue*, 76; Scott, *History of the 67th Regiment*, 15; and J. Woods, *Services of the Ninety-Sixth Ohio Volunteers*, 20.

104. *OR* 24 (1): 41.

105. Ordronaux, *Hints on Health*, 61–63.

106. May 28, 30, 29, 1863, William M. Reid Diary, ALPL.

107. Dana, *Recollections of the Civil War*, 57.

108. Wells, *Siege of Vicksburg*, 63, 79; Philip Roesch Memoirs, 8, box 99, folder 21, Civil War Document Collection, USAHEC.

109. Sherman, *Sherman's Civil War*, 493.

110. September 11, 1862, 31st Mississippi, Lt. Col. M. D. L. Stephens. Featherstone's Brigade, Loring's Division [diary of Dr. Thomas J. Blackwell], box 1, folder 142, Regimental Files, Vicksburg Campaign Series, VNMP.

111. United States Surgeon General's Office, *Medical and Surgical History*, 4:96.

112. Elliot, *History of the Thirty-Third Regiment Illinois*, 45.

113. John Leavy, "Diary of John A. Leavy, MD; Surgeon—Green's Arkansas Brigade," 22–23, box 2, folder 59, Journals, Diaries, and Letters, Vicksburg Campaign Series, VNMP.

114. May 17, 1863, Rowland Chambers Diaries, vol. 6, Louisiana and Lower Mississippi Valley Collection, Louisiana State University, Baton Rouge.

115. J. Smith, "Confederate Soldier's Diary," 316–17.

116. H. M. Compton to Major Reen, June 25, 1863, entry 131, Papers of Various Confederate Notables, box 6, John C. Pemberton, May–July 1863, Letters Received, Record Group 109: War Department Collection of Confederate Records, NARA.

117. *OR* 24 (2): 347–49.

EPILOGUE

1. Simon, *Papers of Ulysses S. Grant*, 9:134.

2. Blake, *Succinct History of the 28th Iowa Volunteer Infantry*, 23; Mason, *Forty-Second Ohio Infantry*, 236.

3. Clampitt, *Occupied Vicksburg*, 32, 49.

4. Mason, *Forty-Second Ohio Infantry*, 236.

5. Clampitt's *Occupied Vicksburg* is the most thorough examination of the Union army's occupation of Vicksburg.

6. Maxwell, *Lincoln's Fifth Wheel*, 265–68; Sherman, *Sherman's Civil War*, 627–28; Sherman, *Memoirs*, 883.

7. H. W. Bellows to R. Bellows, January 2, 1865, quoted in Maxwell, *Lincoln's Fifth Wheel*, 279.

8. Stanton and Hammond's relationship is well documented. See Meier, "U.S. Sanitary Commission Physicians," 19–21, 26; Blustein, "To Increase the Efficiency of the Medical Department"; Rutkow, *Bleeding Blue and Gray*, 242–45; Flannery, "Another House Divided," 494–96; and Shiepko "William Alexander Hammond's Transformation," 90–92.

9. United States Surgeon General's Office, *Medical and Surgical History*, 3:719–21, includes a reprinting of Circular No. 6 as well as excerpts from the reports describing soldiers' condition at Vicksburg. Circular No. 12, "Directions Concerning the Manner of Obtaining and Accounting for Medical and Hospital Supplies for the Army with a Standard Supply Table," entry 63, Central Office Issuances and Forms: Circulars and Letters of the Surgeon General's Office, box 1, RG 112; Stevens, "Seventeenth Annual Session of the Ohio State Medical Society," in *Cincinnati Lancet and Observer*, 417. Maxwell, *Lincoln's Fifth Wheel*, 235–55, offers a thorough discussion of Hammond's court-martial.

10. Rubenstein, "Study of the Medical Support," 40.

11. *OR* 39 (3): 713–14; Maxwell, *Lincoln's Fifth Wheel*, 278–79.

12. C. Riebsame to William T. Rigby, September 16, 1901, Correspondence, 1901, William T. Rigby Series, box 1, folder 33, VNMP.

Bibliography

PRIMARY SOURCES

Manuscripts

Abraham Lincoln Presidential Library, Springfield, IL
    Sylvester Beckwith Letters
    Anthony Burton Diary
    Albert Chipman Papers
    William R. Eddington Memoirs, "My Civil War Memoirs and Other Experiences"
    John B. Fletcher Diary
    Ulysses S. Grant Papers
    John Lindley Harris Letters
    John Higgins Letters
    John A. McClernand Papers
    Thomas Madison Reece Papers
    William M. Reid Diary
    Job H. Yaggy Diary

Alabama Department of Archives and History, Montgomery
    Elisha K. Flournoy Civil War Letters
    Edward Brett Randolph Family Papers
        Edward Brett Randolph Diary
    William Lewis Robert Papers
    E. D. Willett Civil War Papers
Kislak Center for Special Collections, University of Pennsylvania, Philadelphia
    Rare Book Collection
Library of Congress, Manuscripts Divisions, Washington, DC
    Robert Edwin Jameson Diary and Letters
    Abraham Lincoln Papers
        Series 1: General Correspondence and Related Documents, 1833–1916
    James McClintock Signal Corps Messages
    Edwin McMasters Stanton Papers
Louisiana and Lower Mississippi Valley Collection, Louisiana
        State University, Baton Rouge
    Rowland Chambers Diaries
Mississippi Department of Archives and History, Jackson
    Henry C. Davisson Collection
    William A. Drennan Papers
National Archives and Records Administration, Washington, DC
    Record Group 94: Records of the Adjutant General's Office
        Entry 544, Field Records of Hospitals, 1821–1912
            Index to Field Records of Hospitals, 1821–1912
            Register 9, *City of Memphis*
        Entry 621, Medical Records: Reports of Disease and Individual
            Cases, 1841–1893, file A and bound manuscripts
        Entry 624, Medical Records, 1861–1889, file F
        Entry 650, Registers of Deaths of Volunteers, 1861–1865
    Record Group 109: War Department Collection of Confederate Records
        Entry 95, Commissary Papers 1862–1865
        Entry 131, Papers of Various Confederate Notables
    Record Group 112: Records of the Office of the Surgeon General
        Entry 12, Office of the Surgeon General, Letters Received, 1818–1870
        Entry 63, Central Office Issuances and Forms: Circulars
            and Letters of the Surgeon General's Office
Old Courthouse Museum, Vicksburg, MS
    Aquila Bowie Memoirs
    Theodosia McKinstry Memoirs
    Dora Richards Miller Diary, "War Diary of a Union Woman in the South"
    Benjamin Underwood Letters
Reynolds-Finley Historical Library, University of Alabama at Birmingham
    Sanitary Commission Series
State Historical Society of Iowa, Des Moines
    Hezekiah Baughman Diary

    True Morrill Diary
    Seneca B. Thrall Civil War Letters
    Cyrus Wilson Civil War Papers
Ulysses S. Grant Presidential Library, Mississippi State University, Starkville
US Army Heritage and Education Center, US Army War College, Carlisle, PA
    Civil War Document Collection
        George C. Burmeister Diary
        Douglas Ritchie Bushnell Letters
        Schuler Coe Letters
        James Forbis Letters
        Charles Foster Diary
        Ichabod Frisbie Papers
        Woodbury Hardy Letters
        Eugene Harrison Diary
        Orrin Albert Kellam Diary
        Oscar McLouth Papers
        McPheeters Family Papers
        Henry T. Morgan Letters
        Israel Ritter Diary
        Philip Roesch Memoirs
        Isaac Vanderwarker Diary
        James C. Whitehill Memoirs
Vicksburg National Military Park, Vicksburg, MS
    Vicksburg Campaign Series
        Journals, Diaries, and Letters
            Emma Balfour Diary
            Diary of John A. Leavy, MD; Surgeon—Green's Arkansas Brigade
            Theodosia McKinstry Memoirs, Civilian at Vicksburg
        Regimental Files
            31st Mississippi, Lt. Col. M. D. L. Stephens. Featherstone's Brigade,
                Loring's Division [diary of Dr. Thomas J. Blackwell]
    William T. Rigby Series
Wisconsin Historical Society, Madison
    John Barney Papers
    Christopher R. Blackall Memoirs, "In the Tornado: Days of '62–64:
        From the Diary and Letters of an Army Surgeon to His Family"
    Henry Clemons Civil War Letters
    George Hale Diary
    John G. Jones Civil War Letters
    John Wesley Largent Civil War Letters
    Alexander McDonald Civil War Diaries, 1862–1865
    Quiner Scrapbooks: Correspondence of the Wisconsin Volunteers, 1861–1865
    Daniel Ramsdell Papers
    Henry P. Strong Letters

Newspapers and Periodicals

American Medical Times
Boston Herald
Chicago Medical Journal
Chicago Tribune
Confederate Veteran
Harper's Monthly Magazine
Medical and Surgical Reporter

Milwaukee Daily Sentinel
Mobile Register
National Tribune
New York Times
North American Journal of Homeopathy
Sanitary Reporter
Vicksburg Daily Whig

Books

Abrams, A. S. *A Full and Detailed History of the Siege of Vicksburg*. Atlanta: Steam Powered Presses, 1863.

Adamson, A. P. *Brief History of the Thirtieth Georgia Regiment*. Griffin, GA: Mills Printing Co., 1912.

Ambrose, Stephen E., ed. *A Wisconsin Boy in Dixie: The Selected Letters of James K. Newton*. Madison: University of Wisconsin Press, 1961.

Anderson, John Q., ed. *Brokenburn: The Journal of Kate Stone, 1861–1868*. Baton Rouge: Louisiana State University Press, 1955.

Anderson, John Q., ed. *A Texas Surgeon in the C. S. A.* Tuscaloosa: Confederate Publishing Company, 1957.

Andrews, Edmund. *Complete Record of the Surgery of the Battles Fought near Vicksburg, December 27, 28, 29, & 30, 1862*. Chicago: George H. Fergus, Book and Job Printers, 1863.

Ankeny, Henry G. *Kiss Josey for Me!* Edited by Florence Marie Ankeny Cox. Santa Ana: Friis-Pioneer Press, 1974.

Atkinson, Matt, ed. *Lieutenant Drennan's Letter: A Confederate Officer's Account of the Battle of Champion Hill and the Siege of Vicksburg*. Gettysburg: Thomas Publications, 2009.

Barton, T. H. *Autobiography of Dr. Thomas Barton, the Self-Made Physician of Syracuse, Ohio*. Charleston: West Virginia Print Co., 1890.

Beadle, Elias Root. *The Sacredness of the Medical Profession: A Sermon Delivered before the Students at Jefferson Medical College and the Medical Department of the University of Pennsylvania, Sabbath Evening, November 19th, 1865*. Philadelphia: J. S. Claxton, 1865.

Bellows, Albert J. *How Not to Be Sick: A Sequel to "Philosophy of Eating."* New York: Hurd and Houghton, 1868.

Bentley, Lieut. W. H. *History of the 77th Illinois Volunteer Infantry, Sept. 2, 1862–July 10, 1865*. Peoria: Edward Hine, Printer, 1883.

Bering, John A., and Thomas Montgomery. *The History of the 48th Ohio*. Hillsboro, OH: Highland News Officer, 1880.

Beyer, W. F., and O. F. Keydel, eds. *Deeds of Valor from the Records in the Archives of the United States Government*. 2 vols. Detroit: Perrien-Keydel Co., 1906–7.

Billings, John D. *Hardtack and Coffee; or, The Unwritten Story of Army Life*. Boston: George M. Smith & Co., 1887.

Black, Samuel. *A Soldier's Recollections of the Civil War with Supplemental Chapters by Comrades*. Minco, OK: Minco Minstrel, 1911.

Blake, Ephraim. *A Succinct History of the 28th Iowa Volunteer Infantry*. Belle Plaines, IA: Union Press, 1896.

Bringhurst, Thomas H., and Frank Swigart. *History of the Forty-Sixth Regiment, Indiana Volunteer Infantry, September 1861–1865*. Logansport, IN: Press of Wilson, Humphreys, and Co., 1888.

Brinton, John H. *The Personal Memoirs of John H. Brinton: Major and Surgeon, 1861–1865*. Carbondale: Southern Illinois University Press, 1996.

Brockett, L. P. *The Camp, the Battlefield, and the Hospital: Or, Lights and Shadows of the Great Rebellion*. Philadelphia: National Publishing Company, 1866.

Chambers, William Pitt. *Blood and Sacrifice: The Civil War Journal of a Confederate Soldier*. Edited by Richard A. Baumgartner. Huntington, WV: Blue Acorn Press, 1994.

Cooke, Chauncey. *A Badger Boy in Blue: The Civil War Letters of Chauncey H. Cooke*. Detroit: Wayne State University Press, 2007.

Crooke, George. *The Twenty-First Regiment of Iowa Volunteer Infantry: A Narrative of Its Experiences in Active Services Including a Military Records of Each Officer, Non-commissioned Officer, and Private Soldier in the Organization*. Milwaukee: King, Fowle, and Co., 1891.

Dana, Charles A. *Recollections of the Civil War: With the Leaders at Washington and in the Field in the Sixties*. New York: Appleton and Company, 1898.

Edwards, William Henry. *A Condensed History of Seventeenth Regiment S.C.V., C.S.A.: From Its Organization to the Close of the War*. Columbia, SC: Press of the R. L. Bryan Co., 1908.

Elliot, Isaac Hughes. *History of the Thirty-Third Regiment Illinois Veteran Volunteer Infantry in the Civil War, 22nd August 1861 to 7th December 1865*. Gibson City, IL: Regimental Association, 1902.

Estabrook, Charles E. *Wisconsin Losses in the Civil War: A List of the Names of Wisconsin Soldiers Killed in Action, Mortally Wounded or Dying from Other Causes in the Civil War, Arranged According to Organization*. Madison: Adjutant General's Department, 1915.

Folgers, Alfred M. *The Family Physician: Being a Domestic Medical Work, Written in Plain Style, and Divided into Four Parts*. Spartanburg, SC: Cottrell, 1845.

Forman, J. G. *The Western Sanitary Commission: A Sketch of Its Origin, History, Labors for the Sick and Wounded of the Western Armies, and Aid Given to Freedmen and Union Refugees, with Incidents of Hospital Life*. St. Louis: R. P. Studley and Co., 1864.

Grant, Ulysses S. *Personal Memoirs of U. S. Grant*. 2 vols. New York: Charles L. Webster and Company, 1885–86.

Grecian, Joseph. *History of the Eighty-Third Regiment, Indiana Volunteer Infantry for Three Years with Sherman*. Cincinnati: J. F. Uhlhorn, 1865.

Greene, Francis Vinton. *The Mississippi*. New York: Charles Scribner's Sons, 1881.

Gunn, John C. *Gunn's Domestic Medicine*. Cincinnati: Moore, Wilstach, and Baldwin, 1864.

Hammond, William A. *Military Medical and Surgical Essays Prepared for the United States Sanitary Commission*. Philadelphia: J. B. Lippincott and Co., 1863.

Hicks, Robert D., ed. *Civil War Medicine: A Surgeon's Diary*. Bloomington: Indiana University Press, 2019.

Holcomb, Julie, ed. *Southern Sons, Northern Soldiers: The Civil War Letters of the Remley Brothers, 22nd Iowa Infantry*. DeKalb: Northern Illinois University Press, 2003.

Illinois Infantry, 13th Regiment. *Military History and Reminiscences of the Thirteenth Regiment of Illinois Volunteer Infantry in the Civil War in the United States, 1861–1865*. Chicago: Women's Temperance Publication Association, 1892.

Illinois Infantry, 55th Regiment. *The Story of the Fifty-Fifth Regiment Illinois Volunteer Infantry in the Civil War, 1861–1865*. Clinton, MA: W. J. Coulter, 1887.

Ingersoll, Lurton Dunham. *Iowa and the Rebellion*. 3rd ed. Philadelphia: J. B. Lippincott and Co., 1867.

Johnson, Charles Beneulyn. *Muskets and Medicine; or, Army Life in the Sixties*. Philadelphia: F. A. Davis Company, 1917.

Jones, S. C. *Reminiscences of the Twenty-Second Iowa Volunteer Infantry: Giving Its Organization, Marches, Skirmishes, Battles, and Sieges as Taken from the Diary of Lieutenant S. C. Jones of Company A*. Iowa City: n.p., 1907.

Josyph, Peter, ed. *The Wounded River: The Civil War Letters of John Vance Lauderdale, M.D.* East Lansing: Michigan State University Press, 1993.

Kiper, Richard L., ed. *Dear Catharine, Dear Taylor: The Civil War Letters of a Union Soldier and His Wife*. Lawrence: University Press of Kansas, 2002.

Logan, John Alexander. *The Proposed Ohio Senatorial Investigation: Speech by Senator John A. Logan of Illinois in the United States Senate Wednesday, July 21, 1886*. N.p., 1886.

Logan, John Alexander. *Speech of Major-General John A. Logan on Return to Illinois, after Capture of Vicksburg*. Cincinnati: C. Clark, 1863.

Loughborough, Mary Ann. *My Cave Life in Vicksburg with Letters of Trial and Travel*. New York: Appleton and Company, 1864.

Macleod, George H. B. *Notes on the Surgery of the War in the Crimea with Remarks on the Treatment of Gunshot Wounds*. Richmond: J. W. Randolph, 1862.

Mahan, James Curtis. *The Memoirs of James Curtis Mahan*. Lincoln: Franklin Press, 1919.

Marshall, T. B. *History of the Eighty-Third Ohio Volunteer Infantry, the Greyhound Regiment*. Cincinnati: Eighty-Third Ohio Volunteer Infantry Association, 1912.

Mason, Frank. *The Forty-Second Ohio Infantry: A History of the Organization and Services of That Regiment in the War of the Rebellion*. Cleveland: Cobb, Andrews, and Co., 1876.

Morss, Christopher, ed. *Helena to Vicksburg: A Civil War Odyssey; The Personal Diary of Joshua Whittington Underhill, Surgeon, 46th Regiment, Indiana Volunteer Infantry, 23 October–21 July 1863*. Lincoln Center, MA: Heritage House, 2000.

Newberry, John Strong. *U.S. Sanitary Commission in the Valley of the Mississippi during the War of the Rebellion*. Cleveland: Fairbanks, Benedict and Co., 1871.

Oak, William Royal. *On the Skirmish Line behind a Friendly Tree: The Civil War Memoirs of William Royal Oak, 26th Iowa Volunteers*. Edited by Stacy Dale Allen. Helena: Far Country Press, 2006.

Oldroyd, Osborn. *A Soldier's Story of the Siege of Vicksburg*. Springfield, IL: Published for the Author, 1885.

Ordronaux, John. *Hints on Health in Armies, for the Use of Volunteer Officers*. 2nd ed. New York: D. Van Nostrand, 1863.

Parson, Emily Elizabeth. *Memoirs of Emily Elizabeth Parsons: Published for the Benefit of the Cambridge Hospital*. Boston: Little, Brown, and Co., 1880.

Popchock, Barry, ed. *Soldier Boy: The Civil War Letters of Charles O. Musser, 29th Iowa*. Iowa City: University of Iowa Press, 1995.

Porcher, Francis Peyre. *Resources of the Southern Fields and Forests: Medical, Economical, and Agricultural*. Charleston: Evans and Cogswell, 1863.

Porter, David Dixon. *Incidents and Anecdotes of the Civil War*. New York: D. Appleton and Company, 1887.

Puck, Susan T, ed. *Sacrifice at Vicksburg: Letters from the Front*. Shippensburg, PA: Burd Street Press, 1997.

Quiner, E. B. *The Military History of Wisconsin: A Record of the Civil and Military Patriotism of the State, in the War for the Union, with a History of the Campaigns in Which Wisconsin Soldiers Have Been Conspicuous*. Chicago: Clarke and Co., 1866.

Regimental Association. *History of the Forty Sixth Regiment, Indiana Volunteer Infantry, September 1861–1865*. Logansport, IN: Press of Wilson, Humphreys, and Co., 1888.

Report of the Western Sanitary Commission for the Year Ending June 1, 1863. St. Louis: Western Sanitary Commission Rooms, 1863.

Ritner, Jacob B. *Love and Valor: The Intimate Civil War Letters between Captain Jacob and Emeline Ritner*. Edited by Charles F. Larimer. Western Springs, IL: Sigourney Press, Inc., 2000.

Russell, William Howard. *The Battle of Bull Run*. New York: Rudd and Carleton, 1890.

Scott, Reuben. *The History of the 67th Regiment Indiana Infantry Volunteers*. Bedford, IN: Herald Book and Job Print, 1892.

Sears, Stephen W, ed. *For Country, Cause and Leader: The Civil War Journal of Charles B. Haydon*. Boston: Ticknor and Fields, 1993.

Sherman, William T. *Memoirs of General William T. Sherman*. Edited by Charles Royster. New York: Library of America, 1990.

Sherman, William T. *Sherman's Civil War: Selected Correspondence of William T. Sherman, 1860–1865*. Edited by Brooks D. Simpson and Jean V. Berlin. Chapel Hill: University of North Carolina Press, 1999.

Simon, John Y., ed. *The Papers of Ulysses S. Grant*. 32 vols. Carbondale: Southern Illinois University Press, 1967–2013.

Smith, Edward P. *Incidents of the United States Christian Commission*. Philadelphia: J. B. Lippincott and Co., 1869.

Sperry, A. F. *History of the 33rd Iowa Infantry Volunteer Regiment, 1863–6*. Edited by Gregory J. W. Urwin and Cathy Kunzinger Urwin. Fayetteville: University of Arkansas Press, 1999.

Stevens, E. B., ed. *The Cincinnati Lancet and Observer*. Vol 6. Cincinnati: S. G. Cobb, Printer, 1863.

Stillé, Charles. *The History of the United States Sanitary Commission, Being the General Reports of Its Work during the War of the Rebellion*. Philadelphia: L. B. Lippincott and Co., 1866.

Taylor, Jay F., ed. *The Reluctant Rebel: The Secret Diary of Robert Patrick, 1861–1865*. Baton Rouge: Louisiana State University Press, 1987.

Throne, Mildred, ed. *The Civil War Diary of Cyrus F. Boyd, Fifteenth Iowa Infantry, 1861–1863*. Baton Rouge: Louisiana State University Press, 1998.

Tripler, Charles S. *Handbook for the Military Surgeon*. 2nd ed. Cincinnati: Robert Clarke and Co., 1861.

Trowbridge, Silas Thompson. *Autobiography of Silas Thompson Trowbridge M.D.* Carbondale: Southern Illinois University Press, 2004.

United States Congress. *Journal of the House of Representatives of the United States: Being the Third Session of the Thirty-seventh Congress; Begun and Held at the City of Washington,*

December 1, 1862, in the Eighty-seventh Year of the Independence of the United States. Washington, DC: Government Printing Office, 1863.

United States Navy Department. *Official Records of the Union and Confederate Navies in the War of the Rebellion*. 30 vols. Washington, DC: Government Printing Office, 1894–1922.

United States Sanitary Commission. *Documents of the U.S. Sanitary Commission*. 3 vols. New York: s.n., 1856–66.

The United States Sanitary Commission: A Sketch of Its Purposes and Its Work. Compiled from Documents and Private Papers. Boston: Little, Brown, 1863.

United States Surgeon General's Office. *The Medical and Surgical History of the War of the Rebellion (1861–1865)*. 6 vols. Washington, DC: Government Printing Office, 1870–88.

United States War Department. *Revised United States Army Regulations of 1861: With an Appendix Containing the Changes and Laws Affecting Army Regulations and Articles of War to June 25, 1863*. Washington DC: Government Printing Office, 1863.

United States War Department. *The War of the Rebellion: A Compilation of the Official Records of the Union and Confederate Armies*. 128 vols. Washington, DC: Government Printing Office, 1880–1901.

Wafer, Francis M. *A Surgeon in the Army of the Potomac*. Edited by Cheryl A. Wells. Montreal: McGill–Queen's University Press, 2008.

Watson, William. *Letters of a Civil War Surgeon*. Edited by Paul Fatout. West Lafayette, IN: Purdue University Press, 1961.

Wells, Seth J. *The Siege of Vicksburg from the Diary of Seth J. Wells*. Detroit: William M. Roe, 1915.

Willison, Charles A. *Reminiscences of a Boy's Service with the 76th Ohio: In the Fifteenth Army Corps, under General Sherman, during the Civil War by That "Boy" at Three Score*. Huntington, WV: Blue Acorn Press, 1995.

Winschel, Terrence J., ed. *The Civil War Diary of a Common Soldier: William Wiley of the 77th Illinois Infantry*. Baton Rouge: Louisiana State University Press, 2001.

Woods, J. T. *Services of the Ninety-Sixth Ohio Volunteers*. Toledo: Blade Printing and Paper Co., 1874.

Woodward, J. J. *Outlines of the Chief Camp Diseases of the United States Armies as Observed during the Present War*. Philadelphia: J. B. Lippincott and Co., 1863.

Articles

Abernethy, Alonzo. "Incidents of an Iowa Soldier's Life, or Four Years in Dixie." *Annals of Iowa* 12, no. 6 (October 1920): 401–28.

Beach, J. N. "Army Surgeons: Their Character and Duties." *Cincinnati Lancet and Observer* 6 (June 1863): 329–34.

Boos, J. E., and Patrick H. White. "Civil War Diary of Patrick H. White." *Journal of Illinois State Historical Society* 15, no. 3 (1922): 640–63.

Buegel, John T. "The Civil War Diary of John T. Buegel, Union Solder." Translated by William G. Bek. *Missouri Historical Review* 40 (April–July 1946): 307–29, 503–30.

Byers, S. H. M. "How Men Feel in Battle: Recollections of a Private at Champion Hills." *Annals of Iowa* 2, no. 6 (July 1896): 438–49.

Fingerson, Ronald L. "A William Tecumseh Sherman Letter." *Books at Iowa* 3 (November 1965): 34–38.

Frank, Elijah. "E. H. Frank to Catherine Varner, Charlotte, Iowa, 1862–1863." *North Dakota Historical Quarterly* 4 (1929): 186–96.

Halsell, William D. "The Sixteenth Indiana Regiment in the Last Vicksburg Campaign." *Indiana Magazine of History* 43 (March 1947): 67–82.

Hass, Paul H., ed. "The Vicksburg Diary of Henry Clay Warmoth, Part I." *Journal of Mississippi History* 31 (November 1969): 334–47.

Hass, Paul H., ed. "The Vicksburg Diary of Henry Clay Warmoth, Part II." *Journal of Mississippi History* 32 (February 1970): 60–74.

Jones, J. H. "The Rank and File at Vicksburg." *Publications of the Mississippi Historical Society* 7 (1903): 17–31.

Longacre, Edward G., ed. "'Dear and Mutch Loved One': An Iowan's Vicksburg Letters." *Annals of Iowa* 43, no. 1 (Summer 1975): 49–61.

Lyons, Bessie L. "Flashlights on Vicksburg." *The Palimpsest* 8 (1927): 71–80.

Maertz, Louise. "Midland War Sketches IV: Extracts from the Home Letters of One of Miss Six's Nurses in 1863." *Midland Monthly* 3, no. 1 (January 1895): 79–85.

Maynard, Douglas, ed. "Vicksburg Diary: The Journal of Gabriel M. Killgore." *Civil War History* 10, no. 1 (1964): 33–53.

Murray, R. "Report from the Union Medical Director at the Battle of Shiloh." *Journal of Civil War Medicine* 19, no. 3 (2015): 1–3.

Osborn, George C., ed. "A Tennessean at the Siege of Vicksburg: The Diary of Samuel Alexander Ramsey Swan, May–July, 1863." *Tennessee Historical Quarterly* 14, no. 4 (December 1955): 353–72.

Pitts, Florison. "The Civil War Diary of Florison D. Pitts." *Mid-America* 40 (1958): 22–68.

Sanders, J. Y. "Diary in Gray: Civil War Journal of J. Y. Sanders." Edited by Mary Elizabeth Sanders. *Louisiana Genealogical Register* 17, no. 1 (1969): 16–20.

Smith, James West. "A Confederate Soldier's Diary: Vicksburg in 1863." *Southwest Review* 28, no. 3 (Spring 1943): 293–327.

Smith, Thad L. "The Twenty-Fourth Iowa Volunteers: From Muscatine to Winchester, Part 1." *Annals of Iowa* 1, no. 1 (April 1893): 15–37.

Smith, Thad L. "The Twenty-Fourth Iowa Volunteers: From Muscatine to Winchester, Part 2." *Annals of Iowa* 1, no. 2 (July 1893): 111–28.

Smith, Thad L. "The Twenty-Fourth Iowa Volunteers: From Muscatine to Winchester, Part 3." *Annals of Iowa* 1, no. 3 (October 1893): 180–96.

Thompson, J. K. P. "Iowa at Vicksburg and the Vicksburg National Military Park." *Annals of Iowa* 5, no. 4 (January 1902): 272–92.

Williams, G. Mott. "Letters of General Thomas Williams, 1862." *American Historical Review* 14, no. 2 (1909): 304–28.

SECONDARY SOURCES

Books

Acton, Carol, and Jane Potter. *Working in a World of Hurt: Trauma and Resilience in the Narratives of Medical Personnel in Warzones.* Manchester: Manchester University Press, 2015.
Adams, George Worthington. *Doctors in Blue: The Medical History of the Union Army in the Civil War.* Baton Rouge: Louisiana State University Press, 1996.
Alberti, Fay Bound, ed. *Medicine, Emotion, and Disease, 1700–1950.* New York: Palgrave Macmillan, 2006.
Allhoff, Fritz. *Physicians at War: The Dual-Loyalties Challenge.* Dordrecht, Netherlands: Springer Books, 2008.
Anthamatten, Peter, and Helen Hazen. *An Introduction to the Geography of Health.* New York: Routledge, 2011.
Ariès, Philippe. *The Hour of Our Death.* New York: Vintage Books, 1982.
Armstrong, Warren B. *For Courageous Fighting and Confident Dying: Union Chaplains in the Civil War.* Lawrence: University Press of Kansas, 1998.
Ballard, Michael. *Grant at Vicksburg: The General and the Siege.* Carbondale: Southern Illinois University Press, 2013.
Ballard, Michael. *Vicksburg: The Campaign That Opened the Mississippi.* Chapel Hill: University of North Carolina Press, 2010.
Baron, S. *Medical Microbiology.* 4th ed. Galveston: University of Texas Medical Branch at Galveston, 1996.
Bearss, Edwin Cole. *The Campaign for Vicksburg.* 3 vols. Dayton: Morningside Press, 1985–86.
Bearss, Edwin Cole, and J. Parker Hills. *Receding Tide: Vicksburg and Gettysburg: The Campaigns That Changed the Civil War.* Washington DC: National Geographic Society, 2010.
Bell, Andrew McIlwaine. *Mosquito Soldiers: Malaria, Yellow Fever, and the Course of the American Civil War.* Baton Rouge: Louisiana State University Press, 2010.
Beringer, Richard E., Herman Hattaway, Archer Jones, and William N. Still Jr. *Why the South Lost the Civil War.* Athens: University of Georgia Press, 1986.
Berry, Stephen W., II. *All That Makes a Man: Love and Ambitions in the Civil War South.* New York: Oxford University Press, 2003.
Bever, Megan L., Lesley J. Gordon, and Laura Mammina. *American Discord: The Republic and Its People in the Civil War Era.* Baton Rouge: Louisiana State University Press, 2020.
Bollet, Alfred Jay. *Civil War Medicine: Challenges and Triumphs.* Tucson: Galen Press, 2002.
Bourke, Joanna. *Dismembering the Male: Men's Bodies, Britain, and the Great War.* Chicago: University of Chicago Press, 1996.
Brady, Lisa M. *War upon the Land: Military Strategy and the Transformation of Southern Landscapes during the American Civil War.* Athens: University of Georgia Press, 2012.
Brookes, Stewart. *Civil War Medicine.* Springfield, IL: C. C. Thomas, 1966.
Broomall, James J. *Private Confederacies: The Emotional Worlds of Southern Men as Citizens and Soldiers.* Chapel Hill: University of North Carolina Press, 2019.
Brown, Kathleen M. *Foul Bodies: Cleanliness in Early America.* New Haven: Yale University Press, 2009.

Browning, Judkin, and Timothy Silver. *An Environmental History of the Civil War*. Chapel Hill: University of North Carolina Press, 2020.

Bynum, W. F. *Science and the Practice of Medicine in the Nineteenth Century*. Cambridge: Cambridge University Press, 1991.

Carmichael, Peter S. *The War for the Common Soldier: How Men Thought, Fought, and Survived in Civil War Armies*. Chapel Hill: University of North Carolina Press, 2018.

Carroll, Dillon J. *Invisible Wounds: Mental Illness and Civil War Soldiers*. Baton Rouge: Louisiana State University Press, 2021.

Clampitt, Bradley R. *Occupied Vicksburg*. Baton Rouge: Louisiana State University Press, 2016.

Clarke, Frances M. *War Stories: Suffering and Sacrifice in the Civil War North*. Chicago: University of Chicago Press, 2011.

Cooter, Roger, Mark Harrison, and Steve Sturdy, eds. *Medicine and Modern Warfare*. Atlanta: Rodopi, 1999.

Cooter, Roger, Mark Harrison, and Steve Sturdy, eds. *War, Medicine and Modernity*. Gloucestershire: Sutton, 1999.

Costa, Dora L., and Matthew Khan. *Heroes and Cowards: The Social Face of War*. Princeton: Princeton University Press, 2008.

Cowdrey, Albert E. *This Land, This South: An Environmental History*. Lexington: University of Kentucky Press, 1983.

Cunningham, Andrew, and Perry Williams. *The Laboratory Revolution in Medicine*. Cambridge: Cambridge University Press, 1992.

Cunningham, Horace H. *Doctors in Gray: The Confederate Medical Service*. Baton Rouge: Louisiana State University Press, 1993.

Cunningham, Horace H. *Field Medical Services at the Battles of Manassas*. Athens: University of Georgia Press, 1968.

Currie, James I. *Enclave: Vicksburg and Her Plantations, 1863–1870*. Jackson: University Press of Mississippi, 1980.

Davis, George B., Leslie J. Perry, and Joseph W. Kirkley. *The Official Military Atlas of the Civil War*. New York: Arno Press, 1978.

Dean, Eric T., Jr. *Shook Over Hell: Post-Traumatic Stress, Vietnam, and the Civil War*. Cambridge, MA: Harvard University Press, 1997.

Devine, Shauna. *Learning from the Wounded: The Civil War and the Rise of American Medical Science*. Chapel Hill: University of North Carolina Press, 2014.

Dougherty, Kevin. *The Vicksburg Campaign: Strategy, Battles, and Key Figures*. Jefferson, NC: McFarland, 2015.

Dowdey, Clifford, ed. *The Wartime Papers of Robert E. Lee*. New York: Da Capo Press, 1987.

Downs, Jim. *Sick from Freedom: African-American Illness and Suffering during the Civil War and Reconstruction*. Oxford: Oxford University Press, 2012.

Drake, Brian Allen. *The Blue, the Gray, and the Green: Toward an Environmental History of the Civil War*. Athens: University of Georgia Press, 2015.

Duffy, John. *From Humors to Medical Science: A History of American Medicine*. 2nd ed. Urbana: University of Illinois Press, 1993.

Duffy, John. *The Healers: A History of American Medicine*. Urbana: University of Illinois Press, 1979.

Elder, Angela Esco. *Love and Duty: Confederate Widows and the Emotional Politics of Loss.* Chapel Hill: University of North Carolina Press, 2022.

Eustace, Nicole. *Passion Is the Gale: Emotion, Power, and the Coming of the American Revolution.* Chapel Hill: University of North Carolina Press, 2008.

Faust, Drew Gilpin. *This Republic of Suffering: Death and the American Civil War.* New York: Vintage Books, 2008.

Ferrell, James J. *Inventing the American Way of Death.* Philadelphia: Temple University Press, 1980.

Flannery, Michael. *Civil War Pharmacy: A History of Drugs, Drug Supply and Provision, and Therapeutics for the Union and Confederacy.* Baton Rouge: CRC Press, 2004.

Foote, Lorien. *The Gentlemen and the Roughs: Violence, Honor, and Manhood in the Union Army.* New York: New York University Press, 2010.

Foote, Lorien. *Rites of Retaliation: Civilization, Soldiers, and Campaigns in the American Civil War.* Chapel Hill: University of North Carolina Press, 2022.

Foucault, Michel. *The Birth of the Clinic: An Archaeology of Medical Perception.* Translated by A. M. Sheridan Smith. New York: Pantheon, 1973.

Foucault, Michel. *Discipline and Punish: The Birth of the Prison.* New York: Vintage Books, 1995.

Frank, Joseph Allen, and George A. Reaves. *Seeing the Elephant: Raw Recruits at the Battle of Shiloh.* Chicago: University of Illinois Press, 2003.

Freemon, Frank R. *Gangrene and Glory: Medical Care during the American Civil War.* Urbana: University of Illinois Press, 2001.

Gabriel, Richard. *Between Flesh and Steel: A History of Military Medicine from the Middle Ages to the War in Afghanistan.* Washington, DC: Potomac Books, 2013.

Gallagher, Gary W. *The Confederate War.* Cambridge, MA: Harvard University Press, 1997.

Gillett, Mary C. *The Army Medical Department, 1818–1865.* Washington DC: Center of Military History, 1981.

Gordon, Lesley J. *A Broken Regiment: The 16th Connecticut's Civil War.* Baton Rouge: Louisiana State University Press, 2014.

Gordon, Lesley J. *"I Never Was a Coward": Questions of Bravery in a Civil War Regiment.* Milwaukee: Marquette University Press, 2005.

Grabau, Warren E. *Ninety-Eight Days: A Geographer's View of the Vicksburg Campaign.* Knoxville: University of Tennessee Press, 2000.

Grimsley, Mark. *The Hard Hand of War: Union Military Policy toward Southern Civilians, 1861–1865.* Cambridge: Cambridge University Press, 1995.

Haller, John S., Jr. *American Medicine in Transition, 1840–1910.* Urbana: University of Illinois Press, 1981.

Haller, John S., Jr. *The History of American Homeopathy: The Academic Years, 1820–1935.* New York: Pharmaceutical Products Press, 2005.

Haller, John S., Jr. *Kindly Medicine: Physio-Medicalism in America, 1836–1911.* Kent: Kent State University Press, 1997.

Haller, John S., Jr. *Sectarian Reformers in American Medicine, 1800–1910.* New York: AMS Press, 2011.

Hamner, Christopher H. *Enduring Battle: American Soldiers in Three Wars, 1776–1946.* Lawrence: University Press of Kansas, 2011.

Handley-Cousins, Sarah. *Bodies in Blue: Disability in the Civil War North*. Athens: University of Georgia Press, 2019.

Harrison, Mark. *The Medical War*. Oxford: Oxford University Press, 2010.

Hattaway, Herman, and Archer Jones. *How the North Won the Civil War: A Military History of the Civil War*. Urbana: University of Illinois Press, 1983.

Hess, Earl J. *Civil War Infantry Tactics: Training, Combat, and Small-Unit Effectiveness*. Baton Rouge: Louisiana State University Press, 2015.

Hess, Earl J. *The Civil War in the West: Victory and Defeat from the Appalachians to the Mississippi*. Chapel Hill: University of North Carolina Press, 2012.

Hess, Earl J. *Liberty, Virtue, and Progress: Northerners and Their War for the Union*. New York: New York University Press, 1988.

Hess, Earl J. *Storming Vicksburg: Grant, Pemberton, and the Battles of May 19–22, 1863*. Chapel Hill: University of North Carolina Press, 2020.

Hess, Earl J. *The Union Soldier in Battle: Enduring the Ordeal of Combat*. Lawrence: University Press of Kansas, 1997.

Hoehling, A. A. *Vicksburg: 47 Days of Siege*. New York: Fairfax Press, 1991.

Humphreys, Margaret. *Intensely Human: The Health of the Black Soldier in the American Civil War*. Baltimore: Johns Hopkins University Press, 2008.

Humphreys, Margaret. *Malaria: Poverty, Race, and Public Health in the United States*. Baltimore: Johns Hopkins University Press, 2001.

Humphreys, Margaret. *A Marrow of Tragedy: The Health Crisis of the American Civil War*. Baltimore: Johns Hopkins University Press, 2013.

Humphreys, Margaret. *Yellow Fever and the South*. Baltimore: Johns Hopkins University Press, 1999.

Jalland, Pat. *Death in the Victorian Family*. Oxford: Oxford University Press, 1996.

Janzen, John M. *The Social Fabric of Health: An Introduction to Medical Anthropology*. Boston: McGraw-Hill, 2002.

Jensen, Niklas Thode. *For The Health of the Enslaved: Slaves, Medicine, and Power in the Danish West Indies, 1803–1848*. Copenhagen: Museum Tusculanum Press, 2012.

Johnson, Allison M. *The Scars We Carve: Bodies and Wounds in Civil War Print Culture*. Baton Rouge: Louisiana State University Press, 2019.

Kaufman, Martin. *American Medical Education: The Formative Years, 1765–1910*. Westport, CT: Greenwood Press, 1976.

Keegan, John. *The American Civil War: A Military History*. New York: Alfred Knopf, 2009.

Keegan, John. *The Face of Battle*. New York: Viking Press, 1976.

Kett, Joseph F. *The Formation of the American Medical Profession: The Role of Institution, 1780–1860*. New Haven: Yale University Press, 1968.

Kiper, Richard L. *Major General John Alexander McClernand: Politician in Uniform*. Kent: Kent State University Press, 1999.

Kleinman, Arthur. *Patients and Healers in the Context of Culture: An Exploration of the Borderland between Anthropology, Medicine, and Psychiatry*. Berkeley: University of California Press, 1980.

Lang, Andrew F. *In the Wake of War: Military Occupation, Emancipation, and Civil War America*. Baton Rouge: Louisiana State University Press, 2017.

Linderman, Gerald F. *Embattled Courage: The Experience of Combat in the American Civil War.* Oxford: Oxford University Press, 1997.

Long, Lisa. *Rehabilitating Bodies: Health, History, and the American Civil War.* Philadelphia: University of Pennsylvania Press, 2004.

Marvel, William. *Andersonville: The Last Depot.* Chapel Hill: University of North Carolina Press, 1994.

Marvel, William. *Lincoln's Autocrat: The Life of Edwin Stanton.* Chapel Hill: University of North Carolina Press, 2015.

Matt, Susan J., and Peter N. Stearns, eds. *Doing Emotions History.* Urbana: University of Illinois Press, 2014.

Maxwell, William Quentin. *Lincoln's Fifth Wheel: The Political History of the United States Sanitary Commission.* New York: Longmans, Green, 1956.

McNeill, J. R. *Mosquito Empires: Ecology and War in the Greater Caribbean, 1620–1914.* Cambridge: Cambridge University Press, 2010.

McPherson, James. *Battle Cry of Freedom: The Civil War Era.* New York: Oxford University Press, 1988.

McPherson, James. *For Cause and Comrades: Why Men Fought in the Civil War.* New York: Free Press, 1987.

McPherson, James. *War on the Waters: The Union and Confederate Navies, 1861–1865.* Chapel Hill: University of North Carolina Press, 2012.

McWhiney, Grady, and Perry D. Jamieson. *Attack and Die: Civil War Military Tactics and the Southern Heritage.* Tuscaloosa: University of Alabama Press, 1982.

Meier, Kathryn Shively. *Nature's Civil War: Common Soldiers and the Environment in 1862 Virginia.* Chapel Hill: University of North Carolina Press, 2013.

Meyers, Christopher C. *Union General John A. McClernand and the Politics of Command.* Jefferson, NC: McFarland, 2010.

Miller, Brian Craig. *Empty Sleeves: Amputation in the Civil War South.* Athens: University of Georgia Press, 2015.

Miller, Donald L. *Vicksburg: Grant's Campaign That Broke the Confederacy.* New York: Simon and Schuster, 2020.

Morris, Christopher. *Becoming Southern: The Evolution of a Way of Life, Warren County and Vicksburg, Mississippi, 1770–1860.* New York: Oxford University Press, 1995.

Morris, Christopher. *The Big Muddy: An Environmental History of the Mississippi and Its Peoples from Hernando De Soto to Hurricane Katrina.* Oxford: Oxford University Press, 2012.

Morris, David B. *The Culture of Pain.* Berkeley: University of California Press, 1993.

Nelson, Megan Kate. *Ruin Nation: Destruction of the American Civil War.* Athens: University of Georgia Press, 2012.

Noe, Kenneth W. *The Howling Storm: Weather, Climate, and the American Civil War.* Baton Rouge: Louisiana State University Press, 2020.

Nudelman, Franny. *John Brown's Body: Slavery, Violence, and the Culture of War.* Chapel Hill: University of North Carolina Press, 2004.

Numbers, Ronald L., and Todd L. Savitt, eds. *Science and Medicine in the Old South.* Baton Rouge: Louisiana State University Press, 1989.

Payne, Lynda. *With Words and Knives: Learning Medical Dispassion in Early Modern England.* Aldershot, Eng.: Ashgate, 2007.

Petty, Adam H. *The Battle of the Wilderness in Myth and Memory: Reconsidering Virginia's Most Notorious Civil War Battlefield*. Baton Rouge: Louisiana State University Press, 2019.

Porter, Roy. *The Greatest Benefit to Mankind: A Medical History of Humanity*. New York: Norton, 1997.

Rable, George C. *Fredericksburg! Fredericksburg!* Chapel Hill: University of North Carolina Press, 2012.

Rable, George C. *God's Almost Chosen Peoples*. Chapel Hill: University of North Carolina Press, 2002.

Reardon, Carol. *With a Sword in One Hand and Jomini in the Other*. Chapel Hill: University of North Carolina Press, 2012.

Reddy, William M. *The Navigation of Feeling: A Framework for the History of Emotions*. Cambridge: Cambridge University Press, 2001.

Robertson, James I., Jr. *Soldiers Blue and Gray*. Columbia: University of South Carolina Press, 1998.

Rosenberg, Charles E. *The Care of Strangers: The Rise of America's Hospital System*. Baltimore: Johns Hopkins University Press, 1992.

Rosenberg, Charles E. *The Cholera Years: The United States in 1832, 1849, and 1866*. Chicago: University of Chicago Press, 1962.

Rosenberg, Charles E., ed. *Right Living: An Anglo-American Tradition of Self-Help Medicine and Hygiene*. Baltimore: Johns Hopkins University Press, 2003.

Rothman, David J. *The Discovery of the Asylum: Social Order and Disorder in the New Republic*. 2nd ed. New York: Aldine de Gruyter, 1990.

Rutkow, Ira. *Bleeding Blue and Gray: Civil War Surgery and the Evolution of American Medicine*. New York: Random House, 2005.

Saikku, Mikko. *This Delta, This Land: An Environmental History of the Yazoo–Mississippi Floodplain*. Athens: University of Georgia Press, 2005.

Sappol, Michael. *A Traffic of Dead Bodies: Anatomy and Embodied Social Identity in Nineteenth-Century America*. Princeton: Princeton University Press, 2001.

Savitt, Todd L., and James Harvey Young, eds. *Disease and Distinctiveness in the American South*. Knoxville: University of Tennessee Press, 1988.

Schantz, Mark. *Awaiting the Heavenly Country: The Civil War and America's Culture of Death*. Ithaca: Cornell University Press, 2008.

Shea, William L., and Terrence J. Winschel. *Vicksburg Is the Key: The Struggle for the Mississippi River*. Lincoln, NE: Bison Books, 2005.

Sheehan-Dean, Aaron, ed. *The View from the Ground: Experiences of Civil War Soldiers*. Lexington: University of Kentucky Press, 2007.

Shryock, Richard Harrison. *Medicine in America: Historical Essays*. Baltimore: Johns Hopkins Press, 1966.

Smith, Andrew F. *Starving the South: How the North Won the Civil War*. New York: St. Martin's Press, 2011.

Smith, Mark M. *Sensing the Past: Seeing, Hearing, Smelling, Tasting, and Touching in History*. Berkeley: University of California Press, 2008.

Smith, Mark M. *The Smell of Battle, the Taste of Siege: A Sensory History of the Civil War*. Oxford: Oxford University Press, 2014.

Smith, Timothy B. *Bayou Battles for Vicksburg: The Swamp and River Expeditions, January 1–April 30, 1863*. Lawrence: University Press of Kansas, 2023.

Smith, Timothy B. *Early Struggles for Vicksburg: The Mississippi Central Campaign and Chickasaw Bayou, October 25–December 31, 1862*. Lawrence: University Press of Kansas, 2022.

Smith, Timothy B. *The Inland Campaign for Vicksburg: Five Battles in Seventeen Days, May 1–17, 1863*. Lawrence: University Press of Kansas, 2024.

Smith, Timothy B. *The Siege of Vicksburg: Climax of the Campaign to Open the Mississippi River, May 23–July 4, 1863*. Lawrence: University Press of Kansas, 2021.

Smith, Timothy B. *The Union Assaults at Vicksburg: Grant Attacks Pemberton, May 17–22, 1863*. Lawrence: University Press of Kansas, 2020.

Solonick, Justin S. *Engineering Victory: The Union Siege of Vicksburg*. Carbondale: Southern Illinois University Press, 2015.

Sommerville, Diane Miller. *Aberration of Mind: Suicide and Suffering in the Civil War Era South*. Chapel Hill: University of North Carolina Press, 2018.

Starr, Paul. *The Social Transformation of American Medicine: The Rise of a Sovereign Profession and the Making of a Vast Industry*. New York: Basic Books, 1984.

Steiner, Paul E. *Disease in the Civil War: Natural Biological Warfare in 1861–1865*. Springfield, IL: C. C. Thomas, 1968.

Taithe, Bertrand. *Defeated Flesh: Medicine, Welfare, and Warfare in the Making of Modern France*. Lanham, MD: Rowman and Littlefield, 1999.

Thompson, Lauren K. *Friendly Enemies: Soldier Fraternization throughout the American Civil War*. Lincoln: University of Nebraska Press, 2020.

Titus, David. "The Failure of the Confederate Vicksburg Campaign." Strategy research project, United States Army War College, 1996.

Valenčius, Conevery Bolton. *The Health of the Country: How American Settlers Understood Themselves and Their Land*. New York: Basic Books, 2002.

Waldrep, Christopher. *Vicksburg's Long Shadow: The Civil War Legacy of Race and Remembrance*. Lanham, MD: Rowman and Littlefield, 2005.

Walker, Peter. *Vicksburg: A People at War, 1861–1865*. Wilmington, NC: Broadfoot, 1987.

Warner, John Harley. *Against the Spirit of the System: The French Impulse in American Medicine*. Baltimore: Johns Hopkins University Press, 1998.

White, Jonathan W. *Midnight in America: Darkness, Sleep, and Dreams during the Civil War*. Chapel Hill: University of North Carolina Press, 2017.

Wiley, Bell Irvin. *The Life of Billy Yank: The Common Soldier of the Union*. Indianapolis: Bobbs-Merrill, 1957.

Wiley, Bell Irvin. *The Life of Johnny Reb: The Common Soldier of the Confederacy*. Indianapolis: Bobbs-Merrill, 1943.

Williams, T. Harry. *Lincoln and His Generals*. New York: Knopf, 1952.

Williams, T. Harry. *McClellan, Sherman, and Grant*. New Brunswick, NJ: Rutgers University Press, 1962.

Winschel, Terrence J. *Triumph and Defeat: The Vicksburg Campaign*. Mason City, IA: Savas, 1999.

Winschel, Terrence J. *Vicksburg: Fall of the Confederate Gibraltar*. Abilene, TX: McWhiney Foundation Press, 1999.

Wintermute, Bobby A. *Public Health and the U.S. Military: A History of the Army Medical Department, 1818–1971*. New York: Routledge, 2011.
Winters, Harold A., Gerald E. Galloway Jr., William J. Reynolds, and David W. Rhyne, eds. *Battling the Elements: Weather and Terrain in the Conduct of War*. Baltimore: Johns Hopkins University Press, 1998.
Woods, Michael E. *Emotional and Sectional Conflict in the Antebellum United States*. New York: Cambridge University Press, 2014.
Woodworth, Steven E. *While God Is Marching On: The Religious World of Civil War Soldiers*. Lawrence: University Press of Kansas, 2001.
Woodworth, Steven E., and Charles D. Grear, eds. *The Vicksburg Campaign: March 29–May 18, 1863*. Carbondale: Southern Illinois University Press, 2013.

Articles, Dissertations, and Theses

Abbasi, Karman. "Climate, Pandemic, and War: An Uncontrolled Multicrisis of Existential Proportions." *BMJ* 376 (March 2022). https://doi.org/10.1136/bmj.o689.
Adams, George Worthington. "Confederate Medicine." *Journal of Southern History* 6, no. 2 (1940): 151–66.
Alberti, Fay Bound. "Bodies, Hearts, and Minds: Why Emotions Matter to Historians of Science and Medicine." *Isis: Journal of the History of Science in Society* 100, no. 4 (2009): 798–810.
Blustein, Bonnie Ellen. "To Increase the Efficiency of the Medical Department: A New Approach to Civil War Medicine." *Civil War History* 33, no. 1 (1987): 22–41.
Bollet, Alfred Jay. "An Analysis of the Medical Problems of the Civil War." *Transactions of the American Clinical and Climatological Association* 102 (1992): 128–41.
Bollet, Alfred Jay. "The Major Infectious Epidemic Diseases of Civil War Soldiers." *Infectious Disease Clinics of North America* 18 (2004): 296–97.
Bollet, Alfred Jay. "Scurvy and Chronic Diarrhea in Civil War Troops: Were They Both Nutritional Deficiency Syndromes?" *Journal of the History of Medicine and Allied Sciences* 47, no. 1 (1992): 49–67.
Brady, Lisa M. "From Battlefield to Fertile Ground: The Development of Civil War Environmental History." *Civil War History* 58, no. 3 (2012): 305–21.
Breeden, James O. "A Medical History of the Later Stages of the Atlanta Campaign." *Journal of Southern History* 35, no. 1 (1969): 31–59.
Breeden, James O. "States-Rights Medicine in the Old South." *Bulletin of the New York Academy of Medicine* 52 (1976): 348–72.
Brodman, Estelle, and Elizabeth B. Carrick. "American Military Medicine in the Mid-Nineteenth Century: The Experience of Alexander H. Hoff, M.D." *Bulletin of the History of Medicine* 64 (1990): 63–78.
Brown, Michael. "Surgery Identity and Embodied Emotion: John Bell, James Gregory and the Edinburgh 'Medical War.'" *History* 104, no. 1 (2019): 19–41.
Carrigan, Jo Ann. "Privilege, Prejudice, and the Strangers' Disease in Nineteenth-Century New Orleans." *Journal of Southern History* 36, no. 4 (1970): 568–78.

Carroll, Dillon J. "'The God Who Shielded Me Before, Yet Watches over Us All': Confederate Soldiers, Mental Illness, and Religion." *Civil War History* 61, no. 3 (2015): 252–80.

Cooter, Roger. "Medicine and the Goodness of War." *Canadian Bulletin of Medical History* 12 (1990): 637–47.

Dean, Eric T., Jr. "'We Will All Be Lost and Destroyed': Post-Traumatic Stress Disorder and the Civil War." *Civil War History* 37, no. 2 (June 1991): 138–53.

Dror, Otniel E. "Afterward: A Reflection on Feelings and the History of Science." *Isis: Journal of the History of Science in Society* 100, no. 4 (2009): 848–51.

Flannery, Michael A. "Another House Divided: Union Medical Service and Sectarians during the Civil War." *Journal of the History of Medicine and Allied Sciences* 54, no. 4 (1999): 479–510.

Franke, Norman H. "Pharmaceutical Conditions and Drug Supply in the Confederacy." *Georgia Historical Quarterly* 37, no. 4 (1953): 287–98.

Freemon, Frank R. "Lincoln Finds a Surgeon General: William A. Hammond and the Transformation of the Union Army Medical Bureau." *Civil War History* 33, no. 1 (1987): 5–21.

Freemon, Frank R. "Medical Care at the Siege of Vicksburg, 1863." *Bulletin of the New York Academy of Medicine* 67 (1991): 429–38.

Freemon, Frank R. "The Medical Challenge of Military Operations in the Mississippi Valley during the American Civil War." *Military Medicine* 157 (September 1992): 494–97.

Gallagher, Gary W., and Kathryn Shively Meier. "Coming to Terms with Civil War Military History." *Journal of the Civil War Era* 4, no. 4 (2014): 487–508.

Grant, S.-M. "'Mortal in This Season': Union Surgeons and the Narrative of Medical Modernisation in the American Civil War." *Social History of Medicine* 27, no. 4 (2014): 689–707.

Hanson, Kathleen S. "Down to Vicksburg: The Nurses' Experience." *Journal of the Illinois State Historical Society* 97, no. 4 (2004): 286–309.

Harrison, Mark. "The Medicalization of War—the Militarization of Medicine." *Social History of Medicine* 9 (August 1996): 267–76.

Hartley, Heather, David Kenneth Wright, Brandi Vanderspank-Wright, Pamela Grassau, and Mary Ann Murray. "Dead on the Table: A Theoretical Expansion of the Vicarious Trauma That Operating Room Clinicians Experience When Their Patients Die." *Death Studies* 43, no. 5 (2019): 301-310

Hasegawa, Guy R., and F. Terry Hambrecht. "The Confederate Medical Laboratories." *Southern Medical Journal* 96, no. 12 (2003): 1221–30.

Hauser, Jason. "By Degree: A History of Heat in the Subtropical American South." PhD diss., Mississippi State University, 2017.

Hoffman, Bjørn. "On the Triad Disease, Illness and Sickness." *Journal of Medicine and Philosophy* 27, no. 6 (2002): 651–73.

Jones, Gordon Willis. "The Medical History of the Fredericksburg Campaign: Course and Significance." *Journal of the History of Medicine and Allied Sciences* 18, no. 3 (1963): 241–56.

Jones, Jonathan S. "Opium Slavery: Civil War Veterans and Opiate Addiction." *Journal of the Civil War Era* 10, no. 2 (2020): 185–212.

Kemmerly, Phillip R. "Logistics of U. S. Grant's 1863 Mississippi Campaign: From the Amphibious Landing at Bruinsburg to the Siege of Vicksburg." *Journal of Military History* 86, no. 3 (2022): 573–611.

Khamesipour, Faham, et al. "A Systematic Review of Human Pathogens Carried by the Housefly (*Musca domestica* L.)." *BMC Public Health* 18, no. 1049 (2018). https://doi.org/10.1186%2Fs12889-018-5934-3.

King, Joseph Edward. "Shoulder Straps for Aesculapius." *Military Surgeon* 114, no. 3 (1954): 216–26.

Kramer, Howard D. "The Effect of the Civil War on the Public Health Movement." *Mississippi Valley Historical Review* 35, no. 3 (1948): 449–62.

Mammina, Laura. "In the Midst of Fire and Blood: Union Soldiers, Unionist Women, Military Policy, and Intimate Space during the American Civil War." *Civil War History* 64, no. 2 (2018): 146–74.

Marshall, Nicholas. "The Great Exaggeration: Death and the Civil War." *Journal of the Civil War Era* 4, no. 1 (2014): 3–27.

McMurry, Richard M. "'Marse Robert and the Fevers': A Note on the General as Strategist and on Medical Ideas as a Factor in Civil War Decision Making." *Civil War History* 35, no. 3 (1989): 197–207.

Meier, Kathryn Shively. "'No Place for the Sick': Nature's War on Civil War Soldier Mental and Physical Health in the 1862 Peninsula and Shenandoah Valley Campaigns." *Journal of the Civil War Era* 1, no. 2 (2011): 176–206.

Meier, Kathryn Shively. "U.S. Sanitary Commission Physicians and the Transformation of American Healthcare." In *So Conceived and So Dedicated: Intellectual Life in the Civil War–Era North*, edited by Lorien Foote and Kanisorn Wongsrichanalai. New York: Fordham University Press, 2015.

Messner, William F. "The Vicksburg Campaign of 1862: A Case Study in the Federal Utilization of Black Labor." *Louisiana History: The Journal of the Louisiana Historical Association* 16, no. 4 (1975): 371–81.

Miller, John MacNeill. "Composing Decomposition: In Memoriam and the Eco-critical Undertaking." *Nineteenth-Century Contexts* 39, no. 5 (2017): 383–93.

O'Hara, Charles G. "Susceptibility of Ground Water to Surface and Shallow Sources of Contamination in Mississippi." *Hydrologic Atlas* 739 (1996). https://pubs.usgs.gov/ha/739/plate-1.pdf.

Oldstone-Moore, Christopher. "The Beard Movement in Victorian Britain." *Victorian Studies* 48, no. 1 (2005): 7–34.

Parrish, William Earl. "The Western Sanitary Commission." *Civil War History* 31, no. 1 (1990): 17–35.

Percy, Dean B., Lucas Streith, Heather Wong, Chad G. Ball, Sandy Widder, and Morad Hameed. "Mental Toughness in Surgeons: Is There Room for Improvement?" *Canadian Journal of Surgery* 62, no. 6 (December 2019): 482–87.

Petty, Adam H. "Wilderness, Weather, and Waging War in the Mine Run Campaign." *Civil War History* 63, no. 1 (2017): 7–35.

Privette, Lindsay Rae Smith. "'A Hard Place to Be Well': Soldiers' Health and the Environment during the Vicksburg Campaign." *Journal of Mississippi History* 86, no. 3 (2024): 59–84.

Privette, Lindsay Rae. "More Than Paper and Ink: Confederate Medical Literature and the Making of the Confederate Army Medical Corps." *Civil War History* 64, no. 1 (2018): 30–55.

Quinn, E. Moore. "'I Have Been Trying Very Hard to Be Powerful "Nice"': The Correspondence of Sister M. De Sales Brennan during the American Civil War." *Irish Studies Review* 18, no. 2 (2010): 213–33.

Rafuse, Ethan S. "Still a Mystery? General Grant and the Historians, 1981–2006." *Journal of Military History* 71, no. 3 (2007): 849–74.

Rodrigues, Hugo, Ricardo Cobucci, Antônio Oliveira, João Victor Cabral, Leany Medeiros, Karen Gurgel, Tházio Souza, and Ana Katherine Gonçalves. "Burnout Syndrome among Medical Residents: A Systematic Review and Meta-analysis," *PLOS ONE* 13, no. 11 (2018): e0206840. https://doi.org/10.1371/journal.pone.0206840.

Rosenwein, Barbara. "Worry about Emotions in History." *American Historical Review* 107, no. 3 (2002): 821–45.

Rubenstein, David A. "A Study of the Medical Support of the Union and Confederate Armies during the Battle of Chickamauga: Lessons and Implications for Today's US Army Medical Department Leaders." Master's thesis, US Army Command and General Staff College, 1990.

Rutkow, L. W., and I. M. Rutkow. "Homeopaths, Surgery, and the Civil War: Edward C. Franklin and the Struggle to Achieve Medical Pluralism in the Union Army." *Archives of Surgery* 139, no. 7 (2004): 785–91.

Sanchez, Jose L., Michael J. Cooper, Christopher A. Myers, et al. "Respiratory Infection in the U.S. Military: Recent Experience and Control," *Clinical Microbiology Review* 28, no. 3 (2015): 743–800.

Schlagenhauf, Patricia. "Malaria: From Prehistory to Present." *Infectious Disease Clinics of North America* 18 (2004): 189–205.

Shiepko, Jessica M. "William Alexander Hammond's Transformation of the Army Medical Department during the American Civil War." Master's thesis, Sam Houston State University, 2018.

Shryock, Richard H. "Empiricism versus Rationalism in American Medicine, 1650–1950." *Proceedings of the American Antiquarian Society* 79, no. 1 (1969): 99–150.

Smith, Dale C. "'A Burden Too Heavy to Bear': War Trauma, Suicide, and Confederate Soldiers." *Civil War History* 59, no. 4 (2013): 453–91.

Smith, Dale C. "Military Medical History: The American Civil War." *Magazine of History* 19 (September 2005): 17–19.

Smith, Dale C. "The Rise and Fall of Typhomalarial Fever: I. Origins." *Journal of the History of Medicine and Allied Sciences* 37, no. 2 (1982): 182–220.

Starr, Paul. "Medicine, Economy, and Society in Nineteenth-Century America." *Journal of Social History* 10, no. 4 (1977): 588–607.

Stearns, Peter N., and Carol Stearns. "Emotionology: Clarifying the History of Emotions and Emotional Standards." *American Historical Review* 90, no. 4 (1985): 813–36.

Sternhell, Yael A. "Reimagining the Civil War." *Reviews in American History* 44, no. 4 (2016): 581–87.

Stith, Matthew M. "The Deplorable Condition of the Country: Nature, Society, and War on the Trans-Mississippi Frontier." *Civil War History* 58, no. 3 (2012): 322–47.

Weiner, Dora B., and Michael J. Sauter. "The City of Paris and the Rise of Clinical Medicine." *History of Science Society* 18 (2003): 23–42.

White, Paul. "Focus: The Emotional Economy of Science." *Isis: Journal of the History of Science in Society* 100, no. 4 (2009): 792–97.

Willoughby, Christopher. "'His Native, Hot Country': Racial Science and Environment in Antebellum American Medical Thought." *Journal of the History of Medicine and Allied Sciences* 72, no. 3 (2017): 328–51.

Wilson, Leonard G. "Fevers and Science in Early Nineteenth Century Medicine." *Journal of the History of Medicine and Allied Sciences* 33, no. 3 (1978): 386–407.

Index

acute respiratory distress syndrome, 51, 163n69
Allen, George T., 25, 26, 27
ambulances, 2, 20, 75, 77, 90, 95, 96, 97, 103
amputation, 101, 106–10, 114, 118, 173n42
Andrews, Edmund, 32, 106, 108
Army of the Potomac, 5, 7, 20, 99, 152
ars moriendi (good death), 56, 165n103
authority: medical, 3–4, 7–8, 16, 20, 26, 49, 51, 54–55, 64, 72, 124, 147; military, 4–5, 7–8, 15, 18, 19, 35, 39, 51, 58–59, 63–64, 69, 90, 94, 128, 135, 147, 152

bad air (miasma), 35, 42, 45, 84
Ballard's Farm, 44, 52
bayou. *See* topography
Bentley, William, 80, 83
Big Black River, Battle of, 70, 98, 99, 126, 172n16

Black, Samuel, 28, 54, 57
Blackall, Christopher, 1, 116
blackberries, 82, 85, 146, 147
Blair, Frank P., 30–32, 45, 162n24
bluffs. *See* topography: bluffs
Brashear, B. B., 50, 58
Bruinsburg, 70, 76, 97
burial, 55–57, 61, 85, 98
Bushnell, Douglas, 31, 33, 55

calories, 69, 124–25
camps: convalescence in, 69, 72, 136; location of, 50–51, 129, 139, 142–43; and proximity to food and water, 142–47; recreation at, 141–42; sanitation in, 125–26, 129, 132–33, 142; sickness in, 50–52, 129–30, 142–43, 151. *See also* troop health

canal: 1862 construction of, 23–24, 40; 1863 construction of, 8, 39, 40–43, 45; failure of, 64; tensions over, 57–59, 62–64
cane, 42, 77, 110–11, 122, 129; for beds, 110; for shelter, 110–11
Champion Hill, Battle of, 70, 86, 98–99, 103–5, 154
Circular No. 2, 23, 26, 54
Circular No. 6, 153, 179n9
civilian relief organizations: and interference with military operations, 5, 15–19, 34–35; and relationship with US Army, 5, 8, 15, 23, 34–35, 42, 73, 124, 127–29, 139, 152–53. *See also* United States Sanitary Commission (USSC); Western Sanitary Commission (WSC)
civilians, 4, 13, 39, 53, 62, 80, 94, 110, 124, 126, 136, 148
Clemons, Henry, 37–38
climate, in Lower Mississippi River Valley, 6, 9, 24, 35; and health of soldiers, 24, 34–35, 39, 64, 78–79, 124, 129, 133, 140
Coe, Schuler, 12, 28
common continued fever, 51
Complete Record of the Surgery of the Battles Fought near Vicksburg, 32, 106
Confederate soldiers, health of, 147–49
Cooke, Chauncey, 2, 90–91, 131
Crimean War, 14, 102
Crooke, George, 68, 122, 140

Dana, Charles, 77, 81, 115, 144, 146
Davisson, Henry C., 29–30, 35
deforestation, 6
dehydration, 85, 87, 90, 93, 125, 132, 140, 143
De Soto Point, 23, 40, 42, 57, 126, 129, 139
diarrhea, 2, 24, 38, 47, 51–52, 63, 87, 112, 125, 131–34, 142, 147; acute, 63, 125, 134; chronic, 38, 51, 63, 125, 132, 134, 142
donations, 5, 15–16, 19, 22
drought, 40, 79, 121, 125, 143, 151
dust: and combat wounds, 106; and marching conditions, 121, 125; and thirst, 122

dysentery, 2, 4, 24, 56, 63, 125, 126, 132–34; acute, 63, 125, 134; chronic, 63, 125, 134

Eddington, William, 77, 82, 84, 122, 144
emaciation, 1, 148
emotional bonds, 115–16; and detachment of medical officers; 112–13, 115; endurance of, 70, 85; hardships and, 3, 84, 111, 154; resilience of, 95, 111
emotions, xii, 53, 57, 95, 117, 153
environment, 5, 8, 9, 68, 69, 80, 85, 123–24, 139, 154; and challenges to healthcare, 94–95, 102, 133; and disease, 5–7, 42, 53, 78, 130; as enemy or ally, 58, 69, 79, 85, 124; and threats to soldiers' health, 5–7, 39, 40, 51, 58, 59, 62, 68, 71, 75, 79, 84, 85, 88, 93, 129, 133
erosion, 5–6, 122
erysipelas, 33, 55, 138
evacuation, 2, 5, 7, 14, 17–18, 21, 30, 32–33, 44, 55, 101; during campaign, 70, 94, 97–98, 102, 110, 111, 117; at Chickamauga, 100; at Gettysburg, 99; during siege, 124, 135–37

Farragut, David, 23–24, 79
XV Army Corps, 40, 43, 98
54th Indiana, 29, 48, 49, 50, 51
Finely, Clement A., 13, 19
flies, 133
flooding, 12, 44–45, 57
food shortage. *See* hunger
forage, 79–83, 121, 139, 145, 147, 148, 153, 154; comfort of, 83–85, 139; emotional benefits of, 8, 124, 153
Forbes, Williams S., 96, 110–11, 116, 137
Fort Donelson, 15–17, 21–22, 26, 32–33, 60
fresh food, access to, 69, 145–47
furlough, 53–55, 131

gangrene, 33–34
good death (*ars moriendi*), 56, 165n103
Grant, Ulysses S: and soldiers' health, 50, 52, 55, 58, 60, 62–63, 78, 94, 126; and strategy, 25, 40, 67, 71–72, 76–79,

92, 99, 122–23; and US Army Medical Department, 34–35, 55, 58–65, 75, 94, 96, 100, 135; and USSC, 127–29
gratuitous suffering, 8, 38, 124, 127
gullies, 6, 130

Hammond, William Alexander, 19, 84, 89, 132, 153; and Medical Department reforms, 20–23; and Edwin Stanton, 19, 152–53
Hard Times Plantation, 70, 77, 97
heat, 6, 24, 78, 85, 121–22, 124, 140–42, 151
heat exhaustion, 86–92, 140
Hewitt, Henry Stewart, 71, 97
Holston, John, 74, 97–98
hospital boats, 16, 21, 26, 32, 55, 135; *City of Louisiana*, 26, 38; *City of Memphis*, 21, 26, 34, 135–36; *D. A. January*, 21, 135; *Henry Von Phul*, 26, 34, 35; *Nashville*, 21, 44, 73, 135; *R. C. Wood*, 135
hospitals, 1, 7–8, 15–17, 21, 22, 30, 32, 59, 64, 72, 73–74, 94, 100, 127, 132, 134, 137, 141, 147; Confederate, 148–49; sights and sounds in, 102–5, 111, 114–15, 118–19, 138; system of, 2, 27, 43, 97, 99, 135–36, 138–39
hunger, 82, 84–85, 91–92, 93, 122–23, 126, 139
hygiene, 27, 47–48, 50, 52, 132
hypothermia, 46–47

intermittent fever, 63, 125, 130–31, 134
isolation, effects of, on troops, 8, 70–71, 94–95, 99–100, 102, 111, 124, 127

Jameson, Robert, 88, 129, 144
James' Plantation, 70, 74–75, 172n8
Johnson, Charles, 81, 102–3, 105, 106, 113–14, 137, 144

latrines, 52, 132
Letterman, Jonathan, 20–21, 26, 71
levees, as graves, 55–57, 65. *See also* topography: levees
loess, 6, 122, 143
Lower Mississippi River Valley, 5–6, 35, 40, 78, 121, 154; geography of, 5–6, 12, 143.
See also climate, of Lower Mississippi River Valley

malaria, 35, 57, 63, 78, 97, 130–32, 138–39;
malarial parasites, 130
Manassas, Battle of, 13–14, 15, 17, 32–33, 95
Marshall, T. B., 54, 81, 82, 91, 123, 141, 143
Mason, Frank, 11, 27, 54, 56, 122, 125
May 19 assault, 98, 99, 103, 104, 112, 122, 123, 134, 135
May 22 assault, 98, 99, 103, 104, 113, 114, 118, 122, 123, 127, 134, 135, 154
McClernand, John A., 25, 34, 40, 43, 48–50, 52, 58, 64, 67, 74–78, 91, 95, 97, 134
McMillan, Charles, 12, 27, 30, 32
McPherson, James Birdseye, 85, 92, 101, 104
measles, 3
Medical and Surgical History of the War of the Rebellion, The, 7, 51, 63, 112, 125
medical corps, 2–5, 7–8, 12–14, 17, 19–20, 22–23, 26, 30, 33, 34, 62, 70–72, 75, 93–96, 98–105, 110–11, 113–14, 117–18, 124, 126–28, 134–35, 139, 147, 152–54, 156n6; criticism of, 3–4, 13, 14–19, 22, 59–62, 114–15, 117–18, 152; and tension with military commanders, 27, 48–50, 54–55, 58–59, 61–64, 95–96, 163n58
medical reform, 3, 5, 8, 13, 14–15, 18, 19–23, 26, 34, 38, 152–54
miasma, 35, 42, 45, 84
microorganisms, 6, 24, 33, 51, 124, 131
Milliken's Bend, 28, 34, 38, 56, 64, 67, 69, 70–75, 77, 95, 97, 98, 100–101, 121, 124, 126–27, 129–30, 135–37, 139, 143
Mills, Madison, 71–72, 75, 98, 100, 110, 136, 138
Mississippi Alluvial Plain, 5
mosquitoes, 9, 78, 130, 154

Newberry, John Strong, 15–17, 22
Newton, James,
"noble suffering," 8, 82, 85, 117

Ordronaux, John, 52, 84, 88–89, 146
Overland Campaign, 152–53

Pemberton, John C., 25, 79, 98, 148–49, 154
Perkins' Plantation, 67, 70–71, 74–75, 95, 100, 143
Pittsburg Landing. *See* Shiloh, Battle of
pneumonia, 47, 51, 55
Porter, David Dixon, 25, 71, 76, 144
Port Gibson, Battle of, 77, 85, 94, 95–99, 102, 108, 115, 122; landscape surrounding, 78, 80
press, Northern, 4, 14, 34, 39, 59, 63, 126
public criticism: of medical corps, 4–5, 14, 59–61, 117–18; of military leadership, 4–5, 14, 34, 59–61

quinine, 59, 138–39

rain, 6, 12, 32, 39, 40, 42, 44, 46–47, 52, 60, 64, 68, 69, 79, 83–84, 110, 121, 125, 130, 143, 151
Ramsdell, Daniel, 114–15, 136–37
rations, 38, 46, 68–69, 71, 75, 76–79, 80, 82–83, 94, 99, 122, 124–25, 127, 129, 145, 147
ravines. *See* topography: ravines
Raymond, Battle of, 70, 80, 92, 98–99
remittent fever, 125, 131, 134
ridges, 6, 110, 122.

sanitation, 2–3, 27, 60, 127; deterioration of, 51, 124–25, 129, 132–33, 148, 151. *See also* United States Sanitary Commission (USSC)
Scates, Walter, 74–75
XVII Army Corps, 98
shelter, 42–43, 45–49, 51, 69, 83, 90, 110, 118, 132, 135, 141, 151; shebangs as, 141–42
Sherman, William T., 4, 12, 18–19, 25–28, 34–35, 38, 40, 45, 54, 59, 60, 64, 68, 71, 72, 78, 81–82, 85, 88–91, 127–28, 144, 146, 152
Shiloh, Battle of, 17–18, 21, 26, 32–33, 60, 63, 70, 95, 129
sickness, 1–2, 6, 24, 37–39, 51–53, 55, 58, 62–63, 72, 85, 87, 126, 134, 140, 145–46, 151

siege tactics, 123, 129, 139; and effects on hospital system, 135, 139
sleep, 12, 28, 38, 46, 76–77, 83–85, 91, 103–4, 119, 121, 125, 130, 141, 170n83
smallpox, 3, 126
soldiers: and tension with officers, 4, 7, 37–39, 47, 53–54, 90–91; and tension with surgeons, 3–4, 7–8, 60–61, 90–91, 114–16
stamina, 7, 77, 83, 122–23, 139
straggling, 74–75, 90–91
Strong, Henry, 46, 83, 93, 118–19
sun exposure, 2, 6, 12, 14, 28, 40, 68–69, 76, 77, 90, 105, 110, 121, 132, 135, 140
sunstroke, 85–88, 90, 125–26, 139, 140, 170n93
supply distribution, 2, 15, 21, 23, 33, 76, 137–38, 139
surgeons: compared to civilian practitioners, 8, 101–2, 106; emotional detachment of, 113–16; professionalism of, 2–4, 21–23, 71, 95–96, 106, 108, 110–14, 116, 118, 124; shortage of, 13, 27, 58–59, 62, 117; and tensions with soldiers, 3–4, 7–8, 60–61, 90–91, 114–16
swamps. *See* topography: swamps
swimming, 48, 141–42

temperature: body, 46, 87-88, 90, 140; and weather, 2, 46, 68, 85–86, 125, 140–41
XIII Army Corps, 40, 43, 50, 64, 68, 74, 76, 95, 137
33rd Wisconsin, 116, 139, 141
Thrall, Seneca, 42, 43, 47, 118, 130, 137
topography: bayous, 6, 8, 11–12, 21, 26, 28, 30–33, 35, 40, 42, 48, 56, 67–69, 80, 91, 121, 130, 141–43; bluffs, 5–6, 11, 24, 28, 30–31, 34, 39–40, 79–80, 88, 129, 136, 142, 154; deforestation, 6; gullies, 6, 130; levees, 6, 40–43, 45, 47, 55–57, 61, 64–65, 68–69, 76; ravines, 2, 5, 77, 110, 122, 129–30, 136, 139, 141, 144; ridges, 6, 110, 122; swamps, 5–6, 8, 12, 26, 30, 40, 42–43, 45, 57, 65, 79, 130, 143

transportation, 2, 20, 26–28, 70–71, 74–75, 90, 94, 96, 98, 100, 129, 136–37, 152
triage, 2, 7, 103, 111, 136, 153
troop health: and camp locations, 37–39, 42–43, 47, 53, 62–64, 125–26; and camp sanitation, 51–52, 123–25, 132–33, 148; Confederate, 147–49
Trowbridge, Silas, 101, 104–5, 108–9
23rd Wisconsin, 37, 38, 60, 64
typhoid, 3, 24, 51–52, 55, 63, 125, 134

United States Army Medical Department, 34, 116, 156n6
United States Sanitary Commission (USSC), 2, 4, 15–19, 42, 62, 73, 124, 126, 127–29, 141, 152–53. *See also* civilian relief organizations

Van Buren Hospital, 72
Vicksburg, Siege of, 1–2, 7, 8, 111, 116, 118, 122–24, 129, 131–35, 138–40, 142, 145, 147–48, 152, 154
Vicksburg Campaign, xii, 2, 8, 69, 78, 80, 87, 91, 94–95, 97, 100, 102, 110–11, 118, 121, 126, 137, 153
Vollum, E. P., 61–63

Warriner, Henry, 73, 126–28
water, 5–6, 11–12, 17, 26, 28, 30–33, 38–40, 42–47, 61, 64, 67–68, 78–79, 83, 86, 89–90, 151; access to during siege, 121, 130–33, 135, 142–45, 148; contaminated, 38, 51–52, 125, 131–33, 142–43, 147; sources of, 52, 87, 89–90, 130, 135, 143–45
Wells, Seth, 44–45, 81
Western Sanitary Commission (WSC), 4, 15–17, 19, 35, 63, 124, 126, 127–29. *See also* civilian relief organizations
Whitehill, James, 86, 134
wilderness, 11–12, 42, 78, 81, 152
Wiley, William, 46–47, 57, 86
Willison, Charles, 52–53, 56–57
Wood, R. C., 26, 55, 58–59, 61–63, 135
Woods, John, 108
Woods, Joseph Thatcher, 45, 55, 144–45

Yeatman, James, 127–28
yellow fever, 6, 35, 78
Young's Point, 28, 37, 40, 43–47, 56–60, 64–65, 68, 70, 86, 93, 97, 126, 129–30, 137, 139

Index

www.ingramcontent.com/pod-product-compliance
Lightning Source LLC
Chambersburg PA
CBHW021856230426
43671CB00006B/408